BLACKWELL BRISTOL
LECTURES ON
GREECE, ROME
AND THE CLASSICAL
TRADITION

Tales of the Barbarians

Blackwell-Bristol Lectures on Greece, Rome and the Classical Tradition

Series Editors: Neville Morley, Charles A. Martindale, and Robert L. Fowler

The Bristol Institute of Greece, Rome and the Classical Tradition promotes the study of Greco-Roman culture from antiquity to the present day, in the belief that classical culture remains a vital influence in the modern world. It embraces research and education in many fields, including history of all kinds, archaeology, literary studies, art history and philosophy, with particular emphasis on links between the ancient and modern worlds. The Blackwell Bristol lectures showcase the very best of modern scholarship in Classics and the Classical Tradition.

Publications:

Why Plato Wrote
Danielle S. Allen

Tales of the Barbarians: Ethnography and Empire in the Roman West
Greg Woolf

Dionysus Resurrected: Performances of Euripides' The Bacchae in a Globalizing World
Erika Fischer-Lichte

Past Speakers and Lectures:

2013 Mark Vessey, University of British Columbia "Writing before Literature: Later Latin Scriptures and the Memory of Rome"
2012 Bettina Bergmann, Mount Holyoke College "Worlds on the Wall: the Experience of Place in Roman Art"
2011 Colin Burrow, All Souls College, The University of Oxford "Imitation"
2010 Erika Fischer-Lichte, Free University of Berlin, "Dionysus Resurrected: Performances of Euripides' The Bacchae in a Globalizing World"
2009 Greg Woolf, St. Andrews University, "Barbarian Science: Ethnography and Imperialism in the Roman West"
2008 Danielle S. Allen, Institute for Advanced Study, Princeton University, "Philosophy and Politics in Ancient Athens"
2007 Ian Morris, Stanford University, "The Athenian Empire"

Future Speakers:

2014 Andrew Feldherr, Princeton University
2015 Susan E. Alcock, Brown University
2016 Glenn W. Most, The University of Chicago

BLACKWELL BRISTOL
LECTURES ON
GREECE, ROME
AND THE CLASSICAL
TRADITION

Tales of the Barbarians

Ethnography and Empire in the Roman West

Greg Woolf

WILEY Blackwell

This paperback edition first published 2014

© 2014 Greg Woolf

Edition history: Blackwell Publishing Ltd (hardback, 2011)

Registered Office
John Wiley & Sons Ltd, The Atrium, Southern Gate, Chichester, West Sussex, PO19 8SQ, UK

Editorial Offices
350 Main Street, Malden, MA 02148-5020, USA
9600 Garsington Road, Oxford, OX4 2DQ, UK
The Atrium, Southern Gate, Chichester, West Sussex, PO19 8SQ, UK

For details of our global editorial offices, for customer services, and for information about how to apply for permission to reuse the copyright material in this book please see our website at www.wiley.com/wiley-blackwell.

Library of Congress Cataloging-in-Publication Data

Woolf, Greg.

Tales of the barbarians: ethnography and empire in the Roman west/Greg Woolf.
     p. cm. — (Blackwell Bristol lectures on Greece, Rome and the classical tradition)
    Includes bibliographical references and index.
    ISBN 978-1-4051-6073-5 (hardcover: alk. paper) ISBN 978-1-118-78510-2 (pbk.: alk. paper)
    1. Acculturation–Rome.   2. Rome–Ethnic relations.   3. Rome–Culture policy.
    4. Rome–History–Empire, 30 B.C.–284 A.D.
    5.   National characteristics, West European. I.   Title.
    DG272.W66 2011
    9370.07–dc22

                                          2010030303

A catalogue record for this book is available from the British Library.

Cover design by Nicki Averill

Set in 10/12pt Sabon by Thomson Digital, India
Printed in Malaysia by Ho Printing (M) Sdn Bhd

1   2014

Contents

For my mother

Translations Used

Except where otherwise noted, translations are reprinted by permission of the publishers and Trustees of the Loeb Classical Library, Cambridge, MA: Harvard University Press, copyright by the President and Fellows of Harvard College. Loeb Classical Library® is a registered trademark of the President and Fellows of Harvard College. All other translations are by the author.

The Roman History of Ammianus Marcellinus, during the Reign of the Emperors Constantius, Julian, Jovianus, Valentinian, and Valens, trans. C.D. Yonge. London: Bohn's Classical Library, 1862.

Appian's Roman History, trans. Horace White. Loeb Classical Library. London: William Heinemann, 1912.

Dio's Roman History, trans. Earnest Cary and Herbert Baldwin Foster. Loeb Classical Library. Cambridge, MA: Harvard University Press, 1914.

Diodorus of Sicily, trans. C.H. Oldfather. 12 vols. Loeb Classical Library. Cambridge, MA: Harvard University Press, 1933–9.

The Roman Antiquities of Dionysius of Halicarnassus, trans. Earnest Cary and Edward Spelmann. Loeb Classical Library. London: William Heinemann, 1937.

Hippocrates, vol. 1, trans. W.H.S. Jones. Loeb Classical Library. London: William Heinemann, 1923.

Justin, History of the World extracted from Trogus Pompeius, etc., trans. John Selby Watson. London: George Bell & Sons, 1890.

Livy in Fourteen Volumes, trans. B.O. Foster. Loeb Classical Library. Cambridge, MA: Harvard University Press, 1924.

Manilius Astrononomica, trans. G.P. Goold. Loeb Classical Library. Cambridge, MA: Harvard University Press, 1992.

Parthenius of Nicaea. The poetical fragments and the Ἐρωτικὰ παθήματα. Edited with introduction and commentaries by Jane L. Lightfoot. Oxford: Clarendon Press, 1999.

Plutarch's Lives, vol. 2, trans. Bernadotte Perrin. Loeb Classical Library. London: William Heinemann, 1914.

Polybius, The Histories, trans. W.R. Paton. Loeb Classical Library. Cambridge, MA: Harvard University Press, 1922.

Posidonius III, The Translation of the Fragments, trans. I.G. Kidd. Cambridge Classical Texts and Commentaries. Cambridge: Cambridge University Press, 1999.

The Geography of Strabo, trans. H.C. Hamilton and W. Falconer, 3 vols. London. George Bell & Sons. 1903.

Tacitus, Germania, Translated with Introduction and Commentary, trans. James B. Rives. Clarendon Ancient History Series. Oxford: Clarendon Press, 1999.

Vitruvius, On Architecture, trans. Frank Grancer. Loeb Classical Library. Cambridge, MA: Harvard University Press, 1934.

Introduction

Joseph Conrad's *Heart of Darkness* begins with a story, told on the deck of a cruiser moored on the Thames estuary where a group of old friends pass the time as they wait for the tide to turn. As the sun sets over London, the narrator begins his tale of the degeneration of imperial rule and Western rationality in the depths of Africa. '"And this also," said Marlow suddenly, "has been one of the dark places of the earth."'

The phrase is a quotation from Psalm 74, an appeal to God not to forsake his people in the midst of the heathen, a very suitable epigram for this novel. Verse 20 in the King James Bible reads 'Have respect unto the covenant: for the dark places of the earth are full of the habitations of cruelty'.

Neither Conrad nor Marlow follows up that thought immediately. Conrad continues by characterizing this latter-day Odysseus as an inveterate follower of the seas, a man whose wandering mind is untypical of sailors, especially in his yarns, because to him the meaning of an episode was not inside like a kernel but outside, enveloping the tale like a misty halo. Marlow, for his part, continues:

> I was thinking of very old times, when the Romans first came here, nineteen hundred years ago – the other day ... Light came out of this river, you say Knights? Yes; but it is like a running blaze on a plain, like a flash of lightning in the clouds. We live in the flicker – may it last as long as the old earth keeps rolling! But darkness was here yesterday. Imagine the feelings of a commander of a fine – what d'ye call 'em? – trireme in the Mediterranean, ordered suddenly to the north; run overland across the Gauls in a hurry; put in charge of one of these craft the legionaries – a wonderful lot of handy men they must have been, too – used to build, apparently by the hundred, in a month or two, if we may believe what we read. Imagine him here – the very end of the world, a sea the

Tales of the Barbarians: Ethnography and Empire in the Roman West   Greg Woolf
© 2014 Greg Woolf

colour of lead, a sky the colour of smoke, a kind of ship about as rigid as a concertina – and going up this river with stores, or orders, or what you like. Sand-banks, marshes, forests, savages, – precious little to eat fit for a civilized man, nothing but Thames water to drink. No Falernian wine here, no going ashore. Here and there a military camp lost in a wilderness, like a needle in a bundle of hay – cold, fog, tempests, disease, exile, and death – death skulking in the air, in the water, in the bush. They must have been dying like flies here.

The Heart of Darkness was published in 1902, just five years after Kipling's poem 'Recessional', and this opening frame voices a similar consciousness of the imminent end of empire. Rome, as so often for this generation, offered compelling resemblances and contrasts. Marlow goes on at once to provide some of the latter: we are not quite like them, we are more efficient, they were no colonists and barely had an administration. They were mere conquerors, who 'grabbed what they could get for the sake of what was to be got' and he continues in similar vein. The reader is not taken in, of course. What Marlow found up river, at 'the farthest point of navigation and the culmination of my experience', will shatter forever his and our faith in the comforting narratives of the civilizing process. We are no better than the Romans, and our fate will be no different from theirs.

Thinking about the British empire in terms of ancient Rome was perhaps inevitable. So much of the paraphernalia of British rule – titles and slogans, symbols and ornaments – had been created in the Victorian era, when the status of Classics in the education of the British elite was at an all time high.[1] Yet there has been a price for historians in this Romanizing of Europe's imperial adventures. Whenever Britain becomes the new Rome, the ancient Britons, the Gauls and other western peoples become Victorian savages, illiterate tribesmen hidden in the dark forests of an unexplored continent. Rome's penetration of Europe was easy to imagine as a precursor of the Scramble for Africa. Many versions of the analogy have since been presented. There have been noble Britons, and British victims as well as British savages. Scholars have drawn attention to the limitations of the comparison, from at least the beginning of the twentieth century.[2] Yet successive generations of revisionists have found it easier to exchange domination and exploitation for the civilizing process than to decolonize our histories of the Roman West.[3] Post-colonial studies have in many ways only prolonged our double identification with Roman imperialism and its victims.

This book is intended as a contribution to this project of decolonization. Decolonizing does not mean redressing the balance. This is no attempt to give voices to those whom I shall continue to call barbarians, and certainly not to proclaim their ways of life better than (or even merely different from) what replaced them under Roman rule. I am not setting out to 'take their side', as if by affirming solidarity with some of my conquered ancestors, I can expiate the imperialist deeds of my more recent relatives. Nor do I want to tell the story from their point of view. Peoples without History, are usually those who have been deprived of it by force.[4] Pretending to restore it is a condescension that trivializes the original theft. It is in any case an impossible task for antiquity, where it is hard enough to tell a story with any nuance from the conquerors' perspective. Rather this is an investigation of a group of themes that have become central to the history of modern empires in general, but an investigation that has constantly to navigate between analogy and difference.

The subject of this book is the creation of new histories in the Roman West. This new knowledge, and the process by which it was created, I shall term ethnography. What that term might mean in antiquity will need to be clarified in chapter 1.[5] But using it has the advantage that it allows me to connect the various texts in which my stories about barbarians are found to similar texts created in other places and periods. It also allows me to draw on a rich body of debate among modern anthropologists and historians about what happens when accounts of unfamiliar peoples are translated into writing.[6] Their questions have helped me formulate my own. Who was involved in the generation of that new knowledge? How did the circumstances under which they met shape the form taken by the stories they told? How did the prior intellectual preoccupations of ancient writers shape *their* questions and their answers? How far did empire set the terms in which they came to understand each other? Reading ethnographies has its own pleasure – and I have enjoyed dipping my toes into unfamiliar waters – but I do not expect the stories of Roman Europe to be the same as, or indeed different from, those told in the modern world. If my problematic owes everything to current debates among both historians of empire and ethnographers, my answers will not systematically proclaim either the equivalence of ancient experience, or its utter foreignness.

What do I mean by the Roman West? A vast region that Roman armies fought in, occupied and eventually conquered, between the middle of the third century BCE and the end of the first century CE.[7] The term is a conventional one. West, that is, of Italy, itself largely under Roman control before the first campaigns were waged on the larger islands and along the Mediterranean littorals of France, Spain and North Africa. All these territories were conquered by the end of the Punic Wars, that is in the middle of the second century BCE. It took over a century more to make the Atlantic the limit of Roman rule. The final portions of Roman North Africa and Spain, Gaul, Britain and Germany were not turned into provinces until the first century CE. West is also a cultural realm: West in contradistinction to the East of Greek cities and Hellenistic monarchies. Teleologically, this is the half of the empire which, along with Italy, would come to use Latin in its administration and monuments, literature and education. It coincides roughly with the less successful half of the empire after it was divided in the late fourth and early fifth century, the Roman empire that fell, only for part of it to form the foundations of Western Christendom. That West, of course, was not bisected by the Mediterranean: Africa was as much a part of it as the wilder shores of Europe.

The West was not always so different or distinct. When Timaios of Sicilian Tauromenium gave it its first comprehensive history around the beginning of the third century BCE, it was one of a number of peripheries of the Greek core of Mediterranean civilization. Perhaps it might have been compared to the Euxine as another sea seeded with Greek cities in the Iron Age, or even with the newer Greek lands settled by Alexander's veterans and ruled by the descendants of his generals, in Egypt and Anatolia, the Near East and the Hindu Kush. Aristotle had included the constitutions of Rome and Carthage (along with those of some of the western Greek cities) in his political surveys. Eratosthenes wondered if Romans, Carthaginians and Indians should be considered within the civilized core of the world, a core surrounded by barbarian peoples. A much sharper cultural gradient than East/West divided the Mediterranean world, with its centuries and cities and its dense networks of trade, piracy and pilgrimage, from its various continental hinterlands.[8] The Maghreb, the Spanish Meseta and the Massif Central had little in common, except that all were ecologically distinct from the littorals surrounding the western extension of the middle sea.

The West was, in fact, an artefact of Roman power. Part of the aim of this book is to trace how that came about. It was created first by the obliteration of Carthage, and then by devising for Spaniards, Africans and Gauls (and then for others) new means of rule, different from those that Romans were learning to apply in Greek lands.[9] Local memory, whether documented in the Carthaginian libraries – libraries that the conquerors ostentatiously dispersed, translating only one great encyclopaedia of agriculture – or in oral traditions, was treated as worthless. This from a city that had been actively sponsoring the creation of a Latin literature and patronizing Greek scholars for over a century by the time Carthage fell! The early Roman empire stimulated a great recovery and celebration of local memories in the Greek world,[10] but not in the emergent West. Contempt for local traditions in this part of their dominions can be compared to the notorious modern doctrine of *terra nullius*, the designation of territory as legitimately belonging to no one, and so liable to the most extreme forms of colonial remodelling.[11] It is difficult to find explicit statements by Roman writers of such a doctrine, but its application was nevertheless systematic. The Latin West was made, in part, by the effacing of un-Latin and pre-Roman pasts, a process quite different from that applied in other parts of the empire. In their place, new pasts and traditions had to be invented.[12]

Expressed in these terms, the actual violence of Roman conquest might seem to entail what has been called 'epistemic violence'. That term refers to the (usually) colonial engineering of an unbridgeable rupture between the knowledge worlds of pre- and post-conquest societies. Indigenous knowledge – of themselves, their past, their identity and their place in the cosmos – is dramatically devalued, to be replaced by the 'discoveries' of the conquerors, inventions that encode the rulers' gaze and build on their own metropolitan preoccupations. The paradigm for such an approach was that pioneered by Edward Said in his study of what he termed 'orientalism', although more extreme versions of the idea have since gained currency as well as comprehensive critiques.[13] Common ground is that empire exercised a crucial context for the new texts that were produced. Probably most now would assent to some form to Foucault's general proposition that new orders of knowledge are produced by and underpin new orders of power. These ideas have already been influential in Roman history.[14]

More contentious is the extent to which empire is held to *dominate* the intellectual field: Did pre-conquest knowledge make any impact on conquerors? Were there any continuities across epistemic shifts? How far were imperial aspirations to totalizing authority ever realized in practice? Historians of the European empires of the eighteenth and nineteenth centuries are currently locked in sometimes fierce debate over how absolute those ruptures were, and over the extent to which the dominated subjects of European empires actively contributed to the creation of the new knowledge that replaced what was effaced by empire.[15] When the issue is resolved into concrete questions, the answers may vary from one colonial situation to another. This book seeks to ask and answer some such concrete questions, such as: Did western provincials have any input into their new histories? How interested were Roman generals and emperors in gathering and systematizing knowledge? How far did pre-Roman traditions cross the ruptures caused by epistemic violence?

That empire spellbound the Roman imagination cannot be denied. Yet the precise connections remain obscure. Strabo, writing in Augustan Rome, granted that Roman expansion had brought new knowledge, yet his world is arguably Hellenocentric, his foundational text Homer, his predecessors and rivals Polybios and Poseidonios, Eratosthenes and Artemidoros. When Pliny dedicates the *Natural History* to Titus, does he celebrate the imperial frame of the encyclopaedia, or merely seek to appropriate the majesty of empire to his scholarly *magnum opus*? The Roman empire offered various resources to scholars, among them safe passage and all those plundered libraries gathered into the metropolis. But did scholarship pay its dues? Can we credit, as some have, the idea of Caesar guided into the Gallic interior by a battered scroll of Poseidonios? Would merchants exploring the harbours of the empire really find much of commercial advantage in dog-eared copies of Strabo?

The four chapters of this book pursue a sceptical investigation into the connections between empire and knowledge at the turn of the millennia. The first is an attempt to give some specificity to the kinds of knowledge we have of the Roman West in ethnographic writing and considers *en route* questions of genre and tradition, definition and historiography. It also offers an argument about the locations where new knowledge was created. The second chapter is concerned with the intellectual resources available for ordering this information, specifically the scientific paradigms offered by Greek ethnography, and genealogical discourse, also typically if not uniquely Greek. In particular it asks how scientific and mythopoetic modes of analysis were put into relation with each other, and with other ways of ordering the world, and why they did not produce a more systematic theory of human diversity and its origins. The third chapter deals with the imperial context of these investigations, with questions of imperial sponsorship and use of knowledge, questions that have produced a huge literature in relation to modern imperialisms.[16] The fourth asks how this knowledge was employed in the world of the principate, how open to revision it was, and why there seem so few advances in ethnographic knowledge over the course of the empire. Naturally these investigations tangle around each other as they proceed.

One of the many revelations produced by the modern critique of ethnography has been an explosion of the myth of first contact. Someone has always been there before, and very often these forerunners turn out to be essential guides to those who explore territory new to themselves. Writing this book I have been very fortunate in those who have surveyed this territory ahead of me. It will be obvious from my notes how much I depend on those philologists who, over more than a century, have surveyed ancient ethnographic and geographic writing and have teased out its relationship with historiography.[17] Three more recent studies have, however, been both guides into the forest and inspirations. Most fundamental of all has been Arnaldo Momigliano's *Alien Wisdom*, his Trevelyan lectures of 1973, which explored with wit and insight how Greek writers observed and recorded their neighbours as the world was opened up to their enquiries by Hellenistic and Roman imperialisms. Claude Nicolet's *L'inventaire du monde* also started life as a lecture series, in this case the Jerome Lectures of 1986.[18] His rich interweaving of intellectual and administrative history around the theme of space provided a model for historicizing a shift in geographical knowledge at the origins of the principate. Finally, James Romm's elegant volume *The Edges of the Earth in Ancient Thought* (1992) encouraged me to believe it was possible to write a cultural history of geography without doing violence to the literature through which is it now mostly represented.

This book grew within a collaborative project on Science and Empire in the Roman World sponsored by the Leverhulme Trust. I am immensely grateful to the Trust, to my principal collaborators Jason König and Katerina

Oikonomopolou, and also to the many scholars who participated in workshops and conferences held in St Andrews in the course of the project. I seem to have been telling tales about barbarians for a long time now. Audiences in Cambridge, Cologne, Galway, Lisbon, London, Malibu, Minneapolis, Nijmegen, Oxford, Paris, Philadelphia, Seville, St Andrews, Stanford and Sydney have heard and commented on earlier tellings. If they have not improved them more, it is my fault not theirs. Conversations at crucial moments with Kai Brodersen, Michael Crawford, Ton Derks, Mark Harris, Nico Roymans, the late and much missed Dick Whittaker, Jonathon Williams and Fernando Wulff have made larger contributions than any probably realized at the time to the evolution of my ideas.

The invitation to give the Blackwell Bristol Lectures in 2009 provided the perfect opportunity to bring these ideas together. My hosts and discussants at Bristol provided the best audience for which I could have hoped, as supportive and generous as it was critically engaged. For this, and for wonderful hospitality and good company during those two weeks, I am very grateful to Richard Buxton, Gillian Clarke, Bob Fowler, Duncan Kennedy, Charles Martindale, Nicoletta Momigliano, Neville Morley, Ellen O'Gorman, Rosalind Thomas and the Department of Classics and Ancient History as a whole. I am grateful too to Al Bertand, Haze Humbert, Galen Smith, Annie Jackson and all at Wiley-Blackwell for all their help in translating my lectures into this book. The final revisions took place during a fellowship held at the Max Weber College of the Unversity of Erfurt as part of a DFG-sponsored Forschergruppe led by Hans Joas and Jörg Rüpke, and during a period of leave given by the University of St Andrews and sponsored again by the Leverhulme Trust. The staff and collections of the university libraries of St Andrews and Erfurt and of the Warburg Institute have been vital. But neither lectures nor book could have been written without the unparalleled resources of the Joint Library of the Hellenic and Roman Societies at the Institute of Classical Studies in London and the help of its dedicated librarians. My thanks to all.

1

Telling Tales on the Middle Ground

Pliny on Safari

What did Romans know of their western subjects, and how did they claim to know it? Pliny the Elder, in the short account of Africa that makes up the first thirty chapters of Book 5 of his *Natural History*, offers a convenient starting illustration of the texture of ethnographic writing on the Roman West. This is how he begins.

> Africa, the Greeks called Libya, and the sea before it the Libyan Sea. Its limit is Egypt and no other part of the world offers fewer harbours, since the coastline extends from the west in a long curve. The names of its peoples and its towns are mostly impossible to pronounce, except by the natives who live almost entirely in fortresses.[1]

Africa in the middle of the first century CE is presented as remote, difficult either to penetrate or comprehend, and its knowledge begins with the Greeks. Africa remains as unfamiliar as ever, indeed it is in some ways more ungraspable and fabulous for Pliny than for some of his predecessors.[2] I shall return to the apparently irreducible *alterité* of the West in chapter 4. Yet despite these apparent obstacles to comprehension, Pliny has in fact quite a lot to say. As the book proceeds we are introduced to the two Mauretanias, their legendary foundation by the giant Antaeus and his combat with Hercules deftly interwoven with more recent imperial interventions, Caius' reduction of client kingdoms into provinces, the civic foundations of Claudius and Augustus. When Pliny's account reaches the river Lixus he expands on the gardens of the Hesperides – no golden apples now, just some wild olives and the story of the serpent was perhaps based on a serpent-shaped river channel – and then a

Tales of the Barbarians: Ethnography and Empire in the Roman West   Greg Woolf
© 2014 Greg Woolf

sideswipe at Cornelius Nepos for believing all the Greek lies about the region. Details of Roman colonies lead Pliny to the desert, herds of elephants and 'the great mountain of Africa also known as the most fabulous Atlas'.[3] The rugged west-facing crags, the wooded eastern approaches, its abundant springs and fruit and its eery daytime silence that at dusk is replaced by the sounds of dancing Pans and satyrs is indeed most fabulous. Pliny is less critical here than he was of Nepos: 'These things famous authors have reported, alongside the deeds performed there by Hercules and Perseus. An immense and unexplored territory separates it from us.'[4]

From the Atlas, Pliny turns to the coast (ch. 8), citing the commentaries of Hanno the Carthaginian, followed by most Greek and Latin authors, and then going on to the explorations conducted by Polybios in a fleet provided by Scipio Aemilianus. I shall return to this expedition, and others like it, in chapter 3. A long coastal *periplus* follows,[5] punctuated with comments on the animals found in each region. Pliny then turns to the first Roman military expedition into Mauretania during the reign of Claudius, an expedition that did reach the Atlas. Not only did senatorial generals campaign there, but Roman knights now govern the territory.

> There are, as I have said, five colonies in this province and it might seem therefore an area on which it would be easy to gain reliable information. But this – and much else – turns out upon examination to be completely false. For those of high status who cannot be bothered to hunt out the truth, do not wish to seem ignorant and so tell lies. Nothing is so misleading as when an author of repute endorses a false statement.[6]

Pliny again has bad witnesses in his sights, senators corrupted by luxury this time, and corrects them on the basis of local testimony. Then follows (ch. 14) a summary of the report of Suetonius Paulinus, first to cross the Atlas at the head of an army, detailing the unfamiliar flora of the region, the barren desert beyond it, more elephants and a barbarian tribe, the Canari, who eat raw flesh like dogs. Next King Juba, 'more famous for his research than for his rule', is cited, again on the peoples and plants of the Atlas. Then (ch. 17) Pliny passes on to the tribes of Mauretania Tingitana, in which the location of various rivers and mountains is interspersed with historical references, some to the period of the Jugurthine War, others to Augustan and later founda- tions. The accounts of Numidia and Zeugitana are very similar, and Pliny seems a little bored. The land had no interest except as a source of Numidian marble and wild beasts.[7] Both commodities were, of course, of vital interest to the generation that watched the Colosseum rise in the park of what had once been Nero's palace.

Once again, a few places are picked out for their historical interest. Utica is famous for the death of Cato, the colony of Great Carthage lies on the ruins of the Punic city, the boundary of Africa Nova and Africa Vetera is a ditch marking the limit agreed between Scipio Africanus and the kings. The Greater and Lesser Syrtes are described (ch. 26): Pliny provides their dimensions, a desert full of snakes, a forest filled with wild beasts and (inevitably) yet more elephants, then the Garamantes and other peoples of the interior. The place the Lotus Eaters once inhabited and the altars of the Philaeni and the swamp of Tritonis, named by Kallimachos the lake of Pallas Athena, add a slightly mythic air to this last wilderness before the province of Cyrenaica. Chapter 29 summarizes the 516 peoples of Africa, listing Roman colonies, Latin and tributary cities and tribes.

I have summarized Pliny's African ethnography at some length to give a flavour of the sort of things included in accounts of this kind, and in particular to illustrate the very wide range of data he sees suitable for inclusion. Legends of Hercules, Antaeus and Perseus and information about the locations of the Hesperides and the Lotophagoi rub shoulders with turgid administrative detail and detailed itineraries, and with accounts of expeditions, military and otherwise, conducted over a period of half a millennium. How (and how far) ancient writers reconciled mythological knowledge with more scientific accounts will be the subject of chapter 2. But for the moment I want to flag the incommensurability of the data that Pliny gathers.

There is, to be sure, a conventional answer to this sort of disparity when it arises in Pliny's *Natural History* or other compendious encyclopaedic works such as Diodoros' *Library*. This is to claim that the author is a 'mere' compiler, uncritically following his sources, and not particularly interested in the consistency or plausibility of the materials he had gathered. The *Natural History* is particularly liable to such charges since Pliny's own practice of citation makes it rather easier than usual to engage in *Quellenforschung*, the search for the origins of individual data. Pliny constantly represents his great work as a summation of the efforts of countless earlier researchers.[8] Within this portion, the text refers to Nepos, Hanno (at second hand), Polybios, Agrippa, Suetonius Paulinus, Juba and Kallimachos. Pliny certainly also used Pomponius Mela's shorter account of the same area.[9] The final chapter has been shown to derive from an administrative document that may be dated with some certainty to the mid-40s BCE.[10] There are numerous references too to what 'the Greeks' say. The list Pliny provides in Book 1 of the *auctores* consulted for Book 5 as a whole includes fourteen Latin authorities, the *fasti triumphales* and forty-five foreigners, mostly Greeks or writing in Greek. Which were useful for Africa we can only guess – Varro? Poseidonios? Diodoros? Timaios? Many are just names. There are, however, a few surprising omissions. Pliny does not name either Sallust or Strabo.[11] This is a sobering reminder of how incomplete were even the most compendious of ancient synoptic works.

Yet the notion of the *Natural History* as an ill-disciplined and indiscriminate jumble of facts does not convince. Indeed it flies in the face of the most recent readings of that work.[12] Quite apart from the detailed opening exposition of the structure of the work as a whole and the itemized list of sources, and the conventional organization of his geographical section as a tour (*periplus*) of the known world, the *Natural History* as a whole is unified by consistent preoccupations with the nature of the cosmos and the place of man and human history – including that of the Roman empire – within it.[13] The image of Pliny as an indiscriminate, eccentric and obsessive collector of 'facts' derives ultimately from his nephew's epistolary memoirs of him, not from the *Natural History* itself, and these letters had their own agenda.[14]

Besides, Pliny was not unusual in combining materials we would regard as incompatible. Myth and science already rub shoulders in Herodotos and the Hippokratic corpus.[15] Nor, as some of the passages I have quoted show, does he present himself as an *uncritical* compiler. Quite the reverse. Falsehoods and credulity are clearly marked as flaws, and there is an attempt to adjudicate between rival accounts. Autopsy is praised, and his *auctores* are often treated as authorities. The painstaking inclusion of precise distances and lists of civic statuses asserts an aspiration to accuracy. The range of his ethnography cannot be understood simply as a sign of his imperfections as either compiler or critic.

Pliny's ethnography is carefully devised. Notice for example the subordination of history to geography.[16] One effect of his choosing an organizational schema adopted from *periplus* narratives (and not all Pliny's authorities made a similar choice, so his decision to organize his account in this way was a conscious one) was to minimize a sense of change. The ethnographic structure of the world, it insinuates, derives from its overall shape, not from the contingent chance of the moment at which Pliny surveyed it. Pliny has not exactly created an ethnographic present in the modern sense of the term. There is a clear differentiation between a mythological stratum (Hercules and Antaeus), a period from which odd anecdotes may be recalled (Scipio's camp, the death of Cato) and the most recent period characterized by Roman expeditions and interventions, mostly in fact those of Pliny's own lifetime. Perhaps surprisingly there is only a handful of references to republican campaigns, and none at all to Punic Africa before Scipio's sack of Carthage. This too is a deliberate choice, since a great deal of information would have been available on both subjects. Mela's account – which Pliny knew – is quite different in this respect.[17] The issue of the suppression of time in ancient ethnographic writing will recur in chapter 4. Pliny's ethnography is not, then, the sum total of what he knew. It is a selection from a larger body of writing and, we must presume, from an even greater body of knowledge. All this makes the nature of that selection all the more important to understand.

Pliny's account of Africa has offered a convenient starting point for this investigation in several ways. Most important, it illustrates nearly the entire range of materials employed by those who composed passages of what I shall be terming ethnographic writing: Greek myth and Roman military history, accounts of marvels, records of military expeditions and voyages of exploration, administrative documents, and the observations and theorizing of natural philosophers. As my own compilation of stories draws in more examples, they will add speculations based on oceanography and astronomy, medicine, sociology and anthropology; eye-witness accounts of peoples, places and monuments; and the results of the interrogation of priests and other locals.

Pliny's Africa also exemplifies a problem that will recur as I mine Diodoros, Strabo and others for tales about the barbarian inhabitants of Rome's Wild West. Although literary works that were primarily ethnographic and geographic in nature clearly once existed, almost all have been lost. In practice, what we mostly have to deal with are 'compilatory' works, like the *Natural History*. Some were organized as universal histories, some as geographies or as *periplus*, others as miscellanies. Pliny's *magnum opus* is not the only one of these to have suffered a poor reputation until recently among scholars. Compilation has often been seen as a secondary activity, and compilers have sometimes been regarded as secondary intellects. Those prejudices derive partly from the habit of rating ancient works on stylistic and rhetorical grounds, partly from modern views of the primacy of original research, and partly from the problems of credibility posed by works of this kind. At best their procedures of selection, paraphrase and compression stand in the way of our access to original observations and formulations. Hence the search to identify and evaluate the lost sources used by those compilers, like Diodoros, who are less explicit than Pliny about the origins of their information, and to reconstruct their methods of compilation. All this is legitimate even if – like the eccentric travesty of Pliny as a scholar presented by his nephew – all we are after is a list of trustworthy facts.

Yet these compendia, like the universal histories to which they are related, responded to a particular set of desires in the Hellenistic and early Roman periods. However odd it seems to us, there evidently was a need felt to link the myths of Hercules and Antaeus to Paulinus' account of his conquest of the Atlas. Works like Pliny's *Natural History* which fashioned a vast whole out of so many parts, were one way to satisfy this desire. Diodoros and Pliny also explicitly claim that their huge works would save the reader the trouble of consulting so many separate sources themselves.[18] The modern encyclopaedia offers one image of what they tried to achieve: Diodoros preferred the image of a library. The desire to connect up the disparate parts of knowledge, and a sense of the overwhelming quantity of books already written, were both characteristic of the late republic and early empire. This was the intellectual world by which the barbarian West was encompassed. It is not necessarily a disadvantage for us to observe it through these great contemporary effort of synthesis.

Ethnography, Ancient and Modern

It is time, perhaps, to define terms. Ethnography in conventional usage – by which I mean *not* that of classicists – describes both a practice and a genre. The term was first coined in the early nineteenth century, and is now inextricably associated with a profession, a discipline and a genre of exposition. For some practitioners at least, ethnography connotes above all an exercise in recording: the recording in words, pictures, audio- and videotapes and other media, of the distinctive customs, artefacts and bodies of alien peoples.[19] At least some ethnography was envisaged as an exercise in recording primitive ways of life that were believed to be vanishing, and as a result tended to edit out obvious recent intrusions and rely on the testimony of those informants who remembered earlier days. As a mode of collecting, one that purported to be dispassionate and scientific, it had much in common with the taxonomic fieldwork of botanists and zoologists. Like those life-scientists, ethnographers worked in the present day, substituting a tacit evolutionism for historical consciousness.[20] The basic units of analysis in this case might be races. But more often it was the society or culture, either term being treated as an ontologically unproblematic category. The Nuer of Nuerland were a bounded entity, their language and way of life unique to themselves, and so on. More recent critique has highlighted the impossibility of such dispassionate observation, at least in respect of human subjects. The idea of bounded social entities has also come under scrutiny, and ethnographers are now intensely aware of the specific historical context in which each act of observation and recording takes place.[21] Ethnographers were by no means lackeys of empire, but their work has inevitably been located within the accelerating globalization of the twentieth century. Obviously enough, nothing like this ever existed in classical antiquity.

Ethnography for classicists has meant something different.[22] Most influential is the view of Felix Jacoby who made *Horographie und Ethnographie* (glossed as the history of individual places and of individual peoples) one of the central divisions in his taxonomy of Greek historical writing, alongside *Genealogie und Mythographie* and *Zeitgeschichte* (a term that was further subdivided into Universal History, *Hellenika* and the history of particular periods such as the reign of Alexander or the Punic Wars).[23] Convenient as this schema based on subject matter may have been for the classification of fragments, it has canonized a view of the evolution of successive historical genres to which few would now subscribe.[24] More recent accounts of Greek historiography tend to speak of an ethnographic tradition, one that can be traced back to Herodotos and Hekataios and is thereafter more important for some historians than for others.[25] Ethnographic thought itself can be pursued further back via the earliest physicists, notably Herakleitos and Xenophanes, and medical writers to discussions of alien peoples in Homer and Hesiod.[26] One result of these discussions has been to make clear that the content of ethnographic knowledge did not vary significantly between texts that we would consider historical, philosophical or poetic. Put otherwise, there were no genre-specific varieties of ethnographic writing or knowledge. Rather ideas about the diversity of humankind and information about specific peoples circulated widely among those who read and wrote in antiquity. Their familiarity and recognition-value meant they were available for appropriation to ends as various as the philosophical history of Poseidonios and Augustan poetics and triumphal imagery.

All this is very different from our modern notion of ethnography as a disciplinary practice or scientific genre.[27] Expeditions with a geographical aim are occasionally recorded, like Polybios' Atlantic *periplus* mentioned by Pliny. Greek narratives of travel, from those recorded by Herodotos in his *Researches* to the *Periegesis* of Pausanias or Philostratos' *Life of Apollonios*, make connections between the acquisition of knowledge through personal inspection (sometimes termed autopsy) and the practice of *theoria*, a term that ranges semantically from the experience of spectating at sacred games to consulting an oracle or contemplating sacred images. The term 'pilgrimage' captures only a part of these activities.[28] Learning from, as well as about, distant peoples was a common feature of certain kinds of account.[29] From Herodotos onwards, historians, philosophers and mystics occasionally claimed to have acquired knowledge from conversations with priests and other wise individuals in distant lands. But almost no journeys were made specifically to observe and record alien peoples.

The question of genre raises other difficulties. The definition of genres in prose, with no performative contexts to help us out, is in any case problematic. Our own descriptions of particular genres are often based either on later critical accounts like those of Aristotle, and the programmatic statements with which particular writers position themselves relative to their predecessors, or else on the prescriptions of late handbooks like that of Menander Rhetor that speak to worlds in which certain compositional habits and expectations had already emerged. That a notion of universal history existed can be inferred from the different accounts of their predecessors offered by Polybios and Diodoros. That history writing was considered a special domain is evident from Lucian's treatise *How To Write History*. No such critical accounts or prescriptions survive for ethnographic writing. Generic conventions were often anchored on canonized classics – positively or negatively, in the sense that knowing the Homeric epics might establish a set of expectations for the reader of the epic poetry of Apollonius, Ennius or Virgil. Equally the content of a given oratorical genre – panegyric or invective, for example – might be stabilized by educational regimes. Neither consideration can have applied to ethnographic writing, which had no classics (apart from the *Odyssey*)[30] and which had almost no place in educational curricula.[31] There is, to be sure, no reason why particular writing traditions should not develop a tighter and tighter generic definition over time. As it happens our only extant 'pure' ethnographies date from the early second century CE. Attempts have been made to discern the essential structural principles of ancient ethnographies from Tacitus' *Germania*[32] and to a lesser extent from Arrian's *Indica*.[33] But emergent (or convergent) genres of this kind operate in a different way from those orientated from the start on a canonical model. As they proceed in part by refinement, we cannot assume that conventions about what should be included and what excluded from those works would apply to earlier texts. The absence of foundational works is a sure sign that ethnography was never regarded in antiquity as an autonomous discipline. Medicine and mathematics came to be structured around the exegesis of and commentary on sets of classicized texts. Nothing similar happened in ethnography.

The great majority of the passages usually considered as ethnographic or geographic are in fact found within texts of other kinds. This was recognized even in antiquity. So Strabo, beginning Book 8 of his *Geography*, writes

> Since I started out from the western parts of Europe, describing those parts contained between the inner and the outer seas, and surveyed all the barbarous nations in this area up to the river Don and a small part of Greece, namely Macedonia, I propose now to give an account of the remainder of the geography of the Greek world. Homer was the first writer on the subject, and was followed by many others, some of whom composed particular treatises, and entitled them *Harbours* or *Circumnavigations* or *Tours of the Earth*, or gave them some name of this kind, and these included the geography of Greece. Some, included separate topography of the continents in their general histories as Ephoros and Polybios did; while others introduced matter relating to geography in their writings on physical and mathematical subjects, as did Poseidonios and Hipparchos.[34]

Pragmatically, then, we must focus on an ethnographic tradition, considered as a set of writing practices, based on traditions of enquiry and interpretation.

Of what might such a tradition consist? Richard Thomas characterizes it thus, at the start of his *Lands and Peoples in Roman Poetry*:

> With its seeds in the Homeric poems, and continuing into late Latin, the tradition of ethnographical writing is one of the most enduring in classical literature. Behind it lies a function which provides the explanation for such

endurance: by creating a formulaic literary genre to describe the features of other lands and the characteristics of their inhabitants, Greek ethnographic writers, and the Romans after them, were able to depict the diversity of mankind, and thereby to reach a fuller understanding of their own cultures and of their place in the world.[35]

Ethnographic writing for Richard Thomas, then, originated as a response to the perception of human diversity, and subsequently proceeded from its representation to a renewed understanding of local norms. This seems at first to be ground shared with modern ethnography, which sometimes justifies its engagement with the exotic in terms of its capacity to defamiliarize the world from which ethnographers travel out and to which they return.[36] Even if we choose not to regard ethnography as a 'formulaic literary genre', it is clear that the ethnographic mode included formulaic devices, conventional figures, motifs and presuppositions from which barbarian otherness might be generated and elaborated. That this process involved a consequential normalization of the Greek and the Roman has become a *topos* of subsequent writing on the subject.[37] Yet whatever the importance of ethnography in various projects of self-definition, this by no means exhausted its uses.[38]

The tropes of Roman *alterité* have now been well studied.[39] How far they constrained the composition of ethnographic writing is a matter of debate. Some modern accounts stress repeated themes, motifs transfered from one people to another, conventional tendencies to idealization and the like.[40] There is no doubt there was considerable stability in the treatment of some peoples and places, and that certain stereotypes and motifs remained in use over long periods. I shall return to this in the final chapter. Yet part of the argument of this book is that most ethnographic writing is susceptible to historicizing readings, and that many of the discursive strategies created very early on in the tradition were repeatedly put to new uses, uses that related to the lived experience of those involved in cultural encounters. Not all barbarians were alike. The nature and circumstances of these encounters varied. Greek and Roman norms of representation also evolved, even if many of the tools first created for engineering these understandings remained applicable throughout a long history of (mis)communication.

Among these tropes was contained a range of conventional ways of introducing information, among them claims to autopsy, the reported testimony of local informants and so on, many of course shared with history.[41] Other characteristics of the ethnographic mode include a tendency to slow narrative time, to summon up exotic vistas, and to enhance an emphasis on communal – as opposed to individual – identities. These various effects contributed to making the ethnographic mode a useful register for those composing in genres such as history or philosophy. Slipping in and out of ethnographic mode might be a compositional tactic: what resulted were not digressions, but rather intricately plotted diversions. Those diversions served a variety of ends.[42] Most of what we would usually call 'ancient ethnography' in fact consists of passages of this kind.

But if this perspective offers a better understanding of the ethnographic texts and part-texts we have, what are the implications for any investigation into how Greeks and Romans understood their neighbours? Distanced from a discipline of observation, or a genre of recording, and almost always subordinated to larger compositional ends, was ancient ethnography empty of real content? Can we be sure it offers any information comparable either to modern ethnographies or even early modern travellers' tales? It is easy to see why some readings refuse to ask about *Realien*, and why some historians and archaeologists find this style of criticism utterly inimical to their own, rather different, aims.

I wish to argue a more optimistic case. Ethnographic knowledge and texts produced in an ethnographic mode of writing are not the same thing. But the relation between them is not beyond reconstruction. Whether or not Herodotos ever went to the Black Sea, Caesar certainly went to Gaul and at least some of Pliny's many elephants were real. Authors and readers inhabited the world their texts describe. Some at least commuted between textualized exoticism and the often unfamiliar lifeworlds of which the empire was composed (or compiled?). Paulinus went to Africa with ethnography in his head, and some of those who read him would one day find themselves in the Atlas. Besides, although the schematic effects of othering and geographical stereotypes contributed to the structure and contents of ancient ethnographic passages,[43] the variety and detail of these passages is simply too great to be explained entirely in terms of the manipulation of tropes at the centre of the empire.[44]

Getting to Know the Barbarians

Ethnographic knowledge, I take it, is that knowledge we gain of one other in conversation, specifically in dialogues conducted across a gradient of unfamiliarity. Conversations of this kind must have taken place from long before the archaic period. Presumably they increased in frequency as the Mediterranean world and its hinterlands became more and more closely interconnected by trade and settlement, conquest and migration. I am concerned with the latter stages of this process. Most of what was learned in each generation was presumably almost immediately forgotten. But a small amount circulated, became the basis for critical reflection and inspired new enquiries. It is this process to which I most often refer when I speak about the creation of ethnographic knowledge.

Much of this work, I will argue, took place 'on the middle ground'. The phrase was coined by Richard White in his study of the accommodations and relations that developed in the Great Lakes region of North America between the mid-seventeenth and the early nineteenth centuries.[45] It describes a relatively stable world created out of the fragments left over from unplanned consequences of European expansion. Old World diseases, the acquisition of firearms and iron by some but not all indigenous groups, the aftershocks of European wars and the penetration of mercantile entrepreneurs combined to cause massive social dislocation, without putting in its place new systems of government and control. On the middle ground peoples of different ethnic origins – Algonquins and Iroquoians, French and English – cohabited for nearly two centuries in a space transformed but not really ordered or disciplined by European power. Jesuits and fur-trappers, soldiers and refugees all played parts in creating new accommodations. The Roman empire in the West was not entirely like this, but there were similarities.[46] If Roman expansion brought fewer transformative technologies, and nothing like the biological carnage that followed the Columbian Exchange, it did create a world profoundly disrupted by contact yet not, for a long while, intensively assimilated by the invaders. From at least the middle second century BCE traders operated in parts of Spain, Gaul and Africa, far beyond the areas controlled by Roman arms. Usually they only feature in texts when massacres offer a convenient excuse for military action. Yet there is archaeological evidence for the spread of Mediterranean manufactures into selected societies in a vast arc from Romania through Bavaria and Burgundy to the Atlantic. Alongside the artefacts are occasional rare traces of places where entrepreneurs settled, like the Magdalensburg in Austria from where a group of Italians traded in metalware. The opening up of new mines, from the Spanish silver mines described by Polybios to the gold mines in Trajan's newly conquered Dacia, always attracted entrepreneurs from Italy and the interior provinces. From Spain and southern France we know of hybrid communities like Carteia and Lugdunum Convenarum, places that classical writers described as peopled by the offspring of Roman soldiers and local women.[47] 'Roman' soldiers were in any case often local warriors, and many returned home with or without citizenship and beyond notional frontiers. The same was true within the shifting spheres of Roman authority east of the Rhine and north of the Danube, even in the first century CE.[48] Nothing like a stable administrative system emerged before the Augustan age. Even then the power of the Roman imperial state to order society and obliterate local accommodations was much less than that of the new American republic that finally brought White's middle ground to an end. Despite the many differences, there is some point in thinking of the Roman West, especially during the republican empire, as a middle ground on which many different kinds of people met, not always in situations where one side was clearly the master. Those encounters, I shall argue, were generative of new knowledge.

Out of these conversations, taking place in army camps and trading bases, in indigenous settlements and in mining communities, via interpreters on the frontier and envoys in the capital, and perhaps eventually between neighbours on the margins of colonized landscapes, emerged new stories and new understandings. These barbarian tales served in part to connect and co-ordinate world-views, if that is not too grand a way to talk of how strangers satisfied each other's curiosity. And just a tiny portion of these stories found their ways into texts. Once again, we can be absolutely certain that most of the texts that first offered 'pictures from the contact zones'[49] have been lost. Consider all those authorities on Africa that Pliny could read and we cannot. This is the reason we are so dependent on compilations put together at a later date, usually in the imperial metropolis whither all roads led and where authors of all kinds chose to come to work from the middle of the last century BCE. All the same it is occasionally possible to reconstruct or infer the circumstances of those earliest compositions, and behind them the kinds of conversations in which connections were first made. In a few cases it is even possible to date the invention of particular traditions fairly precisely.[50]

Domesticating the Keltoi

Consider, as a first example, this passage taken from Diodoros' account of the wanderings of Herakles in Book 4 of one of the greatest of these compilations, his *Library*.

Herakles then handed over rule over the Iberians to the best of the natives, while he himself gathered up his forces and marched on into Keltike. Travelling up and down the country he freed it from its lawless habits and ingrained hostility to strangers. Now great crowds of people drawn from every tribe flocked of their own accord to follow his army, so he founded a great city and named it Alesia after the wanderings [*ale*] of his army. And he recruited many of the native people too into the city population, and since these predominated numerically eventually all the inhabitants of the city came to be barbarised [*ekbarbarothenai*]. The Keltoi even now honour this same city as the hearth [*hestia*] and mother city [*metropolis*] of all of Keltike. It remained free and unconquered from the time of Herakles up to our own day. But eventually Gaius Caesar, who on account of the greatness of his deeds has been hailed as a god, seized the city by force, subjecting it and all the other Keltoi to the rule of the Romans.[51]

Diodoros then returns to the further wanderings of Herakles. The hero's visit to Gaul and his foundation of Alesia is mentioned again, however, in Book 5 which tells the story of how the eponymous Galates is born after Herakles has sex with the tall and beautiful daughter of the ruler of Keltike.

Once upon a time, so the story goes, a man of striking appearance ruled over Keltike. He had a daughter who was both exceptionally tall and also more beautiful by far than all the other young women. Now her outstanding strength and astonishing beauty made her rather proud and she turned down every man who came seeking her hand in marriage, considering that none of them was worthy of her. But during Herakles' campaign against Geryon, when he invaded Keltike and founded the city of Alesia, this young woman laid eyes on Herakles and was amazed at his prowess and at his splendid physique. After seeking her parents' consent she eagerly welcomed his advances. From her union with Herakles she bore a son named Galates who far surpassed his fellow tribesmen in the force of his character and the strength of his body. When he reached adulthood and took over his ancestral kingdom, he conquered many of the lands that bordered on his own and achieved many military deeds of renown. Famous for his courage, he named those he ruled over Galatai, and the whole of Galatia came in turn to take its name from them.[52]

Much about these accounts is very familiar. Herakles the culture hero, wandering and taming the West, is a familiar figure, as is Herakles the founding father of an ethnic group.[53]

This second story offers an account of how Celts and Gauls are related. Diodoros offers a different solution to this ethnonymic puzzle later on, Strabo offers a third version. Other variants appear in texts composed around the same time.[54] How Galli, Galatai, Keltoi, Keltai and other peoples were connected was clearly a matter of debate in the first century CE as scholars attempted to order and reconcile the various accounts at their disposal. Like scientists today, ancient geographers and historians tried to find a simpler order beneath the diversity of observed phenomena. Discerning a small number of wandering heroes, or a small number of original ethnic groups were alternative (although not incompatible) means to this end.

It also offers an aetiological explanation of the characteristic physiognomy of the Gauls. The princess was distinguished by her *megethos sōmatos* and her *euprepeia*, reiterated almost at once as her *sōmatos rhōme* and *thaumazomenē euprepeia*. She admires Herakles for his *aretē* and *sōmatos hyperochē*. Their son surpasses all those of his ethnos in terms of his *aretē psychōn* and *rhōmē sōmatos*. It is interesting to see how the qualities of the mother play as great a part in explaining the physical superiority of the Gauls as do those of Herakles. The reason, presumably, is that Herakles had so many offspring that differences among them have to be explained as deriving from the variation provided by his brides, notwithstanding the apparent conflict with received medical opinion on the contribution of the mother. It is also interesting to see the interplay in an ethnographic context of physiognomics and genealogy. More on this in chapter 2.

For the moment, however, I want to focus on the story of Alesia. First there is the complex narrative in which the city is first presented as the product of

Herakles' pacification of the lawless and xenophobic Gauls, at the end of the army's great wandering and so a stage in the civilizing process, and is then immediately presented as rebarbarized by the influx of natives. Is this more than the manoeuvring necessary to give the Gauls an ancient Heraklean mother city, and Caesar barbarian opponents? What does it say about Herakles' pacification of the Gauls that Caesar had to do the job again (and what does this say about the prospects for Gallo-Roman civilization if even Heraklean pacification is so easily undone)? Then there is the intrusion into the story of Julius Caesar, moving us abruptly out of the heroic age into very recent history. The gloss, that he was now proclaimed a god as a result of his deeds occurs elsewhere in Diodoros, but it perhaps has an extra resonance in Book 4 which is devoted to heroes and demigods.[55] The Herakles narrative follows an account of the wanderings of Dionysos and precedes the stories of the Argonauts, Theseus, the Seven against Thebes and other heroes. A foundation myth for a Gallic city, in whatever circumstances it was first conceived and spread, has been inserted into a larger narrative about civilization and the passage from myth to history.

Most striking of all, however, is the chronology of the invention of this story.[56] The date of the final revision of Diodoros' *Bibliotheke* is usually put in the late thirties BCE. The foundation of the colony of Tauromenium in 36 BCE is the latest event mentioned that can be dated, and there is no reference to Actium or the supremacy of a single man. Any work of this scale would have taken a long time to compose, of course, and some passages may have been effectively complete long before then, but the mention of Caesar's godhead shows this section was revised as late as 44 BCE. Yet Alesia, was a very minor hill-fort, not even a tribal capital, just the central place of the Mandubii, until Caesar invested it in 52 BCE. The creation of a mythic history for the town, and its elevation to be the mother city of Keltike, had evidently been very rapid indeed.

It is most unlikely that Diodoros invented the story, and we have no reason to think he ever travelled in Gaul. Nor was Caesar the source, since his *Commentaries* employ other means to make the siege of Alesia the culmination of his campaigns, and besides the etymology (Alesia from *ale*) works only in Greek. The exact circumstances within which this piece of ethnographic knowledge was first created are unknowable. But the most likely scenario involves the participation of Greek speakers and Gauls in the decade following the Gallic War, the development of a common story and its transmission via one or more stages to Diodoros. All this had to have happened within twenty years at most. It is a creation of the first generation of Roman Gaul.

Being able to pin down this story so precisely is a rare chance. But it is not without parallels. As will be clear, these tales have a number of family likenesses. They also share a contrast with images of Celts and Gauls created under different conditions. Rome's first encounters with populations from around and beyond the Alps were clearly terrifying, and mediated largely through violence. Unsurprisingly, the dominant themes of the earliest representations are the ferocity and size of their opponents. Polybios and Cato, both writing in the second century BCE, provide views of the populations of the Po valley.[57] Gauls emerge from both as thoroughly warlike. Polybios' Keltoi

> lived in unfortified villages, lacking any permanent buildings whatsover. Sleeping on straw or leaves, eating only meat, they were interested in nothing but war and farming: they lived simple lives without being acquainted with any science or art whatever. And each man's property consisted only of cattle and gold; as these were the only things that could easily be carried with them, when they wandered from place to place, and changed their dwelling as their fancy directed. They made a great point, however, of companionship: for the man who had the largest number of clients or companions in his wanderings, was looked upon as the most formidable and powerful member of his tribe.[58]

The austerity of their martial mobility – which owes something to their Scythian models – is moderated in Polybios' narrative and also in most of the fragments of Cato in which they appear. But the Gauls' obsession with warfare remains manifested in their fascination with weapons, their constant readiness for a fight, and their willingness to engage as mercenaries. For Cato too 'the greater part of Gaul follows two things with the most energy possible, warfare and fine speaking'.[59]

Polybios and Cato were already selecting from an existing literature in Greek that mentioned Celts.[60] This literature was not entirely devoted to their martial characteristics. Timaios, for instance, offered his own etymologically based genealogies for the Keltoi as the descendents of the nymph Galatea. Accounts written after those of Polybios and Cato, such as that of Poseidonios produced in the early last century BCE, would introduce (or reintroduce) information about their more exotic customs, diets, social manners, beliefs, theology and so on.[61] Caesar's Gauls too have their complex ethnographies as well as their ferocious *alterité*. One factor shaping the emphasis on mobility and ferocity in the accounts of Polybios and Cato was certainly the Mediterranean experience of migrations into Greece and Asia Minor in the early third century BCE.[62] But neither the Herodotean model offered by the Scythians, nor accounts of the sack of Delphi compelled imitation.

The reason the ethnographies of Polybios and Cato were so focused on the ferocity of the Gauls is that their accounts were not written on the middle ground. These ethnographies formed part of narratives of conflicts in northern Italy. It is these narratives that elongate the moral distance between

Gauls or Celts and their victims, partly because their authors have chosen to barbarize the Celts to emphasis the threat they posed to Romans, conversely presented as civilized, partly because conflict heightened the sense of difference.[63] It was war, and its narration, that deterred Polybios and Cato from integrating *their* Gauls into the common mythic landscape inhabited by Herakles and the refugees from the Trojan War, a landscape with which both were very familiar.[64]

The production of all these varieties of Celts offered subsequent writers many options. There is no simple line of development that may be followed. Representations of Gauls as ferocious, unpredictable and generally lacking in Roman virtues of discipline and dependability can also be documented in Latin prose of the late republic.[65] Those representations too presumably served the political and compositional needs of the larger projects of which they formed part. The solidification of a sense of Roman identity based on stability, urbanity and rationality made anti-types like the Celts 'good to think with', useful symbols, that is, of everything that the Romans claimed not to be themselves. Conversely, that stereotyping also made it difficult for Romans to think about actual northern populations in more mundane terms, or to recognize the many things they shared with their southern neighbours. It has plausibly been suggested that throughout history the Celts' reputation as unpredictable, labile and contradictory has in part reflected the distance between their normative categories and the presuppositions of those who observed, described and attempted to control them. The familiar was edited out of ethnography because it failed to distinguish them. The construction of more disciplinary ethics of behaviour in the metropolitan centre created the need for an anti-typical Other. The oppositional character that Celts came to embody made this an attractive identity in modern times for various groups who for other reasons felt marginalized by the rational-legal world of European nation states, and contributed to romantic idealisms of different kinds. Greek and Roman Celts would then be the very earliest avatars of this cumulative pattern of representation.[66]

Be this as it may, something new does seem to be emerging in stories like the romances of Alesia created in the decades following Caesar's siege. Here is Parthenios' version, written only a little later

> It is also said of Herakles that when he was bringing the cattle of Geryon from Erythea, his wanderings through the land of the Celts brought him to the court of Bretannus. This king had a daughter called Celtine. She fell in love with Herakles and hid the cattle, refusing to surrender them unless he first had intercourse with her. (2) Herakles was in a hurry to get his cattle back, but he was even more struck by the girl's beauty, and so he did have intercourse with her. When the time came around, a child was born to them, Celtus, from whom the Celts take their name.[67]

The name Bretannos and the interest in the etymology of Celts belongs entirely to the last century BCE but the story of the princess who seduced Herakes by hiding his beasts reworks the story that Herodotos attributed to Greeks living in Pontus about the ancestry of the Scyths.[68] Appropriately enough, given other components of their respective stereotyping, the ancestress of the Scyths hid Herakles' mares, while that of the Celts hid cattle.

The Archaeology of Spain

I am going to leave Herakles for a while with his princess of Keltike, while I consider another set of barbarian tales, these too created on the middle ground. The geographer Strabo gives this account of the researches conducted by Asklepiades of Myrleia who taught *grammatike* in the Spanish interior, presumably in the early last century BCE.

> After this city comes Abdera: this too is a Phœnician foundation. Above these places, in the mountains, can be seen the city of Odysseia with its temple to Athena as Poseidonios relates and also Artemidoros and Asklepiades of Myrleia, a man who taught *grammatika* in Turdetania, and wrote a description [*periegesis*] of the peoples of that region. He says that in the temple of Athena are displayed memorials [*hypomnemata*] of the wanderings of Odysseus, shields and the prows of vessels. And in Callaicia settled some of those who campaigned with Teucer: there were two cities there, the one called Hellenes, the other Amphilochi, for when Amphilochus had died his followers wandered into the interior. It is said that some of the followers of Herakles, and also some people from Messene settled in Iberia, and that a portion of Cantabria was occupied by Laconians, according to him and also others. Here too is the city named Opsicella, said to have been founded by Ocelas, who crossed over into Italy with Antenor and his children.[69]

Strabo's great compilation was organized not as a universal history, like the *Bibliotheke* of Diodoros, nor as a *Historia Naturalis* like that of Pliny, but as a *Geographia*. But if we disregard for a moment the differences in the grand design, the family resemblance is obvious. All three works were written for the most part in Rome, where the libraries first of aristocrats like Lucullus and Piso, and then of the emperors, made the production of great compilations possible.[70] Strabo's work was conducted during the reigns of Augustus and Tiberius, and this passage makes clear how much was already available by that time in those libraries, when he set about collecting barbarian tales for the books that covered the West.[71] Three authorities are cited by named here, each professing to write on the basis of autopsy, or at least on the basis of enquiries made on or near the spot. Unusually we know a little about each one. Artemidoros of Ephesos, who was probably the earliest, had visited

Punic Gades and asked questions of the local merchants there. Perhaps he had also consulted the priests at the temple of Melqart.[72] Most of his references to Spain concern maritime sites, of which a map of his may recently have come to light.[73] Poseidonios had also visited Spain, probably in the nineties BCE. Again a coastal periplus seems most likely. Asklepiades is the hardest to date but is usually considered a contemporary of Poseidonios: the Suda has him teaching in Rome at the time of Pompey.[74] A native of Myrleia in Bithynia, he was a grammarian, wrote commentaries on Homer and a book *On Orthography*. He alone had lived and worked among the peoples of the Guadalquivir valley, perhaps even learned some of their languages in the course of teaching them Greek. All three will have had access to local informants who probably included Greek and Italian traders and settlers and locals of Phoenician origin.[75] Quite possibly there were also Phoenician ethnographic speculations to be sought out, and maybe even Punic texts. Our visitors will also have encountered various Iberian peoples. Most likely their enquiries were conducted in Greek, perhaps also in Latin. Greek was the *lingua franca* across the Mediterranean but according to Strabo the Turdetanoi, who had an alphabet of their own, spoke Latin. Probably some knew more than the languages: it would not be at all surprising if education in *grammatike*, especially from a scholar like Asklepiades, involved the study of Homer.

We are not, in other words, dealing with the ethnographic myth of visitors arriving in a world hitherto unknown, to recover the local knowledge of isolated primitives as expressed in their own language. Rather this is an example of what James Clifford has called 'the Squanto effect', after the Patuxet Indian who met the Pilgrim Fathers when they arrived in the New World in 1620 and greeted them in English acquired during his own earlier visit to Europe, and helped them survive their first winter by acting as a mediator with the local population.[76] There are always Squantos, argues Clifford, and their role as translators and go-betweens is an essential part of cross-cultural encounters, one concealed by narratives of bold explorations of the unknown, or the heroic austerity of the participant-observer methods advocated by an earlier generation of anthropologists. If we ask who guided Artemidoros, Poseidonios and Asklepiades up into the mountains to the city of Odysseia (assuming they made the journey themselves and did not just take their guide's word for it) and who showed them the shields and *rostra* in the temple of a divinity explained to be Athena, our only possible answer is that it was local experts. Maybe those experts had learned about Odysseus in conversation with Greek or Roman visitors. Maybe they had read or listened to the *Odyssey* themselves. Either way the crucial conversations took place on the middle ground, in this case a barely governed Roman province taken from the Carthaginians and then largely left to its own devices. The stories are hybrids in the sense that the elements – Odysseus and Athene, a temple in the mountain – had been contributed by different parties. Even if we were to suppose the interpretative procedures employed to be wholly Greek in origin, there is no reason to think the etymological and syncretistic moves were all made by the visitors. After a while, local informants always know the kinds of answers for which visitors are looking. When Diodoros visited Egypt, the priests in Egypt recounted long lists of eminent Greeks who had consulted them seeking wisdom: the list began with Orpheus and Musaeus and included Homer, Lycurgus, Solon, Plato and Pythagoras.[77] Turdetania was hardly in the same league, but it was not *terra incognita* either.

What Strabo's authorities brought back from Spain were foundation stories couched in the Greek style. These materials were easily accommodated into the schematic master narratives such as the Herakles myth, the wanderings of Odysseus, the stories of the scattering of other Greek and Trojan refugees after the fall of Troy, and the mythology of the Spartan Mediterranean.[78] They were equally amenable to incorporation into universal histories, scientific geographies or other miscellanies. Strabo, who never says he had visited Spain himself, had no direct access to these stories, and although Asklepiades' history sounds as if it was based on his own researches on the middle ground, it is not impossible that both Poseidonios and Artemidoros made used of written accounts as well as what they discovered on their travels. Yet behind all these accounts we can infer conversations in which locals played a part in shaping the tales. Asklepiades may indeed have been gathering traditions, just as he seems to have said he was, rather than inventing them.

Establishing the authorship of Roman Spain's new past would be so much easier if we had Asklepiades' original monograph. But not only do we read him and his colleagues through Strabo's editorializing, but Strabo had his own interests too. The density of prior ethnography in Iberia provided Strabo with a wonderful case study through which to reflect on the methodology of ethnography, not least because so much of what he read of it consisted of earlier polemics. From the opening of the book we have Artemidoros correcting Ephoros and Eratosthenes, and Poseidonios challenging Artemidoros' statements. Artemidoros was clearly on the look-out for traces of Herakles and other heroes. Strabo's own standing as an ethnographer required him to join these arguments. But for Strabo, the real prize of Spanish ethnography was the chance to vindicate Homer. One long discussion[79] offers a quasi-allegorical notion of Homeric geography, equating Tartessos with Tartaris and locating the inspiration for the wandering rocks in both the Straits of Messina and those of Gibraltar. Homer, suggests Strabo, loosely fictionalized information supplied to him by Phoenicians, about their own explorations and about the historical expeditions of Herakles and Odysseus, and the wanderings of Aeneas, Antenor and the rest. What he had learned of the wealth of Spain led Homer to set the Elysian Fields in the west. Strabo knew, however, that this interpretation was controversial. After the account of the researches of Asklepiades of Myrleia, Strabo returns to Homeric geography, praising the work of Krates of Mallos that had made the poet the basis for scientific theorization (*epistemonikas hypotheseis*) and mounting an attack (probably aimed at Eratosthenes) on those who rejected Homer's authority and credulously believed Pytheas' accounts. Unlike the story of Alesia, the mythic history of Spain was being built quite slowly.

Native Wisdom?

Diodoros on Alesia and Strabo on Spain offer vivid glimpses of a process that was occurring much more widely. Sallust attributes part of his complex and bewildering ethnography of the peoples of north Africa to local testimony. It is on the basis of what the Africans say that he finds the ancestors of their various tribes in Persians, Armenians and Medes left over from Hercules' army. He also claims to base part of his account on Punic books written by King Hiempsal, translated for him by the locals.[80] What are we to believe? That we have access to the oral testimony of the indigenous inhabitants? That Sallust transmits Punic scholarship, and if so was it recent conjecture or ancient tradition? Who did the translation? Or are we reading a Roman interpretation of landscapes and peoples that were otherwise incomprehensible? What I have been suggesting is that ethnographic knowledge emerges not from one of these sources, but from an interplay among them. Making connections between Medes and Mauretanians – however bizarre such connections seem – on the basis of ethnonyms and the myth of Herakles' western expeditions, and moreover the expedition of a Herakles who died in the West, depended on combining information derived from different traditions. Where could they be put in contact if not on the middle ground?

One reason to believe this is so is suggested by the question of interest, *cui bono*? Who gained most from these elaborate compositions? This is the old problem of syncretism. Those who compiled great histories or geographies or other kinds of compendia were, at best, secondary beneficiaries. Strabo was able to make use of barbarian tales to advance his own views about the authority of Homer; about how to do geography; about the essential secondarity of the West and its dependence on a series of civilizing encounters, from Homeric explorations to Roman conquest; and to present himself as the latest and most judicious in a series of editorial presences. But this was not what the stories were made for. Their first tellings offered locals a place in a wider world of which they had only just become sensible.[81] By connecting local knowledge to one or another master narrative, barbarian tales anchored a little of what remained important to more powerful and enduring authorities. Seen from the native point of view, barbarian tales were exercises in cultural conservation, in the translation of cultural facts into a medium where their truth would be recognized. Conversely, for visitors from the wider Mediterranean world, the incorporation of local places, names, heroes and legends into the Great Tradition reassured them that the investigation of the West confirmed and reinforced existing truths, rather than challenged them. The conquest of Spain confirmed the authority of Homer, rather than revealing how little he knew. The early modern analogues are obvious.[82] Telling stories on the middle ground was a process of gift exchange, one that created relationships of value to both sides, and in the process created new valuables, new cultural goods that might immediately be appropriated by others and put to new ends.

The convergence of provincial and metropolitan interests in these new histories of the West is beautifully illustrated by one final example, that offered by the last two books of Pompeius Trogus' *Historiae Philippicae*. From the outset this work seems to advertise its hybridity, a Universal History, but in Latin not Greek, yet with a name that alludes to histories of Hellenistic kings. The title does not disappoint, for the centre of gravity is firmly Eastern, and yet when the author reveals himself, towards the very end of his work, we find a definitely western identity[83]

> At the end of the book [thus the epitomator] Trogus relates that his ancestors derived in origin from the Vocontii; his grandfather Pompeius Trogus was given citizenship by Gnaeus Pompey in the Sertorian War; his uncle led cavalry divisions under the same Pompey in the war against Mithridates; and his father served under Gaius Caesar as a secretary and an envoy and was entrusted with his signet ring.[84]

Trogus himself seems to have written in Rome, and to have completed his work during the reign of Augustus. Like Strabo of Amaseia, Timagenes of Alexandria and many others he was a reflective product of a Mediterranean drawn together and torn apart first by Roman conquest and then by Roman civil war.[85] Compilation, in so far as it involved excavating a connected whole out of all the discrepant experiences of those moved about by violence and upheaval, was an immensely topical project, and presumably also a personal one.[86] His work survives only in the epitome of Justin, but originally it was probably composed on the same scale as Diodoros' *Bibliotheke* or Strabo's *Geography* as it consisted of forty-four books and covered the entire period from the empire of the Assyrians and Persians to the Augustan conquest of Spain. Roughly the first quarter dealt with Greek history up to Alexander's conquest of Persia. The remainder followed the various Hellenistic kingdoms, with occasional detours to Carthage, Parthia and other surrounding areas. Romans appeared in the first forty-two books only when at war with other powers.

The final book offered an account of Spain, culminating in what may have been quite a short account of the period of Carthaginian and Roman rule in the peninsula. Assuming the epitome has not distorted the proportions, a large part of this book was concerned with the geography of the peninsula, its fertility derived from its favourable location, and its great natural resources not only of agricultural products, but also of metals, of flax, of horses and even of fish. The inhabitants are prototypes of Tacitus' Germans, sturdy and abstinent, preferring war to peace, and uncorrupted by bathing before the arrival of the Romans. Along with natural wonders, the book also included the same sort of genealogies that Strabo found in his sources. One story recounts the wanderings of Teucer between the fall of Troy and his foundation of the Gallician nation and the Amphilochi. Another group of stories, centred around Tartessos, evoke the Titans and the Curetes as background to an account of how a local king, Gagoris, made several attempts at exposing his daughter's illegitimate son. On each occasion the boy was suckled by different wild animals until, after being raised in the wild, he was recognized as heir to the throne and as king gave the people their laws and taught them agriculture. Trogus comments that the story would be implausible if similar ones were not told of the founders of Rome and of Cyrus the Persian. The myth-history of Spain concludes with a lengthy account of Geryon and Hercules. No sources are specified in the epitome, but it is specified that the three groups of tales relate to three different parts of the Spanish peninsula. Their overlap with Strabo is small. Trogus and Strabo were close contemporaries. We might almost imagine them bumping into each other in the same sections of the Palatine libraries or the *atrium libertatis* as each searched for the same rare copy of Asklepiades' *Iberika*. Yet their selections were evidently different. Who knows how many other Spanish tales were never excerpted and are now lost?

Trogus' personal interest emerges most strongly in the penultimate book of the *Historiae Philippicae*. It begins with a proem to the effect that after a long detour on Parthian and Eastern history, Trogus returns home to deal with the beginnings of the city of Rome, thinking that he would be an ungrateful citizen if, after narrating the history of every people, he was silent only about his homeland. This chapter certainly summarized a longer programmatic statement, and since Book 43 concludes with Trogus' autobiographical notice it is reasonable to read the whole as largely concerned with his self-representation, or what is sometimes called 'autoethnography'.[87] Yet it is a deliberately misleading introduction to the contents. The first part of the book is indeed wholly taken up with Roman antiquities, with the reign of Saturn over the Aborigines, with the legends of Faunus and Evander, of Hercules and Aeneas and the latter's marriage to Lavinia, the war with the Rutuli and the foundation of Lavinium and Alba Longa. *En route* Trogus discusses the origins of the quintessentially Roman festivals of the Saturnalia and the Lupercalia. The second chapter of the epitome is concerned with the story of Romulus and Remus, the third with the foundation of the city, the rape of the Sabine women and the conquest of Italy. So far, so conventional. But at this point, the narrative develops in a more surprising way. During the reign of King Tarquin, a Phocaean fleet suddenly appears, sailing up the Tiber to make an alliance with the Romans before going on to found Marseilles. A long account of the origins of the foundation of Marseilles follows. The Phocaeans' naval pre-eminence had led them to an exploration of the West. Having identified the site of the future Marseilles they sailed up the Rhône to make an alliance with the Segobrigian chief Nannus at just the moment when the latter was about to hold a competition for the hand of his daughter Gyptis. Unsurprisingly, she chose Protis, one of the Greek captains, who received with her hand the land on which to build Marseilles. There followed a war with the jealous Ligurians, but the eventual sequel was the civilizing of the Gauls, the spread of viticulture and oleiculture and the founding of cities. The epitome then provides a long account of conspiracy between the Ligurians and Nannus' successor, but the bravery of a Gaulish woman revealed the plot to her Greek lover and the Massiliots repelled the attack. The last chapter of the epitome relates the rise of the city, its alliances with Spaniards and Romans and its salvation once again, this time through a divine intervention by Minerva which persuades a native prince to make an eternal alliance with the Greeks. The final Massiliot tale has an embassy returning from Delphi hearing of the sack of Rome by the Gauls, and the city collecting gold and silver to recompense Rome. The story ends with honours paid to the Massiliots and an equal alliance with Rome, and the book concludes with the autobiographical notice I cited above.

It would be marvellous to have the full version of this book to see in detail exactly how Trogus wove together the origins of Rome, Marseilles and the early history of Gaul. Many of the motifs are easy to parallel, of course, in foundation literature: the Greek prince and the native princess, the legitimizing grant made by the old king, the need to found a city in violence are all familiar tropes.[88] But the juxtaposition of the myths of Rome and Marseilles invites us to find specific parallels, such as Protis and Gyptis recapitulating the story of Aeneas and Lavinia, with the Ligures playing the role of the Rutuli. There is no warning in the proem that we will have anything but Roman antiquities, so the Massiliot archaeology seems to brusquely interrupt that of Rome, almost as if Trogus was not sure which *patria* really mattered most ... or at least relished the effect of surprise. Then there are the synchronisms. Marseilles is evidently founded around the same time as the Roman republic. Quite possibly the final story connecting Marseilles, Delphi, the Gauls and Rome was worked up into one of those stories that connected the Gallic raid on the sanctuary of Apollo with their attack on Rome and the treasures of Toulouse.

Trogus evidently concluded this tour de force by inscribing himself into the deliberately tangled web of myths he set at the end of the Roman conquest of the world and of his own world history. The effort he put into signing off in this way makes very clear who had the most to gain from all this story-telling. Even if his family had graduated from supplying barbarian allies and aides-de-camp to rival Roman warlords to producing a scholar capable of combing the accumulated mass of Greek ethnography in the imperial libraries, Trogus presented himself as neither wholly metropolitan nor wholly provincial. He and his stories alike were hybrids, created on the middle ground where war and ethnography had opened up new provinces of the imagination.

2

Explaining the Barbarians

A Plurality of Paradigms

> Exceptionally tall and fair haired, almost all the Gauls are red-faced with
> terrible staring eyes, crazy for a fight and arrogant beyond belief. No party of
> foriegners could get the better of a single Gaul, especially if he is reinforced by
> his wife who is mightier than her husband and whose gaze is terrifying,
> especially when she swells her neck and growls, raises her great white arms
> and starts to rain kicks and punches with the force of wind up catapult.[1]

So wrote Ammianus, mixing in uncertain portions the testimony of Timagenes and other writers with his own experience. Comments of this kind were
commonplace. The massive stature of northern barbarians is one of the most
familiar features of their representation in ancient ethnographic writing.[2] We
are now accustomed to seeing this as one aspect of othering, with all the
ideological baggage that term now carries. I have already suggested some
reasons why ancient texts may have othered Gauls the ways they did. Ancient
writers, however, display less agreement about why northerners differed so
much from civilized (that is Mediterranean) norms.

In so far as physical anthropology confirms the tall stature of north
Europeans in antiquity, we are usually inclined to attribute it to differences
in diet. Eaters of flesh and drinkers of milk do tend to produce large children,
and there are some good reasons to believe that ancient Mediterranean
populations often produced small ones.[3] Ancient ethnographic texts show
little awareness of this. Classifying peoples by their diet was another

conventional device ever since Homer wrote of bread-eating mortals and set them in a world fringed by cannibalistic Cyclopes and effete Lotus Eaters. Hellenistic historians and geographers were quite used to differentiating ancient peoples on the basis of what they ate and how they ate it. Athenaios' *Banqueting Sophists* is a rich source of passages of this kind culled from writers such as Agatharchides of Knidos and Poseidonios. The former seems to have written mostly on the eastern part of the known world: his *Periplus of the Erythraean Sea* characterizes various populations of the coasts of Africa and Arabia by what they eat – fish, wild meat, calves – and the fragments of his other works include comments on the debilitating effects of gluttony and luxury.[4] Poseidonios and others wrote vivid accounts of the banquets of the Gauls. But no connection was apparently made between their characteristic diet and their great physical stature. Other answers were preferred to questions such as: Why were the Gauls so big?

The subject of this chapter is explanation. How did ancient accounts make sense of human diversity? Explanations are clearly important to much ethnographic writing, to judge from the space given to them. We should expect this from writing so closely entwined with history and geography, in both of which explanation was as important as description. Ethnography without an explanatory framework is in any case virtually unimaginable. Who could bear to contemplate or inhabit a world of random differences? Yet ancient ethnographic explanations mostly strike us as unsatisfactory. Accounting for difference draws ancient ethnography close to its modern analogues, and at the same time it reveals the distance between them. My aim is not to convict ancient ethnography of unscientific practices. But I am interested in why observation, recording and compilation in this sphere did not lead to the kind of specialized discourse we associate with medicine or mathematics, discourses where the accumulation of consensus and knowledge (some of it incorrect of course) does in some respects seem to resemble that conventionally termed the Scientific Revolution of the early modern period.[5] The explanatory frameworks appealed to in ancient ethnographic writing varied little from the earliest versions we have to the latest. They also seem incoherent and contradictory, even within the same text. How can we account for these deficiencies?

The great size of the Gauls offers a case in point. A variety of explanations was offered, one of which I have discussed already, the story of their descent from Hercules and a local princess of outstanding size as well as beauty. This account appealed to a familiar style of aetiology, one in which genealogy is a prominent element. We are used to calling this sort of explanation an example of myth.

Strabo and others offered a different kind of explanation, one based on the lands in which they lived. He begins his discussion of Keltike beyond the Alps with the tripartite division of its inhabitants into Aquitani, Belgae and Celtae:

Some divide it into three, distinguishing the Aquitanoi, the Belgai, and the Keltai. Of these the Aquitanoi differ completely from the other nations, not only in their language but in their bodies [*tois somasin*], which resemble Iberians more than Galatai. The rest are Galatai in countenance, but do not have a common language, some differing slightly in their speech; nor are their systems of government [*politeiai*] or modes of life [*bioi*] exactly the same.[6]

Strabo then goes on with a geographical account of the boundaries of Keltike, fixing each of its three main peoples in relation to rivers and mountain ranges, before going on to detail the administrative geographies created by Caesar and Augustus, the rivers of Gaul, its great natural fertility, limited only by the fact that the inhabitants of 'outer Keltikê' are warriors rather than farmers. He then proceeds to a survey of each part of the whole, but when this survey returns him to northern Gaul, he resumes his discussion of the temperament and physiology of the Gauls. 'The entire race which is now known as Gallic or Galatic, is mad about warfare, full of passion, and swiftly roused to a fight: yet in other respects they are simple and good-natured.'[7]

Strabo goes on to show how the impulsiveness of the Gauls can be exploited by cunning opponents and to praise the Gauls as easily biddable, and readily persuaded to more profitable pursuits including study (*paideia*) and speech (*logoi*). Their might comes from their large physique and also from their great numbers, as well as their tendency to come to the support of their neighbours when they have been treated unjustly.

Now indeed they are all at peace, for they have been enslaved by the Romans and live according to their commands [*prostagmata*]. But I have given this account of their customs as they were in former times, and also as they exist up to the present day among the Germans. For both in nature and in their form of government [*tois politeumasin*] they are very similar and they are also related to each other. They inhabit adjacent territory, divided by the river Rhine, and are for the most part similar – Germany, being a little more to the north – if we compare respectively the southern and northern parts of the two countries.[8]

Strabo goes on to illustrate their similarities, and to contrast these groups with the Iberians to the south. Just as the Aquitani form an intermediate group between Galatai and Iberians, so the northernmost Gauls – the Belgae – are the fiercest and most Germanic. Strabo then generalizes further about the common characteristics of northern peoples.

Strabo's discussion can be set in a long tradition of writing that asserted a strong connection between the harsh climate of the north and the physical, mental and sociological character of the peoples who live there.[9] By the time Strabo was writing a number of variants had been proposed on the theory that the world was divided into a series of latitudinal zones, *klimata*, each inhabited by a different kind of people. Strabo's own discussion is cast as a commentary on Poseidonios' critique of versions offered by Polybios, Aristotle and Parmenides.[10] It includes the information that Poseidonios named one zone after the Ethiopians and another after the Scythians and Keltoi, and criticizes him for overemphasizing the determinative effect of climate on the species of animals that live and flourish in each zone. These debates have as good a claim as any in antiquity to be termed scientific, with alternative versions judged in terms of how well they accounted for the data produced by observation.

On closer examination, however, Strabo's explanation turns out to be more complex. Germans and northern Gauls are alike *both* because they are kin, *and* because they inhabit the same regions. *Furthermore* they are unlike because the Gauls (nowadays) have become more civilized, while the Germans (still) remain barbarous. Genealogy, geography and history each suggest different patterns of causation. The factors are happily convergent in this case, yet they are notionally independent.[11]

Strabo's text is not at all unusual in tolerating the co-existence of several modes of explanation. This co-existence poses a special case of a problem already noted, that of the coherence of ancient accounts. Why was it considered acceptable to juxtapose mythic and physical geography, eyewitness accounts of exotic flora with the legends of Hercules and Antaeus, the location of Roman colonies and that of the land of the Lotus Eaters? These components seem to belong to different orders of knowledge. Worse, these different orders of knowledge had the potential to undermine each other. Naturally these orders could be made to coincide in particular cases, as Strabo does. But such a fix will not work in every case.

It is easy to imagine an ethnography based entirely on marvels, wonders and monstrosities at the edge of the known world. Much ancient writing fell into this category and myths of wandering heroes and fictive genealogies seem the perfect way of articulating it.[12] Equally, we can imagine an ethnography that grew out of mathematical geography, the researches of Eratosthenes and those strands of historiography we think of as Thucydidean and Polybian. Pliny's *Natural History*, with its grand explicit ordering that offers a systematic account of the world before locating man within it, seems to offer this: in practice monstrosity and historical contingency repeatedly intrude.[13] Yet the combination of the two systems seems unworkable. The inclusion of the fantastic seems to us to reduce the scientific plausibility of the remainder. Conversely, if the aim was to produce an entertaining farrago, why worry about the precise number of zones, or use an administrative record to document in numbing detail the legal statuses of all those tiny north African towns?

The problem is not unique to classical antiquity.[14] But it is a problem none the less. Genealogy and geography each offered general explanatory frameworks within which ethnographic data might be made to make sense. 'Might' is, in fact, too weak. All ethnographers need paradigms to enable them to interpret their harvest of oral testimony and observations. Paradigms of this kind are not only needed at the end of the process, during some period of 'writing up'. Paradigms are also vital during fieldwork, since the hypotheses and generalizations of which they consist serve to direct the gaze of the ethnographer. It is because they tell the ethnographer what to look for, and are also open to challenge by what he or she sees and hears, that fieldwork is often represented as a dialectical process. Education gives the observer insight that mere participants do not have, and the experience of participation allows her to offer an authoritative critique of those grand ideas to which those who have not shared her journey of discovery still subscribe. For these purposes, it does not matter very much whether a paradigm is based on wandering heroes or the effects of meteorology or social evolutionary schemas or a semantics modelled on structural linguistics. Even if they were less aware (or were accustomed to display less self-awareness in their texts) Asklepiades and all those others creating ethnographic knowledge on the middle ground were no different in this respect to modern anthropologists.[15] Without Homer in their heads, and perhaps some knowledge of the critical debate around its exegesis, the physical traces in the temple of Odysseia would have been incomprehensible. But a confusion of paradigms makes the signs less legible, and introduces not only ambiguity about their meaning, but even uncertainty about what counts as data.

Paradigms also contribute to the structuring of knowledge when it is encoded in text. Ethnography, after all, literally means 'writing people'. As a discipline of recording it always involves the translation of people into texts. Paradigms operate in some ways like master narratives, and in others rather like sets of generic conventions. Suppose one's understanding of the origins of the differences between peoples were to place a great emphasis on climatic differences between the lands they inhabit. Would it not be logical to precede ethnographies with accounts of the locations of each people and the climatic conditions of their abode? If, on the other hand, one were to explain the peculiarities of each people in terms of their ancestry, is your text not likely to employ genealogy as a structuring principle? This is, in a sense, the difference between the great compilatory projects of Strabo and of Diodoros. Other texts wrestle with combinations of the two, Herodotos allowing the narrative of Persian conquest to introduce a geographical conspectus of the world, Tacitus in the *Germania* offering but rejecting native genealogy in favour of geographical *ekphrasis* and so on.[16]

The modern critique of ethnography has shown other complexities in the relationship between analytical interpretation and 'writing up'.[17] One concerns the extent to which any written account imposes a certain level of systematization on knowledge. It has been suggested that one solution to the problem of apparent incoherence in pre-modern thought is to accept that knowledge may often, in fact, be held in an unsystematic form without posing intolerable cognitive dissonances. Classicists are most familiar with this through the arguments of Paul Veyne for what he terms *la balkanization des cerveaux* conventionally translated as 'brain-balkanization'.[18] Yet the mental reservations we employ to insulate, for example, our belief in the possibility of miracles away from our beliefs about what promotes road safety, may not work so well on the written page. As theorists of literacy have long argued, writing ideas down exposes them to new kinds of critique.[19] This may be used productively, to create new knowledge, new texts or both.[20] But it also risks making explicit incoherences that were hitherto concealed. For Pliny and others, writing up alien peoples in relation to *both* genealogical myth *and* climatic zones risked producing an incoherent text, even if the ethnographer in the field felt able to work out at any given moment which paradigm made most sense of Gallic head-hunting, and which of the temple at Odysseia in Spain.

Before considering some examples in more detail, let me remove a couple of tempting solutions from discussion.

First, it is not the case that we have two varieties or schools of ethnography in competition. Ancient writers certainly were competitive, and disagreed fundamentally about methods, as Strabo's discussion of Spain or of rival theories of the earth's zones illustrates. But unlike the case in medical or philosophical controversies, there is little sign that the protagonists found it easy to divide their predecessors into different camps. Strabo builds his reputation by correcting the mistakes of all the authorities (except Homer) on the West. Indeed, one key way of inserting oneself into a tradition was to focus one's criticism precisely on those authorities whom one wished to claim as predecessors.[21] Besides many texts blended elements of both these kinds of ethnographical explanation, just as Pliny's and Strabo's did. Nor does social location or formation offer much of an explanation. It is not easy to see why, for example, Diodoros chose to devote a book to wandering heroes, and Strabo one to mathematical geography when their backgrounds, education, working environments, reading matter and presumed audience were so similar.[22]

Second, there is no sign of a gradual encroachment of science into a space occupied by myth. It is possible to trace genealogical modes of argument back to Homer and forwards to Ammianus Marcellinus. Equally accounts of human diversity which related the peculiarities of each group to their location within the cosmos appear in the first Greek prose literature, the *Histories* of Herodotos and famously in the Hippokratic corpus. The only new mode of explanation that does enter, as will become clear, hardly contributes to a narrative of increased rationalization. My solution, then, cannot be cast in the form of a gradually dawning Enlightenment. Ancients certainly did not regard genealogy as less satisfactory than other mode of explanation. For some, the collection and reconciliation of myths of descent and foundation were themselves a systematic enterprise that followed particular rules and procedures. Elias Bickermann went even further in describing genealogically structured accounts of the past, *archaiologiai*, as themselves scientific, and stressed the resemblance between ancient and modern model-building: 'But are modern theories much better? The "Cro-Magnon" race of our textbooks or the "Semites" as the sub-stratum of "Semitic" languages are fictions of a different kind but hardly of a higher value than the Trojan myth of Rome.'[23]

The implicit injunction not to despise ancient research or ancient intellects is well made. Yet there are genuine differences between ancient and modern practice. One of these is that moderns are less tolerant of explanatory incoherence. Our criteria for a good explanation, that is, place considerable emphasis on its consistency with other explanations we hold to be plausible, as well as the goodness of its fit to the data. Unless the romances of Hercules can be shown to be consistent with account of human diversity based on the physical structure of the earth, then most ancient accounts fail that test, and they fail it repeatedly, from archaic Greece to late antiquity.

In the rest of this chapter I shall argue that the long co-existence of contradictory paradigms is related to the different functions they served in the *practice of* ancient ethnography. I shall also argue that this was made possible only because explanations were disciplined into serving complementary functions within individual texts. The price of such disciplining, I shall conclude, was an intellectual stalemate, one that reflects the lack of scientific progress in this field when compared with ancient medicine, engineering or mathematics. Polemics like those of Strabo served to build the authority of those engaging in them, not to refine either the body of knowledge or the methods employed by others. Specifically, such arguments did not result in the successive rejection of unsatisfactory accounts in favour of ones that fitted the data better and/or cohered better with other components of ancient knowledge.

The Uses of Genealogy

Let me begin then with genealogy in practice, and with another story created in the formative period of the empire, this time known to us from the account given in Livy's *History* of the Gallic invasion of Italy.

> About the Gauls' crossing into Italy there is the following story. At the time when Tarquinius Priscus reigned at Rome, greatest power among the Celtae – who form a third part of Gaul – was in the hands of the Bituriges. They provided a king

for all of Celticum. His name was Ambigatus and he was greatly distinguished on account of his talents and his own and the general good fortune. Gaul under his rule was so productive of crops and of people that it seemed hardly possible to control such a great multitude. The king, who was now an old man, wished to relieve his country of a population that might become a burden, and so he announced that his sister's sons, Bellovesus and Segovesus, two energetic young men, would each be sent to whichever new homes the gods granted them by augury. He promised them that they should lead as great a number of emigrants as they themselves wished so that no people might be able to stand in their way. Then, when the lots were cast, Segovesus was given the Hercynian Forest but the gods gave Bellovesus the far easier road into Italy. He set out, taking with him the surplus population of his tribes, the Bituriges and Arverni, the Senones, Aedui, Ambarri, Carnutes and Aulerci, and with great forces of infantry and cavalry marched into the lands of the Tricastini.[24]

Livy goes on to narrate in dramatic terms their crossing of the Alps, a route no one had ever taken before 'unless one is to believe the *fabulae* about Hercules'. They pass the Massilian colonists at war with the Salui, and taking that as a good omen for their own invasion, descend the Taurine pass, defeat the Etruscans on the Ticinus and on the basis of another omen founded a city. 'They called it Mediolanum [Milan].'

Livy's narrative has been much discussed,[25] and I will pick out only a few points. It has been noticed that the designation of the Celtae as a third part of the Gauls, and their location in central France is shared with Caesar, and also that the tribes Livy mentions seem to occupy roughly the locations they did in Caesar's day. As Livy's narrative was written and revised over such a long period, it is more or less impossible to establish a meaningful compositional date for any individual part. But the likelihood is that this story originated around the same time as Diodoros' account of Hercules' foundation of Alesia. Like Trogus' penultimate book it reflects an effort to synchronize Celtic, Massiliot and Roman history: the reign of Tarquin, the foundation of Massilia and the *Volkwanderung* of the Gauls are set alongside each other. So too is the foundation of Milan, which is set at the climax of the narrative. This suggests one possible geographical point of origin for this version, especially given Livy's home town was Padua.[26] Italian communities had been fictionalizing their origins for much longer of course, as the quantity of traditions recovered by Cato the Elder illustrates. But in the Transpadana we might expect this to take place a little later, and the citizens of Milan were described as *Galatai* as late as Plutarch, in an anecdote refering to the Augustan period.[27]

Livy's version of the origins of the Gallic invasion of Italy illustrates a number of features of material of this kind. One is the amount of apparently redundant detail, the significance of which is not always easy to disentangle. Why is Ambigatus king of the Bituriges, not otherwise an especially

prominent tribal group? Do the personal names have particular significances, now lost, or do they simply give the piece Celtic verisimilitude? Some
of this apparent redundancy may derive from a difference between the use to
which Livy put the story and its original intent and context, if it was created
as a legendary origin for Milan. The story also contains an attempt to
connect populations in Gaul, northern Italy and the Danube, at the point
when ancient scholars began to decide that Keltoi, Keltai, Galli, Galatai and
the rest were all essentially one people with a single ancestral heartland.

Livy's narrative reflects a number of ways in which genealogy might be
employed to map ethnic groups. The 'Celtic' populations of central Europe
and north Italy are linked to those of Keltike proper through the relationships
between the leaders. That the leaders of the paired migrations are the
nephews of Ambigatus and not his sons expresses a precise genealogical
distance, that the migrations are synchronized reflects a set of equivalences.
Other accounts exploit those equivalences further to relate the sack of Rome
to that of Delphi, the Pergamene victory to various Roman successes and so
on. But perhaps it also reflects an indigenous – Milanese? Transpadane?
Gallic? – way of thinking about the past.

It is not at all uncommon for societies in which kinship is an important
means of thinking about current social relations, to organize their past
through what have been termed 'genealogical charters'.[28] The study of
genealogies of the Tiv of Nigeria collected over a period of time has shown
how successive versions were often marked by changes in the names and
precise relationships, changes that kept pace with shifts in present-day social
and political relationships. Classicists are very familiar with Greek versions
of this, such as the so-called Hellenic genealogy that gave the eponymous
Hellen three sons, Aiolos, Doros and Xouthos, the latter being father to Ion
and Achaios. These fictions plausibly offered a map of the relationships
between Aeolian, Dorian, Ionian and Achaian Greeks. The three brothers
later acquired a cousin as a means of bringing the Macedonians into the
picture, if at a slightly greater distance, and there were other elaborations.[29]
Then there is Herodotos' account of how a famine in Lydia forced the
division of the people into two, one half staying behind, the other half of the
population being led away by his son to settle Etruria.[30] One of the latest
examples surviving is Tacitus' account of German origins.

> In ancient lays, their only type of historical tradition, they celebrate Tuisto, a
> god brought forth from the earth. They attribute to him a son, Mannus, the
> source and founder of their people, and to Mannus three sons, from whose
> names those nearest the Ocean are called Ingvaeones, those in the middle
> Herminones, and the rest Istaevones. Some people, in as much as antiquity gives
> free rein to speculation, maintain that there were more sons born from the god
> and hence more tribal designations – Marsi, Gambrivi, Suebi, and Vandilii –
> and that those names are genuine and ancient.[31]

It is almost irresistible to compare the successive versions of the myth gathered by Tacitus to the changing genealogical charters that Laura Bohannan documented for the Tiv.

Genealogical myths offer a rather versatile means of relating ethnic groups. First, there is their capacity to create a ranked order of relationships, one through which ethnic groups are not only related but also assigned relative seniority, and through which some relationships are presented as closer than others. Second, by linking these groups to stories of migrations, it is possible to extend a set of relationships over considerable distances. The utility of this in the polydiasporic world of the ancient Mediterranean hardly needs to be underlined. Migration myths of this kind have come to be referred to as a Sacred Spring, a *ver sacrum*, and some historians have even believed this was a genuine Italian custom, a device to relieve actual over-population.[32] More likely Italian peoples had adopted this style of genealogical fiction from the Greeks, regarding it as a merely conventional way to explain and express close relations between distant peoples, and also one which would be acceptable to Greeks.[33] An unexpected benefit for a few who had picked the right ancestors – there are examples from Aphrodisias to Eryx to the Aedui of Burgundy – was the chance to claim kinship with Rome through related myths of origin. The power of genealogy to connect is less often stressed than the capacity of other kinds of ethnography to distance 'other' barbarians. In fact the medium offers the potential to bind together a world of strangers, as much as to put moral distance between antagonistic parties. The world in which Hercules and local princesses could wed and have human children was distinguished from the outer circles inhabited by human–animal hybrids as well as from the inner sphere of ancient peoples.

A final potential offered by genealogy was that of situating particular individuals or families at the centre of an ethnic history. This capability in fact depended on a set of necessary underpinnings to any account that tried to relate entire peoples genealogically. Genealogies were presumably first employed in the way they appear in Homer, as a means of relating individual heroes and establishing their credentials. A powerful case has been made that this sort of 'genealogical thinking' lies at the origin of the notion of a Hellenic people.[34] One could, I suspect, frame a similar argument for the creation of the Celts, if on the basis of much less evidence. When the individual eponyms were located sufficiently far back in mythic time, it was possible to claim that an entire people was descended from one individual or one coupling, like the union of Hercules and Keltike that produced the eponymous Galates. More often the relationship between leaders simply has to stand for that between peoples. So Aeneas and Lavinia express the union of Trojan and Italic strains and Protis and Gyptis that of Massiliots and the Segobrigii. Other myths described mass marriages (or rapes) of indigenous women by male incomers.[35]

Occasionally some care is taken to stress the links between their followers. Bellovesus does not lead out half the tribes but rather a surplus from each of the tribes, rather as if the Celtae had undergone a kind of binary fission, leaving two entities in each of which the same parts were represented. Herodotos has the division of the Lydians bisect families, and has it conducted by lot, another means of making each side in some notional way equivalent to the other. Or the distinction may be deliberately blurred, as when Lucretius dedicates his poem to *Venus Aeneadum Genetrix*, that is, Venus ancestress not just of the Iulian *gens* but of all the Romans. That case is simply the best known of a series of legendary genealogies created at the same time, just as Rome's Trojan foundation myth was just one of many.[36] How fictional was this? The prominence in many accounts of the ancestor of the tribe, the *Stammvater*, has been linked by some to the idea that ethnogenesis in both prehistoric and early mediaeval Europe may have been produced by a process of *Stammesbildung* in which disparate elements 'coagulated' around an aristocratic clan which then provided a unifying identity and story of descent.[37] Whether this was often or seldom the case in reality, the assimilation of dynastic and ethnic lineages had obvious ideological functions.

Those functions changed over time. The interpenetration of a dynastic tradition and that of an entire people might have an original political purpose. Classicists are familiar with the Augustan interweaving of the story of the Julian *gens* with that of Rome in epic, monuments and cult. Presumably such moments were common in prehistory too. Perhaps too, in the chaotic conditions of the early principate, Augustus provided an exemplary model for provincial magnates at the centre of new states, cities and tribes.[38] Subsequently the figure of a *Stammvater* – historical or not – might provide a point of common orientation for different lineages, a necessary organizing point for genealogies designed to claim kinship. Tacitus' account of the variant versions of the story of descent from Mannus suggests he had no illusions about the fictive nature of these genealogies. Only at the very end of all these uses does the common ancestor provided an organizing principle for the ancient ethnographer.

The genealogical paradigm did, however, have clear utility for the creation of ethnographic knowledge. For the ethnographer in the field, whether a Greek schoolmaster or a local *érudit*, it offered a way to characterize any given people. Instead of asking 'Does this people have segmentary opposition?' or 'Are they Bantu speakers?' the ethnographer asks 'Who were their ancestors?' This paradigm directed attention to ethnonyms and toponyms, cults, traditions and just occasionally customs and monuments. Like the objects of twentieth-century ethnography, the locals were not considered to possess accurate knowledge themselves. But they could supply clues on the basis of which the ethnographer, employing his expert training in the linked practices of observation and theorizing, could generate ethnographic knowledge. One might almost say that interpretative paradigms were the main things that ancient ethnographers brought to their encounters on the middle ground. Not entirely, since they also needed facts of their own – the names of Trojan heroes, *nostoi* narratives and the like – with which to connect local names and legends. But while both parties contributed data, it was, to begin with, the Greek and sometimes Roman investigator who knew how to join them up into convincing wholes.

The work of teachers like Asklepiades, of course, meant that soon locals could become their own ethnographers. The stories of Hercules and Odysseus were not difficult to learn, and certainly more accessible than the master narratives of today's ethnography. Trogus was a western example of what was apparently a common type, the local *érudit* who had learned enough of metropolitan conventions to generate home-grown ethnography.[39] That learning included two components: first, a sense of the conventions and methods of ethnographic writing, and second, knowledge derived from classical sources. Homer was an essential but in some cases, at least, more recent works were also consulted. The relationship formed between local histories and compilatory ones was recursive, each informing the other. The process is difficult to trace in detail in the West, but there are suggestive Eastern analogues. Consider the *Babyloniaka* written in the early years of the Seleucid kingdom by Berossos, certainly drawing on written Mesopotamian sources but framed in ways that cohered with Greek historiography. This autoethnography was an important source for the compilatory work of Cornelius Alexander Polyhistor, a Milesian captured during the Mithridatic Wars, freed by Sulla and writing in Rome throughout the middle of the last century BCE. Polyhistor's many writings were then used in turn not only by other authors of compilatory texts, including Pliny and Eusebius, but also by Josephus in his own Hellenizing *archaiologia* of the Jews.[40] As prolific as Alexander Polyhistor was Juba II of Mauretania, whose works, composed in the Augustan period, included books on Arabia and on Libya – which drew on earlier compilations and local traditions and were in turn used by Mela, Pliny the Elder and others – and also a Roman *archaiologia* used by Plutarch.[41] Plutarch was, however, sceptical of the claims of the Tingitani of Mauretania that Juba was descended from Diodoros, the grandson of Hercules, and Tinga the widow of Antaeus, who had established a kingdom there using the remnants of Hercules' Greek army. Behind the story can be dimly imagined attempt by the Tingitani to find links to their new client king, and by Juba to create a respectable Greek and heroic genealogy for himself.[42]

The recovery of the details of descent and migration might be a scientific project, but it was not always really an historical one: the prehistory of barbarian peoples was too uncertain, and so recourse had to be made to rather vague heroic ages and significant synchronizations. But this mattered very little, since for Rome's new western subjects – as for the Tiv – what mattered was the relevance of these relationships to their *contemporary* world. The new knowledge produced was framed in ways that conformed to an international standard, and made use of widely recognized authorities and techniques of authorization. As a result, what genealogical ethnography recovered was often of real use to local communities, as they sought new identities for themselves in relation to the dominant modes of intellectual discourse of the Roman world.

Geographical Understandings

What of the practice and uses of the other main method of ethnography, that which related the peculiar features of ethnic groups to their location in the physical universe, to the territories they occupied and the climatic characteristics of those regions?

The most famous and earliest account of the influence of geography and climate on character is that given in the Hippokratic *Airs, Waters, Places*. The first part discusses in generalizing terms how the medical anthropology of peoples varies according to the winds to which they are exposed, the water supplies they use, and the effect of seasonal weather. No specific locations are mentioned, and attention is focused on characteristic diseases of each environment. The second part (12–24), perhaps originally a separate work, begins with a long comparison of Asia and Europe, arguing for essential differences between the two. A lost portion dealt with Libyans and Egyptians and a long and detailed ethnography survives of the Scythians. At this point the text seems most concerned to show the main causes of the differences in physique and mental qualities between different peoples. Latitude is invoked, but so is elevation, the extent to which seasons differ from one another, and the quality of soil as well as water. Although there are points of difference, the conceptual geography has often been compared to that of Herodotos, especially in the comparison of Asia and Europe and the general sense that some countries naturally breed hardier peoples than do others.[43] At just one point does the author confront alternative paradigms. Discussing in chapter 16 why Asians are less belligerent than Europeans he invokes first the uniformity of the seasons but then goes on to invoke, as a secondary factor, their *nomoi*, specifically the fact that Asians are ruled by kings. This means they have no incentive either to fight or to work hard in the fields since the kings benefit from anything they achieve, the result being that their lands are so poor that even if someone who is by nature brave and full of energy is born there, his character is changed by the local customs.

> Of this I can give a clear proof. All the inhabitants of Asia, whether Greek or barbarian, who are not ruled by despots, but are independent [*autonomoi*],

labouring for their own advantage, these are the most warlike of men. For it is for their own sakes that they run their risks, and they personally receive the rewards for their own bravery and pay themselves the price of any cowardice. You will find some Asians also differ from one another, some being superior, others inferior. The reason for this, as I have said already, is the change of the seasons.[44]

Should we read this a concession that *nomoi* or even Greekness is an independent variable and that climate and geography do not explain everything? Perhaps this is too much to build on one short observation.

It is very striking how many of the ideas employed by the much later writers I have been discussing seem already to be in place in this passage. The theory of the effects of place and climate on lifestyles and physiques was a paradigm that began simple and was increasingly elaborated as a result of being applied to more and more data and criticism.[45] It is true that our information is not good enough to trace the earliest development of these ideas and perhaps it was complex. There is no mention in *Airs, Waters, Places* of the division of the world into five or six zones. But this idea originated in roughly the same period, if Poseidonios was correct that the idea was developed by Parmenides of Elea, and his writings on the cosmos certainly included humans as well as celestial phenomena. Mathematical geography had developed a knowledge of the spherical earth during the early Hellenistic period. It may be, of course, that in Poseidonios' attribution of the notion of *klimata* to Parmenides we are seeing the same sort of move as the recuperation of Homeric geography by Krates of Mallos and Strabo. Perhaps, that is, Poseidonios was attributing to an ancient authority modern geographical ideas that simultaneously protected his status and gave legitimacy to new conjecture. There are plenty of early modern parallels. Perhaps the safest conclusion is that all the components of this style of ethnography can be attested from the fifth century BCE, but that they are combined and formulated in slightly different ways in each extant text. There seems, however, to be neither an emerging consensus nor a consistent trajectory of debate over the centuries within which these texts were composed.

There are in fact striking differences among those authors who make use of what I shall call the climatic paradigm. Some are surprisingly fundamental. Consider the blackness of Ethiopians. The second book of Pliny's *Natural History* offers a whistle-stop tour of the world, taking in astronomy, meteorology and the shape and structure of the earth. A pair of chapters (189 and 90) deal with what follows from heavenly causes.

> For there is no doubt both that the Ethiopians are blackened by the heat of the nearby Sun, and are born as if scorched with curly beards and hair while the cold at the opposite end of the world produces people with white, frosty skins

and long blond hair. These are made fierce by rigour of their climate, while the former wise because of the changeability of theirs.[46]

The effects of climate, Pliny goes on to argue, can also be demonstrated in relation to the legs of southern and northern people, their relative stature, colour, the efficacy of their senses and intellects, and in terms of their social institutions.[47]

Now consider Vitruvius' version at the beginning of his sixth book

> For in those places where the sun pours out his heat more moderately, he keeps the body in good condition. Where he comes closer to earth he scorches it and removes the moisture. On the other hand in those regions that are colder, because they are so far from the south, the moisture is not drawn out from their complexions, but rather the dewy air from the sky pours moisture into the body, leading to greater stature and deeper voices. This is the reason why the northern races are nourished, are taller, fairer skinned and have straight red hair, blue eyes, and plentiful blood, owing that is to the abundance of moisture and the cool climate.[48]

It will come as no surprise to hear that Vitruvius goes on to argue that southerners are parched, short, dark skinned and curly haired, that their blood is thin and although hardy when it comes to withstanding heat, they are terrified of warfare, which northerners of course love. This passage illustrates very nicely the constraints and freedoms allowed by the climatic paradigm. Common ground is that northerners and southerners differ, and the main ways in which they differ are not at issue. But the mechanisms seem quite different. Vitruvius' account depends on an assumption that moisture is the key variable in determining the physical, psychological and social anthropology of each group. Pliny's very short passage also focuses on heat, but here the effects are not mediated through a discussion of moisture but rather of the effects of temperature on the *outside* of the body, singeing southerners black and leaving northerners frosty and pale. The similarity of Pliny's and Vitruvius' statements seem to be literally superficial: that is to say while they have a common notion that latitude is related to human variation, this does not rest on an agreed set of scientific principles or explanatory mechanisms. It is, in fact, possible to find ways to reconcile their accounts but this depends on developing a model of moisture in the growth of the human body and the formation of physignomic and psychological difference. Neither deems it necessary to refer to a model of this kind.

One reason for their differences of emphasis, is that the paradigm is being put to different uses in each of the two texts. Pliny's comments offers human variability as one respect in which the parts of the world differ: others include variable susceptibility to earthquakes (also attributed to celestial influence), the variable number of hours of daylight and the different constellations that may be seen. Pliny's ethnography here, then, is a detail in the depiction of the macrocosm. In Vitruvius' case he is working in the other direction towards a discussion of the need for private residences to be optimized for the weather of the region in which they are built. His capacity to marshall his knowledge of geography and climate to this end illustrates the need for the architect to be learned. Neither is concerned with a general theory of human physiology.

The aims of the author or authors of *Airs, Waters, Places* were different again. The opening claimed a didactic purpose aimed at equipping physicians to take account of local environmental factors, although the Scythian ethnography is hardly compatible with this objective. More importantly, the desire to contrast Asia and Europe exposes some limitations of a paradigm based largely on latitude, given that this does not differentiate the continents. That circumstance compels the author to take into account differences between peoples who occupy the same climatic zone. Other variables such as elevation, aspect and water supply help here. Finally, when the discussion of the Scythians moves from characterizing their commonalities to differentiating individual tribes, environmental factors are increasingly useless.

The climatic paradigm was best at explaining *similarities* between neighbouring peoples. It operates in the present tense. It might offer answers to questions such as 'Why do Gauls and Germans have so many social features in common?' But it would have contributed little to detailed accounts of the tribes of Spain of the kind written by Asklepiades, accounts that sought to uncover historic depth and connections that were not obvious. Climatic ethnography would perhaps have been of little utility to the peoples themselves. Knowing why one was the colour or shape one was, was of little use compared to knowing that you were descended from Antenor or Hercules (or related to Juba or the Romans). No city ever portrayed its climate or typical physiognomy on a coin. Nor was knowledge of this kind of any use in diplomacy.[49] It is unlikely that locals were particularly concerned to develop notions of their own distinctive temperaments: it is a modern idea that the French, English and Germans should have 'national characters' of which they might be proud. The ancient consensus on temperament tended to favour balance, and stigmatized alien peoples from departing from it. Climatic ethnography, it follows, really was of interest mostly to outsiders.

What precisely was the utility of the climatic paradigm for ethnography? Explanations cast in these terms might be useful for discussing ethnographic variability at a very large scale, but would have been of much less use in the field. There were simply insufficient geographic variations between the territories occupied by Rome's new subjects for this method to have been employed by local or visiting ethnographers keen to discover the particularity of Milan, Turdetania or Gaul. Nor was the raw data from which ethnographic knowledge was generated that helpful for this kind of argument. Oral traditions, local customs, cults, place-names and monuments were difficult to explain in these terms. The paradigm instead directs attention to differences of physiology, including appearance, strength and medical susceptibilities, and to a lesser extent to temperament. Most of the populations observed by ancient writers were not sufficiently physiologically varied, nor were the places they inhabited so sharply differentiated from one another climatically, to make local comparison possible. It was quite another thing when comparisons were made between peoples living far apart – Scythians and Ethiopians for example – but few of those writing ethnographic texts will have travelled widely enough to describe them at first hand.

Perhaps the climatic paradigm was most useful to the writers of geographies, universal histories and other synoptic works: as a means of organizing, that is, vast works like those of Poseidonios, Strabo and Pliny. Works composed on such a scale, from Herodotos' *Researches* to the encyclopaedic projects of the Hellenistic and Roman periods, operated with a presumption that the cosmos was an ordered entity. That presumption was common ground in ancient thought.[50] It is natural enough that most of these works discovered human diversity to be patterned in ways consonant with one or another cosmic ordering principle. This could take the form of correlating deviance with distance from a normalized centre, whether Herodotos' Greece or the Italy of Virgil, Strabo and Pliny. It might be a matter of showing how human customs and bodies reflected the different climatic zones of the world from the Arctic to the Equator (and sometimes in one or more opposed mirror-worlds).[51] The earth might be divided into one or into two continents, with lines of symmetry set on the Equator, between Europe and Asia or along the long west–east axis of the Mediterranean. The circularity of the inhabited world might be invoked, or the spherical nature of the globe. Some of these cosmologies look quite scientific to us: the diameter of the globe had been calculated with some accuracy by Eratosthenes; the Arctic Circle and the Equator are still key components of our geography; dividing the space between into zones characterized by particular climates is also familiar.

Other cosmological orders strike us as utterly mythological. The idea that at the edges of the earth the boundary between humans and animals broke down with the occurrence of satyrs and dog-headed peoples is a good example. Yet this latter cosmology found favour from Herodotos to the high Middle Ages.[52] None of these cosmologically orientated ethnographies is easy to reconcile with those based on descent from culture-heroes, but the boundary between them is not one between science and myth. The key difference was whether a given people was to be situated in relation to its physical location in the present-day cosmos, or rather to its place on a genealogical tree that extended back to the heroic age. Diodoros, Dionysios and perhaps Trogus show it was not impossible to order universal history on genealogical principles. But cosmology offered the prospect of connecting human to other kinds of diversity: perhaps the growing sense of the exotic difference of the non-Mediterranean world made that all the more attractive. Improving ethnography often took the form of finding new ways to relate human difference to the structure of the cosmos.

The major intellectual advance in this respect, during the Hellenistic period, was the arrival of astrology. Our main exemplar of the interpenetration of ethnographic and astrological discourse is provided by the *Astronomica* of Manilius written in the late Augustan or early Tiberian period.[53] Astrological methods and knowledge based on Babylonian practice spread through the Mediterranean world, in part thanks to Berossos as it happens, during the early Hellenistic period. The fundamental basis of the system was the notion of a celestial sphere on which the fixed stars were located, and which rotated relative to the earthly sphere which had been measured and described by Eratosthenes and Poseidonios. Fitting the celestial objects around existing models of the cosmos was a relatively easy task. In so far as this represents the astronomical elaboration of a geocentric cosmos this seems quite scientific to us; in so far as it implied sympathetic connections between earth and the heavens it seems the reverse. But our distinction between astronomy and astrology was not shared by Greeks and Romans, any more than it was by early modern scientists like Newton.[54] Babylonian astrologers had observed the wandering movements against this sphere of the seven planets – the sun, the moon, Mars, Mercury, Jupiter, Venus and Saturn – which they regarded as divinities, and also of other transient objects such as comets. The movement of the sun defined the zodiacal constellations. The movements of the other planets were sufficiently complex to allow any given moment of time to be characterized by their unique combination: significances might then be given to the combinations on particular days, such as birthdays (in the casting of natal horoscopes), moments of crisis (such as the murder of Caesar) or particular signs (such as comets). Manilius' poem, unusually, paid little attention to the planets which allowed ancient observations to be mobilized as a system of divination. Instead, the text as we have it seems more concerned with presenting the intricate structure of the cosmos and the mathematical interrelation of its parts. Zodiacal geography is a natural component of this exposition, showing how the diversity of human physiologies and customs can be considered in microcosmic relation to the grand structure of the heavens.[55]

Manilius in Book 4 follows a detailed account of the zodiac with a short survey of the world, introducing his explanation of how each part is ruled by a different constellation. The cardinal points are outlined and the winds that blow from them, the land (*tellus*) is located in the midst of the sea, and the shape of the Mediterranean is described in a clockwise *periplus* in which each land is briefly characterized by products or historical events. The three continents are then characterized: Libya has its complements of serpents, poisons, elephants, lions and apes; Asia is wealthy, vast and exotic; and Europe is 'the greatest land for men and most fertile in noble cities'. Unsurprisingly, after noting the huge stature of Germans, the wealth (*census*) of Gaul and the ferocity of Spain, Manilius' geography concludes with Italy and Rome.[56] Manilius then claims that the creating deity has assigned to each zodiacal *tutela* one part of the world to watch over, along with its cities and peoples, over which the constellations should assert their special powers, just as each *tutela* does over a separate part of the human body.

> For this reason the human race is so arranged that its practices and features vary: nations are fashioned with their own particular complexion; and each stamps with a character of its own the like nature and anatomy of the human body which all share. Germany, towering high with tall offspring, is blond; Gaul is tinged to a less degree with a near-related redness; hardier Spain breeds close-knit, sturdy limbs. The Father of the City endows the Romans with the features of Mars, and Venus joining the War-god fashions them with well proportioned limbs. Quick-witted Greece proclaims in the tanned faces of its peoples, the gymnasiums and the manly wrestling-schools.[57]

And so on. Manilius goes on to decode the differences.

What he offers, however, is not an alternate explanation for human diversity, but rather an *additional* set of factors. His Ethiopians are still burnt by the sun, with Indians and Egyptians less burned because their climates are more moderate. Humankind varies in language and customs. Their foods vary with the different products of each part of the earth. Exotic spices and animal species illustrate how differentiated the world is. At the very general level, Manilius asserts, this variation reflects the different influences of different zodiacal constellations. More specifically, however, the relationship between signs and peoples are left vague. Libra rules over Italy, Gaul and Germany under Capricorn. Libra is appropriate because the balance represents the fact that it measures all things, because the equal length of days and nights makes it the normalized centre, because Rome raises and depresses the fortunes of peoples placed in the scales. Capricorn is appropriate for Germany because it is a hybrid of man and beast (like all barbarians) and because it is ambiguous between land and sea, like Germany itself with its tides. Like Strabo's *Geography* the *Astronomica* offers a topical account of an apparently static system, a vision of the enduring cosmos normalized for the Roman empire of his day.[58]

Manilius was not a lone voice. Another account of the influence of the stars on the physiology of the inhabitants of different *klimata* is contained in the second book of the *Tetrabiblos* of Ptolemy, a Greek account of astrology in prose composed in the second century CE, but sometimes thought to depend on much earlier texts, even perhaps on Poseidonios.[59] Ptolemy's Ethiopians are shrivelled and blackened by the southern heat, and his Scythians are pale, tall, long-haired because they have more moisture and savage on account of the cold. Peoples who live between them, close to the zodiac, are intellectually superior, better able to pursue mathematical and astrological calculations; those in the east (where the sun rises) are more masculine, those in the west more feminine. Plants and animals in each region follow the same tendencies, in so far as they can. Each part of the world is under the influence of different stars. So the north-west quadrant, that includes *Keltogalatia* and may be equated to Europe, is under the influence of the constellations Aries, Leo and Sagittarius and the planets Jupiter and Mars: this explains why the men who live there are warlike, lovers of liberty who are endowed with qualities of leadership, cleanliness and magnaminity (*megalopsychia*) but also why they prefer sex with other men to sex with women. Places and nations within this quadrant can be further differentiated. Britain, northern Gaul, Germany and Bastarnia are under Aries and Mars so their inhabitants are fiercer and more bestial than those of Italy under Leo and the sun.[60] Ptolemy continues to subject each of the other quadrants to the same treatment, systematically laying down a general baseline of behaviour before going on in the next book to explain how the stars affect the character of individuals. Yet the mechanisms of explanation, in which the planets as well as the zodiacal constellations play a major part, are quite different from those employed by Manilius nor is there any allegorical argument from the character of the lions, scales and so on. There is a similar sense, however, of new science wrapped around a very old image of the world.

Astrology, in both Manilius' *Astronomica* and Ptolemy's *Tetrabiblos*, operates to reinforce that paradigm through which ethnographic difference is made meaningful by contextualizing it within the greater structure of the cosmos. Or is the relationship, at least in Manilius, the reverse? Are tropes of ethnography deployed to differentiate the zodiacal constellations and reinforce the connectedness of heaven and earth which is the real theme of his poem? Neither move (and they are not mutually exclusive) looks to us much like a real scientific advance. No older ideas are rejected to make way for new explanations, and the potential for incoherence seems to have been increased. Yet the application of astrological observation is one of the few new developments in the theorization of ethnography that can be observed throughout Greco-Roman antiquity.

Avoiding Debate

It has become a truism to assert that ancient science was intensely agonistic. The contests for authority staged by Polybios and Strabo with the texts of their predecessors, and the polemic tone of so many of the discussions from which I have quoted, seem to support that case. The *agon*, the zero-sum competition for *kudos*, in the sense of publicly recognized primacy, pervades passages like these. And yet, contradictory and incompatible forms of explanation seem never to be matched against each other. Genealogy and astrology seem natural opponents, better matched than Rhetoric and Poetry. Yet great care seems to have been taken to avoid such a showdown.

Consider how all these different paradigms *might* have been put into relationship with one another. One factor could have been given priority: climate perhaps might be treated as the main influence on human physiology, with genealogical factors shaping how each population responded to it. This sort of multi-factorial explanation is very familiar to us, and we employ it in some of the same terrain. Understanding why some people are more susceptible to particular medical conditions often requires us to consider the interplay of genetic and environmental factors, and perhaps lifestyle too. But there is little attempt in ancient ethnographic writing to develop arguments of this kind.

Another tactic would have been to use different kinds of explanation for different kinds of terrain: the outer edges of the world might have been dealt with in terms of their exotic environments, the civilized interior in terms of genealogy. One model might have been the contrast between the way Herodotos deals with the *logoi* of alien peoples, collected in one part of the text and ordered systematically, and his portrayal of individual Greek cities and families, typically dispersed across a complex web of narratives articulated by memory. Yet this path was not consistently followed either.

In just a few passages of a very few texts, it is possible to read some consciousness of inconsistency and some attempt to reconcile it. I have already discussed the implications of the observation in *Airs, Waters, Places* 16 that both the Greeks and the barbarians who live in Asia and are not subject to kings, are warlike, which could be read as a claim for the priority of *klimata* and/or *diata* over *genos*. Then there is Strabo's criticism of Poseidonios for overstressing the influence of *klimata* relative to what we would probably term cultural factors.

> For the various distributions [of plants, animals and weather (*aeron*)] do not come about by design [*pronoia*], any more than do differences between nations or languages, they all depend on accident and chance. Most of the arts, capabilities and institutions, once someone has invented them, will flourish in any one of the *klimata*, and even despite their influence. Some local peculiarites derive from nature, others from institutions and education [*ethos* and *askesis*]. For it was not due to a peculiarity in their nature that the Athenians cultivated eloquence, while the Lacedæmonians and even the Thebans, who lived even nearer still to them, did not do so: the key variable was the different *ethos* of each. Nor are the

Babylonians and Egyptians philosophers by nature, but by reason of their *askesis* and *ethos*. Equally the qualities of horses, oxen, and other animals, are not determined only by their habitat, but also from their training. Poseidonios confounds all these distinctions.[61]

Strabo does, in fact, in several places seem aware of different paradigms running alongside each other. The issue of whether Germans are like Gauls because of propinquity or common descent does not need to be resolved, but one of these explanations is clearly redundant. Equally his sensitivity to change over time – notably the civilizing of the West and the abolition of ancient institutions in Greece, both under Roman rule – might have raised questions about any explanation of customs purely framed in relation to environment. How could the manners of the Allobroges or Turdetanoi be so transformed if they were shaped predominantly by their environment? This awareness, however, is expressed rarely and more in juxtaposition and comment than in sustained argument. Strabo's aim seems to have been to provide an account of the inhabited world, not a consistent theory of how it came to be. The timelessness of geography as opposed to history offered him cover here.

One could easily imagine debates over whether genealogy or abode mattered most, debates that might have eerily prefigured modern ones over the relative influences of heredity and environment on individual character. It would have been easy to make comparisons between populations held to be related but now living far apart; Lydians and Etruscans, say, or Italian Celts and those of northern Europe. But this does not seem to be something ethnographic writers were concerned with either.

A combinations of factors might have been used to introduce greater differentiation or precision into ethnographic accounts. Differentiation among larger ethnic groups was certainly often attempted but by and large without introducing a more complex notion of causation. Caesar provides a famous example in the opening of the *Gallic War*, the model for the tripartite differentiation of the Gauls used by Livy and Strabo in the passages already discussed.

Gaul as a whole is divided into three parts: the Belgae inhabit one part, the Aquitani another and in the third part live that people who in their own language are called Celtae and in ours Galli. Each of these groups differs from the others in their language, their institutions and their laws. The river Garonne separates the Galli from the Aquitani, while the Marne and the Seine separate them from the Belgae. The Belgae are the most ferocious of all these peoples, because they are the most distant from the culture and civilization of the Province; and because they are least visited by merchants bringing those goods that tend to effeminize the spirit; and because they live closest to the Germans who dwell across the Rhine and with whom they are constantly at war.[62]

There is a good deal that might be said about this passage.[63] Note for example Caesar's solution to the problem of nomenclature between Celts and Gauls; also his naturalization of ethnic groups within territories marked by rivers, and how this contributes to an *ekphrasis* of the terrain; then there is the central role in his definition given to *lingua*, *instituta* and *leges* which some have seen as Poseidonian in origin; and finally the connection he draws between trade and creeping effeminacy. But for the moment I want to point out what is absent from this account, viz. any mention of genealogy, climate, or astrology. The Belgae are fiercest not because of whom they are descended from, nor because they are related to the Germans, nor because of the kind of land they inhabit, nor because of the stars that rule their skies . . . but because they are furthest from Rome. Caesar's Rome is, for these purposes, represented with the conventional tropes of corrosive luxury and infectious decline.[64] An austerity of explanation best suited the contingent purposes of this passage. No complex explanatory scheme was needed to indicate the north in general as untamed and pristine – the moral antipodes of Rome – and its extremes of ferocity located in regions into which only a Caesar would dare to venture.

What can we conclude from this panorama of paradigms? First, that those who wrote ancient ethnography had a range of interpretative frameworks from which to choose. Second, they tended to choose them to suit their immediate needs: whether they were writing at a smaller or larger scale, whether their data were physiological or etymological, whether they were trying to grasp the whole or characterize the part, and so on. Third, although texts were created in which paradigms might have been allowed to compete, ancient writers rarely if ever took advantage of this opportunity to develop a generalizing science.

It might be objected that this is an unfair expectation to impose on the ancient world. That would be a reasonable objection, if my complaint were that science did not drive out myth, and that reasonable causation did not displace irrational ones. But the proper standard of comparison is neither the European Enlightenment nor the Scientific Revolution of the seventeenth century, but rather developments in parallel fields of intellectual endeavour over antiquity. Mathematics offers one example of a road not followed in ethnographic discourse. In that case it is clear that in the early Hellenistic period a set of foundational texts and principles, associated with the name of Euclid, were established by superceding earlier work. Although the *Elements* remained central to the teaching of geometry, and much new work proceeded through commentary on and engagement with them, new work continued to be done. Mathematicians represented themselves, if only to each other, as forming a sort of virtual community united by particular concerns and methods, even if widely dispersed over space.[65] It is possible, too, to write a history of medicine over this period, one that begins with the composition of the Hippokratic corpus and assigns key innovations to particular groups at different periods. If there was less consensus about the way forward, and more public competition to win esteem among Galen and his rivals, there was nevertheless a strong sense of a field of study in which ideas could be disposed of and new ones set in their place.[66] Here at least agonistic urges were expressed in intellectual debate. Naturally it is possible to oversimplify both stories, and yet a definite sense of movement can be discerned in each, whether or not we wish to call it progress.

Ethnography, however, displays no such sense of movement, unless connected with the trope of conquest bringing new knowledge. That trope is the subject of chapter 3 but without anticipating my conclusions, it can be said that even those claims referred to increases in information, not in understanding. Only astrology differentiates the range of explanations offered for human diversity in the early empire from that imagined in classical Greece. Yet it would have been easy for those engaged in ethnographic writing to compare different sets of explanations to one another, or indeed to explore their intersections.

What of those texts that did deploy more than one framework? In a slightly perverse way these paradigms might in fact be made to be complementary, *so long as each was kept in its place*. Genealogy and migration might account for differences between neighbours, for example, while climatic factors might explain similarities between them. It is no surprise that this sort of enquiry is a feature of those classical Greek texts that were interested both in accounting for the dispersal of peoples around the Mediterranean and in the macro-structure of the inhabited world, the *oikoumene*. Yet there seem no clear conventions about which aspects of a group had to be explained one way rather than the other. Was temperament influenced by descent (Gauls, like Hercules, are quick to anger) or environment (southern peoples are more placid)? The suspicion must be that writers typically selected whichever paradigm suited the case concerned. On other occasions, as I have illustrated, they deployed multiple explanations to explain the same data.

What anchored the explanations were the *explananda* – that Ethiopians were always black and Gauls always big. It is the refusal to allow rival or explanatory frameworks to be placed in overt competition that I refer to as disciplining their presence in the text. Given that ethnographic passages were generally subordinated to other rhetorical aims, it is perhaps not surprising that ethnographic theorizing was kept firmly in its place.

Let me illustrate with one last example, Sallust's ethnography of Africa, included in chapters 17–19 of the *Jugurtha*.[67] The ethnographic passage is located, as so often in historical texts, just before a critical point in the narrative, in this case the immediate origins of the war between Rome and its erstwhile client king. The primary rhetorical function, then, is an example of what is sometimes termed 'narrative retardation': the digression operates to build tension and also punctuates the stream of events, although the stated reason is the need to provide background to the races of Africa and Rome's history with them.[68] Africa, rather than Numidia, is stressed, giving Sallust a broader palette as well as making this little war into a clash of continents. The text was written within just a few years of that dry administrative source employed by Pliny for his own African ethnography.

Sallust begins with geography – heat, inaccessibility, the desert – and then the definition of the continent as a third part of the earth. Africa is wild, and so are its inhabitants.

> The sea is savage, harbourless, the land fertile in crops, good for stock-raising but inhospitable for trees. Neither heaven nor earth supplies much water. The people who live there are healthy, energetic and hardworking. Most die of old age – except those who perish in battle or are killed by wild beasts – for disease rarely gets the better of them. But the country abounds in ferocious animals of all kinds.[69]

So far the ethnography emphasizes climate, this time mediated through the harshness which since Herodotos had bred hard people, but also with attention to the peculiar flora and fauna that appeared in Pliny too. Sallust then moves into genealogical mode.

> What I have to say about who the first people to inhabit Africa were, who arrived later and how natives and incomers mixed together, differs from the accounts given by most other authorities. My version is based on books written in the Punic language, allegedly by King Hiempsal himself, and then translated for my use. It fits with the beliefs of those who now cultivate this land. I will tell the story briefly, its trustworthiness depending on these authorities.[70]

Sallust then tells how Africa was originally inhabited by Gaetulians and Libyans who conformed to the classical stereotypes of wild nomads by hunting and gathering, and had no laws or customs or political institutions.[71] Not that these original Africans are considerably more barbaric than any of Caesar's Gauls, as described only a decade or so earlier. These indigenous peoples were then joined, Sallust goes on, by the remnants of Hercules' army after the latter died in Spain. Medes, Persians and Armenians each settled in different areas, intermarrying with different groups of Africans and eventually producing the two populations what will be central to the narrative of the book as a whole, the Moors and the Numidians. Last, and very briefly, Sallust details the arrival of the Phoenicians and the creation of Carthage and the other Punic cities, and (skimming over the Punic Wars) the scene is set for the Jugurthine conflict as a time when Romans already rule the Punic cities. Again, as in Caesar's Gaul, the most remote peoples – here the Gaetulians in the south – are the most barbaric, while those who have been most exposed to trade, the Moors, built towns and were the most civilized.

Sallust's recording of these myths of origin coincides in time, of course, with those of Diodoros on Keltike, of Livy on the Gallic sack, and so on. The theme of explaining particularities in terms of the intermarriage of indigenous peoples and incoming figures with a longer mythic genealogy is also familiar, indeed Sallust also employed it in the *Catiline* in the Roman ethnography that begins with the union of Trojans and Aborigines.[72] His sources and what he say of them have, naturally, been much debated. Are we to take Sallust at face value when he draws (if extremely selectively) on local sources, oral and written? None of this is implausible in terms of what little we know of Punic literature. Scipio had given the libraries of Carthage to the local client kings, which implies a taste for scholarship long before the literary career of Juba. Despite the supposed isolation of Africa it is clear from the narrative that follows that Italian traders were well established in north Africa soon after the fall of Carthage if not before. The mention of Hercules' death in Spain strongly suggests a genuinely Punic element. Sallust has, naturally, selected from and arranged his material for his own and contemporary needs.

But the feature of this account to which I particularly want to draw attention is how the geographic paradigm and the genealogical one are skilfully juxtaposed without actually interacting. What the geographical opening does is provide colour, making Africa wild and its people formidable enemies. How far Persians, Medes and Armenians had been transformed by the climate is never addressed. Nor is it clear how far trade could counteract the influence of locality. Genealogy serves to differentiate and characterize the Numidians and Moors, and to give them a depth of history. Perhaps too this particular genealogy offers suggestive parallels with Roman wars in the East in Sallust's own day.[73] Their mythic time-depth certainly offers an alternative past to that of the Punic Wars, and so allows Sallust to slide over Rome's long prior experience of Africa, recitation of which might have familiarized what he intended to keep wild. His continent is darkened and made more unfamiliar by this tactic. It evidently works since Tacitus imitated it to other the Britons. Sallust is not so much dodging questions about causative factors as not posing them, and the ethnography works as a whole, despite its scientific incoherence, because it is strictly disciplined to the large aims of the text.

The scientific underpinnings of ancient ethnographic writing were rich and various. Not only were there several paradigms available, but they were evidently generative of many hypotheses. They provided a vital resource for those creating new ethnographic knowledge in the Roman West, and offered several routes for the invention of traditions. The barbarian tales thereby created were at once available to be employed for all the various purposes of

Diodoros and Caesar, Sallust and Strabo and many others. What they were not used for, however, was to advance a generalizing science of humankind, the aim of all modern anthropologies. Perhaps it is not surprising that they rarely clashed in the field, on the colonial middle ground. But it is a little surprising and even disappointing that, given the attention paid to the cognate sciences of mathematical geography and medicine, ancient ethnography was always kept on so tight a leash within texts through which it might have transcended those limits.

3

Ethnography and Empire

Greek Ethnographers and Roman Generals

Pliny the Elder describes the expedition of Polybios of Megalopolis into the vast Atlantic:

> At the time when Scipio Aemilianus was waging war in Africa, Polybius, the great historian, took command of a fleet given him by the general, and set out on an expedition to investigate that part of the world. He reported back that west of the Atlas for 496 miles as far as the river Anatis there are forests teeming with wild animals of the kind that Africa brings forth in such profusion.[1]

Polybios, hostage-scholar, documenting a world being transformed by conquest, has seemed to many to provide the very model of the imperial ethnographer.[2]

The idea that Greek scholars regularly gathered new ethnographic and geographical knowledge as they travelled in the company of Roman generals has become a commonplace. Yet Polybios is in fact almost unique: the only other certain example is that of Strabo accompanying Aelius Gallus into Arabia.[3] Other scholars and litterateurs certainly travelled with generals. The historian Theophanes of Mytilene accompanied Pompey against Mithridates and may have written an account of it later. Fulvius Nobilior, in an earlier age, had taken Ennius on campaign with him in Ambracia, and on his return had been celebrated by him in drama and in epic. But the presence of men of letters in the entourages of Roman conquerors generated surprisingly little new information about foreign peoples and places. Much of their activity was perhaps more like that of Quintus Cicero, who composed tragedies

Tales of the Barbarians: Ethnography and Empire in the Roman West   Greg Woolf
© 2014 Greg Woolf

during the longueurs of campaigning in Gaul. The close relationship between military reconnaissance and scientific research epitomized by the voyage of HMS *Beagle* or the expeditions of Captain Cook, a Fellow of the Royal Society and also a naval captain, offers a misleading analogy for the Roman experience.

The Greek scholars who documented Rome's westward expansion were based, for the most part, in Rome. Some were captured on campaign and brought back as slaves. Alexander Polyhistor of Miletus came to Rome after the Mithridatic Wars. Timagenes was brought from Alexandria by Gabinius in 55 BCE.[4] Both were soon freed and set about recording the newly conquered world from the comfortable position of clients. Diodoros, Dionysios and Strabo did not come to Rome in chains. All these benefited from the flood of new information available and the research facilities in the capital funded indirectly by empire. But it does not follow that their work was directed by imperial priorities, nor that their view was formed by the experience of world rule more, say, than of the library. The impact of empire on their work was more complex and less direct than has sometimes been suspected.

My aim in this chapter is to explore the connections between Roman imperial power and Greek ethnographic knowledge. The dyad of Greek scholar and Roman general modelled by Polybios and Scipio represents only one of a range of possible relationships between empire and ethnography in this period. More often, I shall suggest, the relationship between conquest and scholarship was rather remote. When Roman writers began to write in an ethnographic mode,[5] it came first from the styluses of conquerors themselves, men like Caesar and Suetonius Paulinus, rather than those of tame intellectuals (if that is what Polybios and Strabo really were). As for the imperial gaze that recently has been claimed for Strabo's *Geography* and Pliny's *Natural History*, among other works, I shall argue that if empire informed their great compilations, it did not really shape or constrain it.[6]

Most of the barbarian tales I have been considering up to now originated in the middle of the last century BCE. That coincides with the period of Rome's most rapid territorial expansion, for which the conquests of Pompey, Caesar and Augustus are a convenient shorthand. Not coincidentally, the period after the Mithridatic War was also that in which a number of Greek scholars made Rome their home.[7] The historians and geographers I have mentioned were just one division of a great army of Greek scholars benefiting from the patronage of the new masters of the world. The complex exchanges of cultural and economic capital that characterized this age have been illuminated by two decades of research into the works of Philodemus, mostly recovered from the Villa of the Papyri at Herculaneum where he was patronized by Calpurnius Piso.[8] Many recent studies have emphasized the formative character of this broad central period of Roman history.[9] Like all other transformations of Roman high culture, this one entailed new

receptions of Greek thought.[10] Ethnographic writing was, naturally, implicated in these processes in all sort of ways.[11]

Yet Polybios' Atlantic Odyssey is a helpful reminder that Greek investigations of the West dated back much further, just as did Rome's wars of
conquest in the same region. The question of how we insert a history of
ethnographic expansion into a narrative of Roman imperialism must be
posed across more than three centuries. Let us begin with Polybios.

The story of Polybios' African exploration is told by Pliny and usually
presumed to come from the lost thirty-fourth book of the *Histories*, a book
that interrupted the narrative in the 150s BCE and was perhaps a survey of the
Mediterranean world on the eve of the final confrontation between Rome
and Carthage. The fragments assigned to that book come almost entirely
from Strabo, with Pliny and Athenaios adding most of the remainder.
Reconstructing a book from fragments is always hazardous. But if most
have been correctly assigned, we see Polybios in his familiar pose standing in
judgement on his predecessors, Eratosthenes, Dikaiarchos, Artemidoros and
Timaios above all, and behind them Pytheas, Euhemeros and Homer. Strabo
himself cites these disagreements largely in order to build his own reputation
as a critical geographer.

Perhaps the overall tone of Polybios' book was less esoteric. The disputes
recorded by Strabo often concern Polybios' views on various distances, the
locations of particular places and his opinion on the number of *klimata* into
which the world should be divided. But there are also a few stories that hardly
fit the slightly uncharitable characterization of him as 'the prototype of the
historian who never marvels, just as Herodotus is the prototype of the
historian who always marvels'.[12] What else, except as marvels, are we to
make of the underwater oak trees off Lusitania on which tuna allegedly
graze,[13] the house of the Iberian chief that rivals that of the Phaeacians except
that the silver and gold bowls are filled with beer instead of wine,[14] or the
animal unique to the Alps with the form of a deer but the pelt and bristly neck
of a wild boar?[15] Polybios' engagement with the conventional debates of
ethnographic discourse is also shown by his discussion of the relative
influences on ethnic character. On that same people among whom Asklepiades of Myrleia had taught *grammatika*, Strabo writes

> Because of the fertility [*eudaimonia*] of their land, the manners of the Tourde-
> tanoi enjoy are polished [*hemeron*] and urbane [*politikon*]. The same is true of
> the Keltikoi, either through proximity, as Polybius says, or else through kinship:
> but they possess these qualities to a lesser degree, for they live for the most part
> scattered in villages.[16]

The passage conveniently illustrates once again the association of prosperity
with pacific lifestyles, and the lack of debate over the relative influence of

geography and genealogy. The presentation of variant views on the relationship between Turdetanoi and Tourdouloi recall the long discussion of how
Keltoi, Keltae, Galli, Galatai and the rest were to be put together. Polybios'
interest in the fertility of western lands is also evident: he provides accounts of
the natural *eudaimonia* of Lusitania[17] and of the silver mines of Cartagena,
which produced a daily revenue of 25,000 drachmas for the Roman state.[18]

My point in citing these ethnographic commonplaces is not so much to
rescue Polybios' reputation, as to show how easily he can be fitted into the
ethnographic tradition as it had developed through the classical as well as
Hellenistic periods. It is clear enough that Polybios located himself in relation
to Eratosthenes as the latest great geographer, just as he located himself in
relation to Timaios as the latest great historian of the West. Poseidonios, first,
and then Strabo would make the same sort of use of Polybios themselves. But
it is also difficult to see what new elements have appeared (or old ones
disappeared) as a consequence of Rome's unification of the Mediterranean
world. Strabo has sometimes been described as particularly orientated on the
economic productivity of Roman provinces.[19] But this is already present in
Polybios' survey, or indeed in that of his predecessors. Since Foucault and
Said we are collectively rather committed to finding a connection between
an expansion of knowledge and the expansion of empire. But how would we
answer the sceptic who asserted the essential continuities between Timaios
and Eratosthenes on the one hand, and Polybios, Poseidonios and Strabo
on the other?

Greeks had, after all, been exploring a world of empires since the
researches of Hekataios of Miletos and Herodotos. Herodotos' influence
on Hellenistic historians, both on those who followed him and on those who
defined themselves in opposition to him, has been well mapped.[20] Prominent
as the personality of Herodotos is in the first half of the *Histories* he is reticent
on his own experience of travel within the Persian empire. *Pax Persica*
arguably made easier his travels to Egypt and also within the Near East. Yet
frontier guards, garrisons and the satrapal governmental of the late fifth
century Achaemenid empire are all effaced in his account of his travels. The
post-Salamis world through which Herodotos travelled has had most traces
of contemporaneity – and continued Persian overlordship – removed from it.
The arrangement of his world ethnography around the narrative of Persian
conquest exaggerates the extent to which those places are presented in their
pre-conquest, pristine condition.[21] There is an obvious point of comparison
with the ethnographic present of twentieth-century anthropology, from
which first all traces of colonialism, and later the signs of global context,
were silently omitted, so that we might know each culture or society in its
original and uncontaminated state. Colonial rule and then globalization
were, all the same, among the necessary preconditions for modern ethnographic research. The same might perhaps be true for ancient enquiries.

The limits of empire never completely constrained the field of enquiry. The longstanding ancient interest in India preceded and survived the relatively brief period of direct contact that followed Alexander's campaigns. Accounts of India feature in Diodoros' *Bibliotheke*, Strabo's *Geography* and Pliny's *Natural History* despite the fact that it had now effectively receded out of reach, so far that Arrian in his *Indika* had to rely largely on the early Hellenistic accounts provided by Megasthenes.[22] Besides, the exotic had its own attraction, one that drew ethnographic writers into areas that empires rarely penetrated, regions such as Ethiopia, Scythia and Germany.[23] Greek geographical and ethnographical researches had been conducted in the vicinity of empires from long before Rome's conquest of the Mediterranean world. Their subject was defined first by the totality of the world, the *oikoumene* or *orbis terrarum*, and second by the traditions in which they were composed. The limits of any given empire came a poor third.

Why, then, do we read the *Histories* of Polybios so differently from those of his predecessors? One reason is that he tells us to do so, in a passage that interrupts the narrative of the Hannibalic War at the point when Hannibal and Scipio have each arrived at the Po valley. This would be a conventional place for an ethnographic digression, but what Polybios actually offers is a lengthy apology for not providing one.

> Perhaps some readers may wonder why, given that most of what I have said relates to Africa and Spain, I have not said more about the mouth of the Mediterranean at the Pillars of Hercules, nor about the Outer Sea and its peculiarities, nor about the British Isles and the method of obtaining tin there, nor even about the gold and silver mines in Spain itself, all matters concerning which previous authors have disputed at great length.[24]

Polybios's excuse is not a rejection of paradoxography. Instead he says that he prefers not to interrupt the narrative, but will reserve such matters for their proper time and place. Readers who object are like the worst kind of picky eaters at a feast who want to try a little of everything instead of enjoying and digesting properly one dish at a time. That said, however, Polybios goes on to characterize Greek geography as a discipline in progress, each generation surpassing earlier ones. Polybios lays particular stress on the difficulties facing his predecessors when describing the edges of the world. Travel was dangerous, the barbaric nature of the lands made it difficult for them to see much for themselves, and the strange languages made it hard to understand what they were told. It was hard for them to resist lapsing into accounts of marvels.

> Given it was almost impossible in their times to give a true account of the regions I speak of, we should not find fault with earlier writers for their

omissions or mistakes. In fact we really ought to praise and admire them, considering the times they lived in, that they managed to find out anything at all on the subject and so advanced our knowledge. But nowadays, owing to Alexander's empire in Asia, and that of the Romans in other parts of the world, nearly all regions have become accessible by land or sea, and since our own men of action in Greece are relieved of the ambitions of military or political careers and so have ample means for inquiry, we ought to be able to arrive at a better knowledge and something more like the truth about lands formerly little known. That is what I myself will do when I find a suitable place in this work for introducing the subject, and I shall then ask those who are curious about such things to give their undivided attention to me, in view of the fact I underwent the perils of journeys through Africa, Spain and Gaul, and of voyages on the seas that lie on the farther side of these countries, expressly to correct the errors of former writers and to make known to the Greeks those parts of the world too.[25]

At which point Polybios returns to the narrative of Hannibal versus Scipio.

If we wish to find a statement about scientific progress linked to empire, this passage seems at first sight to offers a splendid text, one that explicitly links conquest to exploration. But as usual there is much more going on. Its location in the text – like that of so many ethnographic 'excursuses' – serves to enhance the dramatic moment, in this case Hannibal's final and much deferred penetration of Italy. Equally conventionally, the passage contains a claim for the superiority of Polybios' work over that of his predecessors: he can say more, because they simply could not have known so much. The claim that the Greeks now have to do research because the Romans monopolize power looks back to the opening chapters of this book that emphasize the totality of the control the Romans exercise over the known world. There is more than a little of Thucydides here too, the statesman who writes now he can no long act, and is not distracted by marvels. Polybios' boast about his own travel – not perhaps as dangerous as he represents, given that he was accompanying a Roman army – is a familiar autopsy claim. What is new is the claim that what had transformed the world 'in our time' was the conquests on the one hand of Asia by Alexander, and on the other of everywhere else by Rome. The careful chronicling of *histoire événementielle* gives way for an instant to a more geological vision in which 'their times' are set against 'ours'. The periodization is pretty close to our division of classical from Hellenistic, although ancient readers may have been struck by this early example of paralleling Alexander and Rome.[26] But the big claim is clear. The conditions of ethnography have changed fundamentally, and Polybios is the first beneficiary. Empire, in other words, has been pressed into the service of building Polybios' authority, and raising his text above those of his predecessors. We shall see much more of this stratagem.

Perhaps one reason we have been inclined to accept Polybios' self-positioning at face value is the effect of his deliberate and repeated insertion of himself into the text, so often in the company of powerful Romans. Apart from the most famous incidents – watching Scipio weep at the fall of Carthage, seeking Cato's advice on approaching the Senate for reparations after his exile – a few of these do relate to ethnographic enquiries. Alongside the Atlantic exploration, there is his testimony to being present when Scipio questioned peoples from Marseilles, Narbonne and the city of Corbilo at the mouth of the Loire about Britain.[27] Then there are two notices reported by Pliny the Elder, the first that Polybios and Scipio had together seen the crucified bodies of lions hung up outside African towns as a deterrent to other man-eaters, the second that Polybios had repeated a story told him by a petty African king, that on the borders of Ethiopia houses and stockades were built out of elephant tusks.[28] Up to a point this is merely conventional autopsy, but for Polybios it really does seem to matter who else was present at the spectacle. Polybios deliberately aligns his ethnographic gaze with the gaze of the conquering general.[29] His own *theoria* models a cultured and sensitive response to conquest. There is no doubt that many Romans were curious about the world they conquered, and even occasionally appalled at aspects of their success. Polybios offers himself to us as a fascinated spectator of their wonder and horror.

The other reason we believe him, of course, is our own expectations about the effect on knowledge systems of imperial ventures. Long before discussion centred on Napoleon and Egypt, and on the intellectual corollaries of European political and military hegemony in the Near East and India, these expectations were generated by a sense of the profound shock delivered to established regimes of knowledge in the fifteenth century by the discovery of a New World.[30] Polybios seems for a moment like a precursor of the Genoese and Portuguese adventurers who first explored the west coast of Africa in search of slaves, and then made the great leap across the Atlantic. There was however, a world of difference between Polybios' travels and the royally sponsored explorations of early modern Europe.[31] There is no sign of any Roman effort to create better maps, to locate harbours for subsequent use, or to seek new sources of key commodities such as precious metals, spices, fish or timber, let alone new markets for Roman merchandise. It is true that places are often characterized by their unique products – hunting dogs from Britain, yellow marble from Numidia and so on – but the geographies stop short of providing usable directions, or notes on prices or preferred exchange goods. Rather this is part of a tradition of viewing the parts of the world as differentiated by their products, another tradition that can be traced back to the fifth century BCE, before it became part of the ethnographic register of Agatharchides and others. Virgil's *Fourth Eclogue* characterizes the Golden Age as one in which every land will bring forth every product and it will be unnecessary to cross the seas for trade. This is a very different fantasy to that of the rival mercantile nations of the early modern period.

Ethnographic enquiry must, of course, have been made a little easier and safer by the expanding power of Rome. Not much can be known of the travels of Artemidoros and Poseidonios in the West during the early part of the last century BCE.[32] Although they moved in a world shaped by the collapse of Carthage and the subsequent Roman wars in Spain, Gaul, northern Italy and Africa, there is no particular reason to suppose they travelled with Roman armies or patrons, and certainly no evidence that they were recruited by Roman generals to help document and describe the newly conquered terrain.[33]

It was not, in any case, a New World. Polybios' comments on the obstacles to travel, autopsy and understanding at the edges of the world were wild exaggerations, at least as far as the western Mediterranean was concerned. Those coasts had been settled by Phoenicians and Greeks for half a millennium before his day. The seaways and harbours, peoples and places had become well known in the archaic period. The relative silence of Herodotos on western barbarians was a matter of choice, not necessity: his account makes clear that the western Greeks were well known, and if he characterized other regions as 'places without peoples and peoples without ethnography' that was part of his design.[34] Scattered references to Keltoi, Tartessians, Tyrrhenians and even Romans can be collected from fifth- and fourth-century texts. If they were marginalized within historical writing it was not because they were either unknown or unknowable. It was simply that the great narratives of Greek and Roman imperial histories had not yet touched them.

The Libraries at the Centre of the World

Probably the most important western locale visited by Greek ethnographers was the city of Rome.[35] Educated Greeks of high social status had been coming to Rome regularly from at least the third century. But they seem rarely to have stayed for long. The visit of Krates of Mallos in 159 BCE and the philosophers' embassy of 155 BCE are often cited. The prominence of philosophers on diplomatic missions suggests that some Greek cities had already identified this as a special interest of the republican aristocracy.[36] But there is no sign that Greek scholars regularly resided in Rome in this period either to teach or to study. After the return of the Achaean exiles there were perhaps no significant Greek writers living and working in or around Rome for about two generations.

The implications for ethnography are clear. Rome, in the second century, was an object of ethnographic enquiry, but not a centre of it. It is easy for us to put too much stress on narratives of travel and *theoria*. Ethnographers, then as now, spent most of their time working with books, and in the

Hellenistic era there were only a few places one could find them. Timaios of Sicilian Tauromenium had opened up the history of the West with researches conducted in Athens.[37] Agarthachides probably wrote his works on Europe and on Asia and his account of the Red Sea in Alexandria, before he moved to Athens in the middle of the second century BCE. The western travels of Artemidoros and Poseidonios must have been relatively short interruptions to largely sedentary lives based in the major urban centres of the eastern Mediterranean. Embassies brought both men to Rome in the early first century. Both returned East to write up their travels, Poseidonios in Rhodes, and Artemidoros in Alexandria.

This, then, is the significance of the new atmosphere in Rome that followed the Mithridatic Wars.[38] Rome moved, as it were, from being part of the ethnographic field, to become part of the academy. Greek scholars were kidnapped and otherwise enticed into the households of the Roman aristocracy. A few of those houses were provided with spectacular libraries, many of them snatched from Eastern capitals. The movement of libraries was essential, but it does not entirely explain the change. After all, Polybios had had access to books brought back from the royal libaries of Pella by Aemilius Paulus after the defeat of Macedon, and the work of Cato and Ennius is scarcely imaginable without access to some quite *recherché* Greek books, presumably consulted in Italy.[39] We need to identify the creation of conditions in which scholars were willing to voluntarily spend most of their lives in Rome. No public institutions recruited or supported them, there were no public libraries before the Augustan age (and even then it is unclear how truly public they were). It was members of the Roman elite, enriched by empire and with the broader horizons that empire brought, who supported all this activity. The Mithridatic Wars may have provided an opportunity to acquire books and scholars, but the key factor was the decision to support scholarly activity in Rome. Such support took many forms. It might include offering scholars accommodation and a stipend, employing them as teachers or simply giving them access to books. The exact relationships probably varied, as the social status of the Greeks involved certainly did, from those with aristocratic or even royal connections to those whose capital was mainly cultural. Over the course of long residences in Rome, these relationships presumably sometimes evolved. Some scholars really did spend decades in Italy. Philodemus arrived in the mid-70s and stayed for nearly forty years, based in Herculaneum with Calpurnius Piso's library, but interacting with a wide circle of Latin poets and other Roman writers from at least the 50s BCE until the early Augustan era. Nothing ethnographic has yet appeared from his writings. A number of historians and geographers stayed similar lengths of time. This is perhaps not surprising given the scale of the compilatory projects on which some of them were engaged.

Diodoros provides an unusually well-documented example. The autobiographical note with which he prefaces his *Bibliotheke* states that after he had decided to write a history of the entire world, from the earliest times to the present day, and had realized what an immense project that would be, he travelled widely in Asia and Europe visiting the locations of key historical events, and spent in total thirty years in research.

> As for the resources on which I depended in this labour, they were first of all that enthusiasm which enables anyone to bring to completion a task which seems impossible, and secondly the great supply of materials relevant to this study which is provided by the city of Rome. For the supremacy of this city, a supremacy so powerful that it extends to the bounds of the inhabited world, has provided me in the course of my long residence there with many resources in the most accessible form. For I am a native of the city of Argyrium in Sicily and since through mixing with the Romans in that island, I had acquired a special familiarity with their language, I was able to acquire an accurate knowledge of all the events of the empire from the records [*hypomnemeta*] which have been carefully preserved by them over a long period of time. I have set the start of my history with the myths of Greeks and Barbarians, after examining to the best of my ability the records each people keeps of ancient times [*archaious chronous*].[40]

There is much one might say about Diodoros' self-representation on the basis of this passage. The affairs of Greeks and barbarians point back to Herodotos and Thucydides, and his insistence on the importance of autopsy to correct the errors of his predecessors recalls Polybios. But the emphasis on the importance of knowing Latin, and the references to the resources available in Rome and a voluntary residence of thirty years are quite new. The exact thirty-year period Diodoros means is not clear. But the *Bibliotheke* covered world history from the beginnings to 59 BCE, Diodoros was in Egypt in the 180th Olympiad (60–56 BCE) and the latest event certainly mentioned is the foundation of the Roman colony at Tauromenium, conventionally 36 BCE. Caesar is frequently referred to as deified in recognition of his achievements, but there is no mention of Actium in a number of places where it might be expected. Diodoros arrived, then, some time after the arrival of Alexander Polyhistor and other Mithridatic War captives but before Timagenes, and he wrote in a Rome spellbound by the conquests of Pompey and Caesar. The whole of that period would have been treated in the last of the *Bibliotheke*'s forty books, which began in 70 BCE.

That level of biographical detail is unusual. Timagenes, who arrived in 55 BCE, was patronized successively by Sulla's son Faustus, Augustus and Asinius Pollio. The date of his death is unknown. The time it took Trogus to complete his *Historiae Philippicae* is also unknown, but the terminal date is 25 BCE and his father served with Caesar, presumably in the 50s. The biography of

Strabo is notoriously obscure, but he studied in Rome under Tyrannio of Amisos, another scholar captured in the Mithridatic Wars whose own career in Rome, under the patronage of Pompey, included work on manuscripts that had been captured by Sulla from Athens. Strabo too was patronized by at least one member of the imperial elite, Aelius Gallus, whom he accompanied on campaign in Egypt, and he too spent long periods in Augustan Rome.[41]

Only one other writer of *archaiologia* does give us more precise details about his research career and that is Dionysios.

> I arrived in Italy at the very time that Augustus Caesar put an end to the civil war, in the middle of the 187th Olympiad. Having lived at Rome from that time to this present day, a period of twenty-two years, and learned the language of the Romans and acquainted myself with their writings, I have devoted myself during all that time to matters bearing on my subject. Some information I received orally from men of the greatest learning with whom I associated. The rest I gathered from histories written by the most respected Roman authors – Porcius Cato, Fabius Maximus, Valerius Antias, Licinius Macer, the Aelii, the Gellii and the Calpurnii and many others of note; basing myself on these works, which are like the Greek annalistic accounts, I set about the writing of my history.[42]

Dionysius will have arrived in 30 or 29 BCE and completed his work around 7 BCE.

Diodoros and Dionysios both represent a knowledge of Latin and access to libraries as essential prerequisites of their researches. This does not mean, however, that their historical and ethnographical work drew heavily on works in Latin. Few works of that kind yet existed. Elsewhere, Dionysios' opinion of them was not especially complimentary: 'The Romans, to be sure, have not so much as one single historian [*syngrapheus*] or chronicler [*logographos*] who is ancient; however, each of their historians has taken something out of ancient accounts that are preserved on sacred tablets.'[43]

Dionysios goes on to give a virtuoso demonstration of the incoherence of Roman traditions, and the lack of consensus over which of Rome's three foundations was genuine: this passage incidentally preserves precious testimony of traditions that did not make it into the mainstream.[44] Dionysios then returns immediately to the authority of Greek historians, beginning with Timaios. This was a familiar move, and one that Roman scholars had had to make since Cato the Elder if they wanted to know about remote antiquity. Roman scholars of the Ciceronian and Augustan ages – men like Varro, Nepos, Atticus and Verrius Flaccus – seem to have had to invest a great deal of effort into establishing even such basic data as consular *fasti*. When Cicero and his contemporaries sought documentary evidence they often looked not in the *aerarium* nor the *tabularium* but in the privately held records of those aristocratic families with consular and censorial ancestors.[45]

Ethnographic writing always depended on access to works in Greek. Neither Diodoros nor Dionysios devoted much attention to those periods for which Latin texts were of most use: Dionysios concluded his account where Polybios began his, in the late third century BCE, and much of Diodoros' work concerned very early periods, and then Greek and Hellenistic history. The same was true of Trogos and probably Timagenes. The boast of linguistic competence might well be simply a claim to authority as interpreters of Roman knowledge to Greek readers.

Access to libraries, however, was a much more serious matter, even for access to texts in Greek. That meant cultivating connections with the small number of Roman aristocrats who possessed libraries and gaining access to the residences where they were kept, many outside the city in the luxurious retreats the richest kept in the hilltowns around Rome or in Campania. Plutarch offers an account of Lucullus' library at Tusculum.[46]

> But what he did in the way of establishing a library deserves real praise. He got together many books, and they were well written. The way he used them did him more credit than the way he acquired them. His libraries were thrown open to all, and the arcades surrounding them, and the study-rooms were accessible without restriction to the Greeks, who constantly visited there as if it were a hostelry of the Muses [*hosper eis Mouson ti katagogion*], and spent the day with one another, happily escaping from their other occupations. Lucullus himself also often spent his leisure hours there with them, walking about in the arcades with their scholars, and he would assist their statesmen in whatever they desired. His house was in general a home and *prytaneium* for the Greeks who came to Rome.
>
> He was fond of all philosophy, and well-disposed and friendly towards every school, but from the first he cherished a particular and zealous love for the Academy, not the New Academy, so called, although that school at the time had a vigorous representative of the doctrines of Carneades in Philo, but the Old Academy, which at that time was headed by a persuasive man and powerful speaker in the person of Antiochus of Ascalon. This man Lucullus hastened to make his friend and companion, and arrayed him against the disciples of Philo, of whom Cicero also was one.[47]

Plutarch offers an image of a kind of Roman Museum, not simply a collection of texts but also a sort of *ersatz* philosophical school, equipped for peripatetic debate and with a clear philosophical allegiance. Lucullus is portrayed patronizing on a grand scale, civic or regal rather than aristocratic. The library survived his death and was the setting for two of Cicero's philosophical dialogues: the opening to *De Finibus* offers a picture of it continuing to be open to scholars seeking rare Greek works. In the Hellenistic world it was kings that assembled great libraries and cities that entertained honoured individuals with meals and hospitality in *prytaneia*. The philosophical library of the Villa of the Papyri at Herculaneum was less grand, but it too was equipped with open spaces for ambulatory discussion, and gardens with appropriate statuary. Cicero's philosophical retreat – his 'Lyceum' also at Tusculum – had Greek statuary, and a clear if different philosophical allegiance.[48]

A number of great homes in and around late republican Rome contained collections of various sizes, mostly comprising Greek texts, a few alluding in their design and ethos to the philosophical schools of Hellenistic Athens which many of their Roman owners had visited on the kind of grand tour popular in the last generation of the republic. The collections placed by Pollio in the *atrium libertatis* and Augustus in the Palatine library and the Porticus Octaviae were presumably modelled on these. It is in settings like this that we may imagine our Greek ethnographers rubbing shoulders not only with other Greeks writing on every subject under the sun, but also with Romans such as Varro and Cicero, Caesar and Sallust, Vitruvius and Livy, all of whom had their own interests in ethnographic discourse.

Should we conclude that in these encounters Greek scholars acquired precious new oral testimony about the newly conquered lands, or that they somehow absorbed the conquerors' perspectives, or even influenced the way Roman generals thought about the world and its peoples? Greek and Roman writers certainly exchanged views and read or listened to each other's work, as Cicero's references to Antiochos of Ascalon, Philodemos of Gadara and other luminaries make clear. But did ethnographers pick the brains of generals or brief them about the provinces they had been assigned? This seems unlikely for several reasons. First there was an essential incommensurability between the kinds of knowledge needed and created on the ground, and the traditional subject matter of Hellenistic geography. I shall return to this in a little while, but for now let me simply state that this encompassed differences of scale, different interests in the currency of information and different concerns over precision. Together these combined to rob most geographical writing of any utility on the ground.

But the second reason to think these encounters led to little communication of different perspectives is already evident in Plutarch's account of Lucullus' library. Greek high culture was enclosed, for the republican aristocracy, within a particular cultural space. This might be expressed architecturally. Vitruvius' description of the grandest and most elaborate houses gives some kinds of rooms Greek names, such as the *oecus* (reception room), the peristyle garden space and, inevitably, the *bibliotheca* (for the library). It matters little that these categories did not correspond to Greek categories.[49] Cicero's Tusculan Lyceum had a *gymnasium* and was equipped with appropriate statuary supplied from Athens.[50] Or it might be expressed by keeping one's books and Greek friends in Tusculum or Herculaneum, while meeting clients and political allies in a traditional mansion by the Forum. Conceptually it might take the form of a distinction between *otium* (leisure) and *officium* (duty, business, work) with Greek culture located primarily in the former sphere. The same segregation operationalized within scholarly and literary fields has given rise to the idea of a 'Greek province of the brain'.[51] Scholarship and generalship were located on opposite sides of this line. Debating the merits of the Old Academy with his Greek friends clearly belonged in this province of Lucullus' mind, part of the wide space marked out for his *otium*. Campaigning in Asia was another world.

One thing that emerges from these observations is how very unusual Polybios was, a statesman, travelling on campaign with a Roman general, and also interested in matching his experiences against the geographical and historical accounts offered by Eratosthenes and Timaios. A century later there were very many more Greek scholars in Rome, yet in a way they were less close to the centre of power. The space they occupied was an informal, dispersed and barely institutionalized clustering of books and scholars. It had been assembled by Roman imperialism and sponsored by its proceeds. There was no institutionalised scientific establishment to lobby for exploration and discovery, and there is little sign that the Senate or the emperors saw synergies between geographical research and the wider interests of the Roman people. Rather it formed a specialized and differentiated academy, one from which ethnographers looked out over the Roman Mediterranean and the lands and peoples beyond it that had, almost by coincidence, been conquered by some of the same rich patrons who relaxed from their labours in the company of Greeks.

The World Viewed from the Library

If we ask how empire impacted on the work of those who produced ethnographic writing, we need to consider less direct connections.

Empire perhaps encouraged a sense of the possibility of writing a common history or geography. The idea was not new but perhaps came to seem increasingly viable. Polybios traced universal history back to Ephoros writing in the fourth century BCE: Diodoros claimed Herodotos as the originator.[52] Modern commentators tend to reject such genealogies and use the term to refer only to the great Hellenistic and Roman compilations.[53] Perhaps this is inevitable, if we follow Jacoby in seeking to create a taxonomy of genres. But those claims are not so ridiculous or so unusual – after all Strabo had geography begin with Homer – nor was it simply a question of enhancing the status of a work by setting it in an ancient tradition. What these works shared, and shared too perhaps with Hekataios' *Genealogies* and some works in the Hesiodic corpus, is a sense of openness to the wider perspective, to the widest geographical, genealogical and cosmological contexts in which particular wars or sequences of events became meaningful. That mode of explanation was, as I argued in the previous chapter, one that was important to ethnographical enquiries too. The real contrast is with accounts that accentuate the particular or the local. As a result, almost any account that went beyond the local might draw in characteristics of the universal, common or global. Empires, by definition, created this kind of history, but this was true of Persian and Athenian imperialism long before it was true of the Hellenistic and Roman eras. Imperial expansion or imperial failure might provide a grand unifying narrative for history, and a set of metaphors for the efforts of the compiler. Empires connected people, generated diasporas, facilitated travel. They created conditions in which even local history marked itself as not global, not common and not universal.

Perhaps the major practical contribution made by Roman imperialism was the distribution of people and the tales they told. The backwards and forwards pullulation of soldiers, colonists and traders between Italy and the provinces was coupled with the centrifugal forces attracting ambassadors, hostages, refugees and slaves to the centre, some temporarily, others for good. Only a small part of this movement is visible, in military campaigns, in the mercantile settlements of Delos and Cirta, in the centring of Greek as well as Latin literary activity in Rome, in the well-documented travels of the Roman aristocracy. One effect was a Roman diaspora.[54] Another was the growth of the city of Rome as a great cosmopolitan centre.[55] Both of these movements had implications for the historian's craft, within which we must include the ethnographer's.

Empires have occasionally been described as vast redistributive systems, drawing goods into the centre and pumping them out to the peripheries – not just material goods, but people too. And with the human ebb and flow moved information, some more and some less reliable. A little of it was predigested, in the form of local histories penned on the middle ground, or rare memoirs like those of Paulinus. There were no great officially sanctioned surveys like those through which we know India under the British Raj, and no scientific papers like those of Joseph Banks. The great mass of information must have been less organized, travellers' tales and the like. Of the vast quantity brought in each generation, most was lost. But while it was in circulation it might be harvested. A Polybios or a Strabo might, if he wished, join the circulation of warm bodies for a while, and get a sense of the flow. But it was sufficient to stand at the right points of the system and gather ethnographic knowledge as it passed by, like a coral polyp fixed on some reef, selecting some titbits and rejecting others from the rich currents, according to some prior design. The mass of accumulated books and scholars had made Alexandria and Athens convenient locations for a while. Soon only Rome would do.

Wherever the historian was based, the stories that arrived were flavoured by empire. A case in point is offered by the stories of migrations told about different barbarian groups from Herodotos' Cimmerians to the Huns. Many of the stereotypes applied to these peoples concerned their mobility. Difficult to pin down in any sense at all, this kind of barbarian offered a particular anti-type to the inhabitants of the classical city, peoples without fixed places or pasts, confronting civilizations built on ancient and localized traditions.[56] Barbarians emerged into the light of history for brief moments before disappearing back into the darkness. Tribal identities were in any case apparently highly unstable – at least during periods of migration, and perhaps more generally – undergoing periodic fission, fusion and intermingling.[57] Even if the 'same' peoples re-emerged, their names and grouping might be different. To literate civilizations built on myths that gave some cities and peoples an immense depth of history, this must have been profoundly disturbing.[58] Joining up these episodes in an attempt to create barbarian histories was an enterprise that faced the same kind of difficulties as were posed to mythographers like Diodoros and Apollodoros when they tried to develop an authorative version of the Herakles tradition. Once these barbarians were observed, from the imperial capital with its great collections of *testimonia*, patterns did seem to emerge.

Consider, for example, the much retold story of the gold of Tolosa. The facts, as far as they can be ascertained, are straightforward enough. A Roman consular army, led by Quintus Servilius Caepio, was sent into southwest Gaul in 106 BCE against the Tectosages whose main *oppidum* was at Vielle-Toulouse, ancient Tolosa. The expedition is often associated with the Cimbric Wars, but other contexts are possible, such as the foundation in 118 of the first transmarine colony at Narbonne, at the Mediterranean end of the Gallic isthmus. A great quantity of gold was plundered from Tectosagan sanctuaries, but it mysteriously disappeared in transit. Caepio was blamed. Three years later he was tried and convicted by the tribune Gaius Norbanus, went into exile in Smyrna and never returned. Presumably it was in the context of the trial that he was also accused of not having done enough to help his colleagues against the Cimbri and Teutones. So far so conventional, a routine act of pillage compounded by a hardly less unusual act of alleged peculation. The case is well attested only because Caepio was an enemy of Marius, Norbanus was a dynamic *popularis* tribune and the trial had scandalously been carried out only after a threat of violence had been issued against other tribunes who threatened to prevent it.[59] Presumably many similar acts of brigandage went more or less unnoticed in the age of the Jugurthine War. But the case became notorious and was mentioned several times by Cicero in passing. Perhaps more interesting are the stories that wound around the incident in ethnographic texts. They need, as so often, to be excavated from later compilations, in this case Strabo's *Geography* and Justin's epitome of the *Historiae Philippicae* of Pompeius Trogus.

Here is Strabo's version, which appears in a long discussion of the Tectosages which includes the story that their land was rich in gold, that they were once so numerous and powerful that after a civil war a large part of them migrated, picking up allies from other tribes, and that this expedition was the origin of the Galatian settlement of Anatolia. Strabo found supporting evidence in the ethnonyms of Anatolian Galatia, puzzled over where in Keltike the other Anatolian tribes originated, and made a comparison with the obscurity of the origins of the Brennus who led the Gallic attack on Delphi of 278 BCE. This brings him back to the Tectosages.

> It is said that the Tectosages took part in the expedition against Delphi, and that their treasure, found by the Roman general Caepio in Tolosa, contained part of that booty, although the people had added to it from their own personal property, trying to propitiate the god with their dedications. Well, Caepio, they say, laid his hands on it and consequently ended his life in misfortune, banished for sacrilege from his fatherland, and leaving as his heirs only two girls who turned to prostitution, so Timagenes said, and so perished in disgrace.
>
> Poseidonios' account is more convincing: that the treasure found at Tolosa, amounting to 15,000 talents, stored partly in sacred enclosures, partly in sacred lakes, was unworked gold and silver bullion. But the temple of Delphi by those days was empty of treasure *of that sort* because it had been stripped by the Phocians in the Sacred War. And even if there had been any left, it was distributed over a large number of men; and they were unlikely to have reached their homeland safely, as they got away in miserable plight after the retreat from Delphi and scattered in different directions through dissension.
>
> No, as Poseidonius has said, and many others too, the country itself was rich in gold, the people were both superstitiously god-fearing and not extravagant in their way of life, and so all over Celtica, treasure amassed. And it was their lakes in particular which preserved the inviolability of their treasure, for they sank great masses of gold and silver in them.[60]

Strabo goes on to add that when the lakes were auctioned off by the Roman state, their new owners found in them millstones of hammered silver!

Strabo's archaeology of the Tectosages has drawn on a rich mass of stories, most presumably gathered in Rome. Caepio's notorious crime has receded into the background noise. Why should a Greek writing under Augustus and Tiberius care *which* Roman had robbed which Gallic temple, especially given the general trawling of sacred lakes that followed? Strabo's account of the Greek world offers many more examples of temples stripped of their treasures by Roman generals.[61] The traditional theme of terrible punishments visited on those who plundered temples is deployed by Timagenes in relation to Caepio, and apparently also by Poseidonios to the Gauls who attacked Delphi. Timagenes was reputedly a ferocious and consistent critic of Rome. It is no surprise to see him seizing on an incident about which some Romans already felt guilty, indeed perhaps part of his attraction to Roman patrons was his capacity to articulate a dark and critically inflected account of their rise to world dominion. How far Poseidonios attributed the wretched experience of the raiders of Delphi to their crime is less clear. Was he rationalizing some earlier, moralizing account in order to explain the wider scattering of homonymous tribes in his own day? It is not always easy to discern exactly what patterns were being found in barbarian history, but it is certain that pattern finding was a key goal of all these accounts. Poseidonios' narrative of the original Tectosagian migration from Gaul to Asia via Delphi after a civil war bears obvious resemblances to the various narratives accounting for the Gallic invasion of Italy. Like the Livian version I discussed in chapter 2, this one seems also to have elements of a set of local traditions about Tolosa. It is impossible to say, of course, whether such local traditions had been brought to Rome by native ambassadors or returning teachers, whether stories were told orally or were already encoded in books, or whether they were gathered, perhaps even by Poseidonios himself, on the middle ground. But for the moment I want to consider the imperial contexts of compilation.

What I want to draw special attention to, are the efforts invested by both Poseidonios and Strabo in combining these traditions. The compilatory enterprise here is not a matter of amassing information about a particular place or theme. Rather, both writers seem to be striving to build a narrative that correlates and establishes the relations between distant places and events distant in time. They were clearly not alone in doing so. Poseidonios' version presupposes at least one earlier account in which the gold of Tolosa had been linked to Delphi. His history may have been left unfinished at his death in 51 BCE, but certainly preceded Timagenes' *On Kings*. Strabo, Trogus, Timagenes, Poseidonios and all their unnamed predecessors were engaged in projects of connection. An imperial perspective was not essential for this task. Indeed the task of connecting the Galatai of Asia to the inhabitants of southern France may have begun as early as the third century BCE, with Caepio's disgrace a late addition.[62] All the same, Roman conquest promoted a global view of the Mediterranean and its past, and Roman imperialism provided the facilities for scholars to gather, compare and reconcile the scattered notices of barbarian atrocities.

The same impulse to recover connections beneath the chaotic impact of barbarian invasions appears in the attempts by geographers to make sense of the migration that had most recently threatened Roman control of Italy, that of the Cimbri and Teutones. Strabo begins his account of the Cimbri lamenting the many implausible tales told about them, including the stories that it was a great flood tide that started the migrations and that the Cimbri took up arms against the sea. Ephoros is criticized for claiming the Keltoi submit to periodic inundations of their land as a way of conquering their fear, losing their homes and great numbers of casualties on each occasion. Kleitarchos is ridiculed for describing them trying to outrun the tide on horseback.[63] Both were evidently writing Celtic ethnographies long before the Cimbric Wars, but their work provided material. Poseidonios is then introduced by Strabo as a voice of reason. In place of their accounts he had offered the speculation that the Cimbri, being a wandering people, were the origin of the Cimmerians and had given their name to the Cimmerian Bosporos, the modern Crimea.

> He likewise tells us that the Boioi formerly inhabited the Hercynian Forest, and that the Kimbroi invaded that region and were driven off by the Boioi towards the Danube and the country occupied by the Skordiskoi, a Galatic tribe, and were then driven towards first the Teuristae, or Taurisci, another people of Galatic origin, and then to the Helvetii, who were at that time a rich and peaceful people. But when the Helvetii realised that the wealth the Kimbroi had won from robbery was greater than their own, they – and especially the Tigureni and the Toygeni – joined in their expeditions. But both the Kimbroi and their allies were defeated by the Romans, the one part when they crossed the Alps and descended into Italy, the others on the other side of the Alps.[64]

All this seems perfectly reasonable, until we remember that it is based on nothing but guesswork. It is simply that we find stories of *Volkwanderung* more plausible fictions than stories of warriors fighting the sea. Yet the desire to pin these movements down and arrange them in a rational pattern was doomed to fail. Strabo was not the only author to express despair at tracking down the origins of various peoples. These professions of despair, of course, along with the failure of successive grand theories of barbarian history, only reinforced the notion of barbarians as ungraspable, impossible to fix.

Pompeius Trogus offers a final example, which brings us back to the gold of Tolosa.[65] Trogus certainly had access to the versions offered by both Poseidonios and Timagenes, and perhaps his original account explained why he rejected their versions: we have no real idea of what Justin removed in making his epitome. Or perhaps he simply wanted to weave his own web of connections, wider and more wonderful than those of his predecessors. In Trogus' version, the story of Caepio at Tolosa is inserted into a narrative of events leading up to the Third Macedonian War, and is apparently triggered by mention of the Scordisci, with whom Philip had allegedly made an alliance just before his death and whom he had planned to use against Rome.

> The Gauls, after their disastrous attack upon Delphi, in which they had felt the power of the divinity more than that of the enemy, and had lost their leader

Brennus, had fled, like exiles, partly into Asia, and partly into Thrace, and then returned, by the same way by which they had come, into their own country. Of these, a certain number settled at the conflux of the Danube and Save, and took the name of Scordisci. The Tectosages, on returning to their old settlements about Toulouse, were seized with a pestilential distemper, and did not recover from it, until, being warned by the admonitions of their soothsayers, they threw the gold and silver, which they had got in war and sacrilege, into the lake of Toulouse; all of which treasure, 110,000 pounds of silver, and 1,500,000 pounds of gold, Caepio, the Roman consul, a long time after, carried away with him. But this sacrilegious act subsequently proved a cause of ruin to Caepio and his army. The rising of the Cimbrian war, too, seemed to pursue the Romans as if to avenge the removal of that devoted treasure. Of these Tectosagi, no small number, attracted by the charms of plunder, repaired to Illyricum, and, after spoiling the Istrians, settled in Pannonia.[66]

Even in epitome, Trogus' account shows some familiar features. First there is the desire to link up tiny localized stories into a great pattern: Philip versus Rome, the raid on Delphi, the gold of Tolosa and the Cimbric Wars are all shown to be part of a greater whole. Second the use of narrative tropes to give meaning: the anger of the gods against temple robbers expressed in pestilence and military disaster, migration as flight. Lastly, the use of this narrative to explain the observed scattering of the Keltoi, from Asia Minor to the Danube and south-west Gaul. Trogus was himself, of course, from the Rhône valley. At least in part these complex acts of synthesis have generated a locally owned tradition.

Roman expansion, I suggest, did not set an imperial vision at the heart of ethnographic writing. At best it gave a new importance to some interpretative issues already present in earlier histories and geographies cast on a grand scale. The political unification and centralization of the Mediterranean world had transformed both the field and the academy. Those who wrote ethnographic texts were well aware of this, and used the fact it for their own purposes. Strabo is a case in point.

I can hardly be blamed for having taken on a subject often treated before unless it seems I have done nothing more than copy out the works of my predecessors. But in my opinion, although their treatment of some matters is excellent, there remains much to be done. If I can add even a little information then that is sufficient justification for this project. And indeed the empires of the Romans and the Parthians nowadays have added much to our knowledge, which had already been considerably increased by the campaigns of Alexander, as Eratosthenes rightly observed. For Alexander laid open to our view the greater part of Asia, and the whole of northern Europe as far as the Danube. While the Romans have made known the entire west of Europe as far as the river Elbe, which divides Germany in two, and also the country beyond the Ister as far as the river Dniester. The country beyond this to the Mæotis, and the coasts extending along Colchis, was discovered by Mithridates Eupator and his generals. And the Parthians have made known to us the regions around Hyrcania, Bactriana, and the land of the Scythians lying beyond, territories of which our predecessors knew but little.[67]

Those who wrote ethnographic texts were well aware of the actual and ideological effects of Roman expansion, and were not above making rhetorical use of it for their own purposes. The passage recalls Polybios' claim that the edges of the world were now knowable because of the conquests of Alexander in Asia, and the Romans everywhere else. Trogus too had offered a world unified – and divided – by the empires of the Romans and the Parthians.[68]

Comments of this kind were both true, and yet not the whole story. Expansion certainly brought new information in from the edge, and centralization gathered it in the metropole. But whatever parallels were hinted at between military expansion, and extension of geographical knowledge, these texts were never presented as merely filling a space created by empire. Geographers and historians never claimed the identity of world and empire suggested by some Roman propaganda.[69] The Scipio brothers might portray themselves as conquerors of the continents of Africa and Asia, and the orb might be a potent suggestion of world conquest in Augustan art. Scholars always knew there was another world beyond the imperial frontiers. Should we see Polybios, Trogus and Strabo as displaying cultural resistance in declining to write geographies and histories that set the Roman empire unambiguously at their centre, or in acknowledging the conquest of Alexander and Mithridates and the Parthians as well as those of their Roman patrons? Do their texts deliberately surpass the reach of empire to show the superiority of Greek enterprise over Roman, or of scholarship over military expansion? A lot depends of course, on what sense is given to the notoriously capacious term 'resistance'.[70] But it seems hard to sustain readings of that sort, however appealing they might seem to those listening hard for subaltern voices. The matching question of what Roman generals made of Hellenistic geography and history is even more difficult to answer. What Scipio hoped to get out of his friendship with Polybios is both obscure and mediated mainly via Polybios. Yet on the face of it Greek scholars seem to have been valued for their learned companionship rather than for any particular works that they produced. Rather than seeing them as resisting an implicit contract to map the world as Rome conquered it, it seems more plausible to see their work as orientated on a bookworld that did not quite coincide with the territorial reach of Rome. Empire opened some doors. But there was no genuine homology of power and knowledge, and little imperial imprint on their works.

The Wondering Generals

Scipio marvelled at the strangeness of Africa, questioned merchants in the port of Corbilo somewhere in Atlantic Gaul about the distant tin islands, and sent Polybios off to sail south of the straits of Gibraltar. But he left no memoir of his own. It was not until the last years of the republic that Roman generals and governors began to record their own ethnographic observations. These are the last, or perhaps the first, place to look for a closer alignment of the imperial and the ethnographic gaze, an alignment of the kind that others have found in the Napoleonic *Description de l'Egypte* or the great surveys conducted by some of the governors and lesser functionaries of British India.

Latin ethnographic writing first appears in the middle of the last century BCE,[71] around the same time as Cicero represents himself in the *Tusculans* as part of a self-conscious movement to create a prose Latin scientific litera-ture.[72] In fact, a series of letters shows him in 59 BCE at Antium rather miserably contemplating the writing of a *Geography* based on that of Eratosthenes.[73] Nuggets of information about the barbarian West are con-tained elsewhere in his writings, like the testimony of Divitiacus, the Aeduan nobleman, about the teachings of the Druids.[74] Geographical fragments survive from Nepos and Varro, probably also written in the 50s, and the ethnographic passages of Caesar and Sallust are close to these in date. All show a broad knowledge of the work of their Greek predecessors and contemporaries.

Not all texts in Latin were composed so close to the centre of power. I have already mentioned Trogus, often considered a representative of provincial perspectives even if he was descended from generations of cultural mediators serving Roman generals in Gaul, and Mela, in whose *Chorographia* a local, Punicizing perspective has been detected.[75] Livy, too, in a history of Rome which had much in common with universal histories, gathered and made use of *archaiologiai* like the stories about the Gallic invasion of Italy. Of all these texts only Caesar's can really be claimed as an ethnographic text penned by a conqueror. The language of composition is not, of course, the real issue so much as the role played by the author within the complex politics of empire. Arrian's *Periplus of the Black Sea* and Dio Cassius' account of the wild Britons[76] provide samples of ethnographic writing penned by senatorial writers, and both are in Greek. Both wrote in classicizing modes that look as much to classical Greek historiography (Xenophon and Thucydides in particular) as to their experience as Roman aristocrats. Both also display a sensibility shared with the new Latin ethnography of the early principate. The most distinguishing feature of that sensibility, however, is not so much the administrator's concern for precision and utility, as a sense of astonish-ment and wonder.

Nowhere is this more clearly displayed than in the ethnographic portions of the *Natural History* of Pliny, at once polymathic compiler and member of the new equestrian administrative cadre created at the start of the principate.[77] Many of the authorities cited by Pliny the Elder as *nostri*, Latin writers, that is, as opposed to *externi* (usually meaning Greeks), were clearly men like himself, whether of senatorial or equestrian status. Pliny has plausibly been seen as speaking for an early imperial generation of educated functionaries who brought back to Rome stories about the wonders and peculiarities of the provinces in which they had served.[78]

Pliny's eclecticism has made his text a prime location for the investigation of different kinds of geographical and ethnographical exposition, and their interpenetration. An archaeology of the *Natural History* will easily uncover traces of Greek paradoxography and Roman triumphs, as well as philosophical cosmologies from Plato to the Stoics. None of this is surprising given his compilatory techniques, which apparently involved extensive note-taking and rearrangement of the parts into a new whole. But the design of the whole is his own; his work is a microcosmic record of a world conceived on philosophical lines. Pliny cannot be taken entirely as representative of the ideas of his age, if only because there was so little scientific consensus he might represent. Even if his interests and starting assumptions were not terribly new, the project as a whole entailed processes of selection and especially of arrangement that were unique. Put otherwise, the parts of the *Natural History* may have been common currency, but the relationships Pliny establishes between them were not. If further proof were needed, we just need to consider the immediate reception of the *Natural History*. Pliny the Younger sums it up as 'a work wide-ranging and erudite, and one that shows no less variety than nature herself'.[79] Gellius represents it as a Latin counterpart to the Greek paradoxographers whose fabulous, unheard-of and unbelievable notices he guiltily gobbled up.[80] Solinus mined it extensively for his *Collection of Memorable Things*, a periegesis like that of Mela but one fascinated by marvels. Isidore used it as a source for the *Etymologies*, a work ordered on completely different principles.[81] Their own selections and combinations shattered Pliny's design: had the text of the *Natural History* not survived, there would be no indication from these notices of the elaborate organization of the whole.

All this means that we need to consider separately Pliny's whole, and the parts of which it is made. So does Pliny's grand *design* reveal an 'empire in the encyclopaedia'?[82] The *Natural History* is dedicated to Titus and the prefatory epistle addressed to him. When epic poets do this we suspect them of appropriating some of the majesty of the dedicatee to their work. A good deal of play is made of opposition to the work of the Greeks, and the hero of the preface is Cato the Elder. So far, then, we are offered a book worthy of an imperial prince and utterly Roman.[83] There are a small number of much-quoted passages distributed across the work that in apostrophe praise Rome and Italy, declare the majesty of the Roman peace and attribute to Rome the expulsion of magic to the edge of the world. Pliny makes both explicit and unacknowledged use of information from military expeditions and administrative documents. Yet his subject is the totality of nature, not just that portion of the earth controlled by Rome, and the master, overt, organizing principle of the thirty-three books is cosmological. Pliny begins with the world in the heavens, goes on to geography, then treats humans in Book 7, before going on to systematic surveys of animals, vegetables and minerals. A long section on medicines develops out of the books on plants. That section is just the most evident feature of a secondary or implicit organizing principle based on a set of thematic connections that in the end give the work a different kind of unity.[84] Chief among these connections is a concept of nature that is both teleological and anthropocentric. Mankind is both part of nature and provided for by it, yet human activity also threatens the natural through illegitimate uses of the world's bounty, notably expressed in excessive consumption.[85] The tension between these two ordering principles is manifested in numerous ways. The overt model of the world is a static one, but the thematic concerns, especially regarding human action, often introduce time and change. Moral commentary often seems to have the character of diversion from the announced order of subjects, as if Pliny editorializes himself, drawing attention to topical peril in an account orientated on the vast and unchanging patterns of the cosmos.

Ethnographic passages are specially implicated in all this, since the overt differentiation between Books 3–6 on geography and Book 7 on anthropology constantly breaks down. Ethnographic material can intrude almost anywhere, as when an account of the German Chauci appears at the beginning of Book 16 on forest trees.[86] Pliny's world owes its physical order to Plato, Aristotle and the Stoics, supplemented by the geographers, but its moral character to conventional concerns. Those concerns are usually taken to have arisen out of Roman world conquest.[87] Yet even this is not wholly or uniquely Roman, since Pliny would have found much on luxury and decadence in Hellenistic writers such as Agatharchides and Poseidonios. Empire and its effects are noticed then – how could they not be? – but empire is not central to Pliny's vision of the world. Although there is no book of the *Natural History* for which Pliny cannot find Roman authorities, they have no particular authority over the writings of the despised Greeks. What Pliny has done with the *enkyklios paideia* of the Greeks is not push it into an imperial mould, so much as fit it into his own physical-cum-ethical conception of a bountiful living world centred on mankind.

So much for the whole. What about the parts? The *Natural History* might be thought of as a kind of Lucretian behemoth, a great structure created by the coming together of many tiny components – facts standing for atoms –

doomed to the same disintegration at the hands of Pliny's successors, as that to which he had subjected the work of his predecessors. Pliny's famous boast, that he had gathered into thirty-six books some 20,000 facts collected from 2,000 books written by 100 authors,[88] perhaps suggests he was prepared to let us envisage composition in these terms, as if his main engagement with his predecessors was with the material they had gathered. If the imperial flavour of the work is not to be found in the principles that governed the arrangement of its parts, perhaps we should seek it in the editorial process of selection, in the gathering up of precious information for the pleasure of the rulers of the world.

The collection and description of marvels can been traced back to the origins of Greek literature. Works that were primarily devoted to their presentation are usually said to begin with Kallimachos who apparently used his cataloguing of the Alexandrian library to produce a book of wonders (*thaumata*) arranged by place. Collections of this kind continued to be produced into late antiquity and beyond.[89] Wonders form a capacious category. They might include fabulous human–animal hybrids, such as centaurs and dog-headed men, and also very rare if perfectly natural creatures such as the tallest tree or the smartest elephant. For Pliny, even some human creations like the pyramids qualify.[90] Wonders have no uniform moral or religious significance: they might be *prodigia* (portents), monstrosities or neutral. They are certainly not intrusions of the miraculous or supernatural into an otherwise mundane or scientifically explicable world. What unites them is the fact that they are unusual – extraordinary, standing out against the normal and expected – and the emotions that they evoke in those who see them, hear them or read about them. The mediation of the human observer was vital. Pliny writes of *mirabilia*, *miracula*, *mira* and Varro and Cicero had both composed works on *admiranda*. Author and reader share in this response, like Scipio and Polybios in Africa.

The contemplation of marvels may be a guilty pleasure, and one criticized by philosophers.[91] But it was a pleasure nonetheless, to be distinguished from that other kind of fascination, horror. The sense of wonder evoked by the bones of giants, by the waves of Ocean, by one-eyed men and by giraffes and rhinoceroses, expresses excitement and pleasure at the inexhaustible strangeness of the world. After Romanticism it is enormously tempting to take these evocations of wonder as faithful portrayals of how the ancients viewed the world around them. Was this the sensation that was produced by travel and *theoria* in strange and unfamiliar places? And is this the particularly Roman response to empire here, a marvelled contemplation of all they had won? Pliny, after all, was not the first to wonder. It is not possible to gauge the tone of all those texts by *nostri* (other Latin writers), but some at least did collect stories and anecdotes of this kind. Best known is the work of Pliny's contemporary and perhaps patron Mucianus, cited more than fifty times in the *Natural History* for all sorts of marvels, some at least of them observed while he held office in the provinces.[92]

There are, sadly, enormous problems with such a naïve reading of the wonder of Pliny and his readers. First, it is difficult to find a clear border between Greek and Roman wonder. Was Alexander Polyhistor really doing something so different from Pliny? Did Polybios and Scipio see the same spectacles but understand them differently, one as Greek hostage, the other as Roman general? Gellius' anecdote asks precisely this question, moving us from Aristeas, Isigonos, Ktesias, Onesikritos, Philostephanos and Hegesias to Pliny's seventh book (and through him incidentally Mucianus) – all telling similar tales of animal–human hybrids and hermaphrodites. Recounting his reactions on casually finding, buying and then devouring the Greek texts, Gellius ironically models disgust for their nonsense, fascination with them, and exaggerated respect for the same stories when Pliny tells them, posing first as a cultural mediator, before indulging in a pseudo-Plinian lament on how hermaphrodites, once honoured as prodigies, are now treated as sex-toys in these degenerate times. We are not so different from the Greeks, Gellius suggests, or if we are perhaps it is nothing to be proud of. Paradoxography was, in fact, an interest that united the Greek and Roman *literati* and their many readers. Wonder did not belong to conquerors alone.

Second, wonder does not emerge in breathless apostrophes throughout Pliny's text but is carefully disciplined. The hybrid monstrosities are confined and organized within the opening chapters of just one book, the seventh, which opens with a pageant of human, and semi-human, diversity.[93] Half-humans are arranged around the edge of the world, and other kinds of information about those regions are suppressed.[94] A second catalogue of wonders, later in the *Natural History* focuses on those created and accumulated in Rome, marking it as the centre of the world.[95] Wonder, in other words, can be turned on and off. It was a register of exposition, one that might be employed to add particular colour to particular portions of the *ekphrasis* of the world. Like ethnography, its place in ancient texts is carefully disciplined. Other genres made use of some of the same devices. Lucian's *True History*, Philostratos' *Life of Apollonios*, Pausanias' *Periegesis* and a whole series of other narratives deploy wonder and marvels to different effects.[96]

The exotic had many other uses outside prose literature. The poetic, erotic and aesthetic potentials of the alien do not need to be rehearsed here. But it is worth commenting on the relationship between propaganda, in various media, and ethnography, if only because some influential recent studies have argued for a particularly close relationship between ethnographic discourse and the art and ceremonial with which first generals, and then emperors, asserted and celebrated their military achievements. Ceremonial and monumental art did, on occasion, try to represent the exotic diversity of the empire, often in connection with triumphal imagery.[97] There was, however, little precise overlap between the content of those representations and that of ethnographies. Marvels in particular are virtually absent. Many other components of ethnographic representation – descent and customs for example – were not amenable to visual representation, just as details of dress were rarely a prominent part of textual representations of aliens. Triumphs, and the monuments they generated, needed the visually arresting: red hair for Germans, the vivid coloured costumes of Persians that might be depicted with exotic marbles, distinctive headwear and weapons, however stylized and stereotyped. The overlap with textual representations was therefore partial. Equally there is no doubt that some of the many sources used by Pliny originated not only in memoirs composed by Roman generals and governors and in administrative lists produced by and for them, but in lists of conquered peoples and peoples that were first compiled, carried on placards, and inscribed on monuments in order to glorify particular generals. But this does not make the *Natural History* into a triumphal geography[98] any more than its use of medical texts for that third of the work concerned with remedies and poisons makes it a pharmocological geography. At best what can be detected are basic similarities in the ways that space was imagined and described – as areas divided by rivers and mountains for instance – and a sense that Rome and Italy were at the normal centre of the world. But it would be surprising if this were not the case.

The analytical blurring of the boundaries between ethnographic, administrative and propagandistic orderings of space is a bad idea for several reasons. For a start there is a consequent lack of precision that can only be dealt with by resorting to suggestive juxtaposition in place of argument, and a selection of examples that emphasizes only resemblances. More importantly, the eliding of distinctions makes it difficult to appreciate genuine appropriations from one distinct sphere to another. Appropriation clearly did go both ways. Augustan triumphal art makes much of the globe, an image of the world it owed to Hellenistic astronomy.[99] Polybios and Strabo did use the fact of imperial expansion to claim the superiority of their information and syntheses. Caesar did naturalize his conquests to assert their range and completeness. Yet appropriation, like metaphor, requires a certain distance between the two realms concerned. If our analytical techniques collapse scientific geography into ethnography and both into monumental art we lose the capacity to see how, and where, those appropriations were effected.

I have been arguing in this chapter for a certain distance between the ethnographic enterprises of the late republic and early empire and the military ventures encompassed in the term imperialism. The point is not that Greek scholarship continued regardless of the rise of empires. It is simply that the relationships were more complex, and a good deal less schematic, than those that are sometimes envisaged. This is, I suspect, true of the politics of all ethnography. The autonomy of an academic discipline, whether sustained by intertexts and tradition building or by institutionalization, pulls against other contemporary contexts. The relationship between ethnographic knowledge and administrative control is evidently quite variable from one culture to another.[100] Curiosity, after all, is hardly a cultural constant. Perhaps because we are used to the participation of figures like Macaulay and Lord Cromer in the histories of our own imperial adventures,[101] we forget quite how unusual this sort of combination of governmental and intellectual interest is. Persian satraps, Spartan harmosts, the mercenary captains and local governors of Hellenistic empires seem to have brought back a poorer fund of travellers' tales or else failed to commit them to writing. The aristocracy of Rome was unusually literate from the middle republic to the fall of the western empire. Their personal involvement in literary production did not diminish with the transition from republic to principate. Perhaps only a few of the equestrian and senatorial figures who spent time in the provinces were genuinely well read, and only some of these wrote about their experiences on their return. The cumulative efforts of these wondering generals was significant. Ethnographic curiosity took its place alongside inquiries into meteorology and agriculture, animals, vegetables and minerals. Yet almost none of this was of practical use for ruling the world.

Conquerors and administrators did, of course, need maps and information of various kinds.[102] But when we catch glimpses of Caesar finding out about routes into the interior it is through the (sensible) expedient of asking local allies and sending out reconnoitring parties. Roman military records of the principate suggest some more formal information-gathering. A few *periplus* texts look as if merchants or soldiers might have been able to use them. But most of what was in Strabo's geography was too imprecise or of limited relevance, either to soldiers or traders. At best it reflects a general sense that conquest and trade were among the uses that might be made of alien territory. Debates like those over the geometrical shape of the Alps or Britain, to which Polybios, Strabo and others devoted so much attention, mattered very little. Worse, the intense engagement of each text with its predecessors created palimpsested accounts of the world in which changes over time became blurred. Strabo, in particular, combines material of many different periods, occasionally signalling change 'recently', 'in our time', 'under the rule of the Romans' but almost never giving these notices of transformation any chronological precision. Information that has no markers of currency is worse than ignorance. How would the prospective visitor to the Turdetanoi know whether he was prepared for second- or first-century realities? The attentive reader of Strabo's accounts of the West would be prepared only for change.

Accurate lists of harbours and a comparison of mountain passes would be more useful. The *Periplus of the Red Sea* has some information of this kind.

Ptolemy transmitted some limited data. But if you really wanted to be forewarned, the questioning of local sources on the ground was a routine activity, one that could reasonably enough be set alongside other pragmatic exercises such as the census, and also the work of *agrimensores* and others concerned with planning colonial settlements, urban expansion, roads and military camps.[103] The occasional records that do survive – such as the agrimensorial notices of Merida or the colonial cadastres from the Rhône valley – have little in common with the texts I have been discussing. There is little wonder here. Knowledge created for fiscal purposes was very different from the ethnography created on the middle ground, just as it would be in the Great Lakes area when the westward advance of the American state swept away the imprecision of hybrid understandings.

Nowhere is the gap between the soldier's knowledge and that of the ethnographer clearer than in the contrast between what is of interest to Caesar in his Gallic and German ethnographies, and what matters to him elsewhere in the *Gallic War*.[104] His account of the Gauls begins by stressing their propensity to factionalism, then goes on to describe the dominance exercised by Druids and knights over the plebs. A long passage on the Druids establishes their pre-eminence not only in ritual but also in dispute resolution, describes a pan-tribal organization and hierarchy, their arcane teachings and privileges, the twenty years of training they undergo, their use of Greek letters to encrypt their accounts and the doctrine of the transmigration of souls. The knights, on the other hand, are described merely as devoted to war and surrounded by bands of clients.[105] Caesar returns at once to religion, human sacrifice, the gods of the Gauls and then a collection of curiosities concerning childraising, dowries, funerals and the secretive ways of magistrates. The description of the Germans that follows surveys in turn religion, sexual habits, agriculture, their warlike nature and their absence of political institutions. Caesar's own essay into barbarian history describes a time when Gauls invaded and colonized Germany, the capture of the best parts of Germany by the Volcae Tectosages and the relative decline of the Gauls since that date owing to their closeness to the Roman provinces and their access to luxury. The passage ends with a description of the Hercynian Forest and its most distinctive fauna.

Much has been written on Caesar's motives for insisting on the contrast of Gauls with Germans, and the reasons he may have wished to present the latter as more ferocious than the former.[106] Comprehensible Gaul had institutions that – although alien – could be equated to Roman ones, while ungraspable Germany was a world in which land and water, tribes and territories were fluid. It is also easy to see why the description is placed here in the text, immediately before the crossing of the Rhine. Like Sallust's deployment of ethnography in the *Jugurtha*, Caesar's virtuoso account of Gauls and Germans serves to punctuate the narrative, to signal the importance of the narration that is being deferred, the never-before attempted invasion of Germany, and the high drama that it will produce. Ethnography is again kept in its place.

Perhaps it is no surprise that marriage customs do not intrude into *commentarii*. But the absence of Druids is more of a problem. It has often been noticed that, despite their alleged authority and quasi-political role, they play no part at all in the narrative of events. Over the course of the *Gallic War*, Gaul in fact becomes increasingly familiarized. Magistrates, councils, factions and *popularis* politicians are there from the start, of course. By the siege of Alesia it is a world of city states – the word *urbs* occurs with increasing frequency – and the exotic is penned up beyond the Rhine and the Channel. It is tempting to think that, just for a moment, Caesar was overcome with wonder at the strangeness of the world into which his headlong military advance had brought him, and that he could not quite resist the spectacle offered by the elks and aurochs of the great forest at the heart of unconquered Europe. Yet, as ever in the *Gallic War*, the subjectivity of Caesar is occluded and discipline is maintained.

4

Enduring Fictions?

Irreducible Barbarians

My focus, so far, has been on tales of the barbarians created during the Roman conquest of the West. The first chapter considered the new mythic histories created on that middle ground where barbarian *érudits* and Greek grammarians rubbed shoulders with Roman conquerors across a vast and variegated contact zone. The second surveyed the interpretative frames available to those creating this new knowledge, both older paradigms of geography and genealogy employed by Greek writers since the fifth century and even earlier, and also newer schemas, astrological, ethical and cosmological. The third set this cultural work in the context of empire, looking back to earlier imperial ventures but centring on the creativity of those who compiled vast universal histories, geographies and encyclopaedias in the greatest libraries of Rome and central Italy around the turn of the millennium. This final chapter asks what happened to these stories in the centuries that followed. Did barbarian tales fade away as provincial populations became better known and better integrated into the Roman world? Did the middle ground close up, like its North American analogue, as rational-legal institutions overtook the messy world of hybrid negotiation? Were the stories created in the formative period of contact retold or revised, forgotten or memorialized? Whatever happened to the barbarians?

One of the best-known passages of ethnographic writing from the second century CE is contained in Tacitus' *Agricola*. This is how his description of the Britons begins:

> The location and peoples of Britain have been recorded by many writers. I shall relate them here not in a spirit of competition with their diligence and skill, but

because it was at this time that Britain was for the first time totally conquered. Subjects which my predecessors had to embellish with eloquence, because they were not yet known for certain, I may describe on the authority of the facts themselves.[1]

Tacitus' British ethnography seems at first sight quite conventional. Ethnography is deployed, once again, to slow the narrative and generate a sense of tension just before the climax of Agricola's career. Equally familiar is the claim that new conquest has brought new knowledge, or rather in this case new certainty: just as Agricola surpassed his predecessors as governors, so Tacitus will surpass earlier geographers of the remote Britons. New twists are given by Tacitus' *faux* modest claim that the superiority of his account depends not on his own greater *cura* or *ingenium* but on Agricola's achievement. Plain facts will replace *eloquentia*. We are persuaded. And just in case not, the text launches into a miniaturized and corrected geography, clarifying the location of Britain (between Germany, Spain, Gaul and the vast unbounded northern Ocean), acknowledging the accounts of its shape in Livy and Fabius Rusticus (subtly damned as the most *eloquent* of recent writers) . . . at least as far as Caledonia, where their knowledge and accuracy ran out along with the pre-Agricolan province. At this point the circumnavigation of the island ordered by Agricola is abruptly introduced, along with the discovery of the Orkneys and the sighting of distant Thule. The ethnographic digression has been interrupted by an historical one, and Agricola himself has waded into the text to correct, with plain facts, the eloquence of Tacitus' predecessors. The next chapter offers an account of the Britons' habits, physiognomies, language, triangulating them among other barbarian peoples. Tacitus continually stresses the limits of knowledge. The origins of the peoples are in fact unknown. Tacitus links the Caledonians to the Germans and the Silures to the Iberians on physiognomic grounds, perhaps the result of a migration?

> Those who live closest to the Gauls resemble them, either because they still show signs of a common descent, or because when countries are extended towards each other from opposite directions, the climate [or the heavens? *caeli positio*] has produced similar results in the adjacent regions.[2]

Tacitus' credentials as an ethnographer are established – almost every conventional paradigm has been deployed, or rather evoked – but the indeterminacy and fluidity of Britain has not been significantly reduced. Tacitus strengthens the case for a Gallic settlement of Britain by pointing to similarities of cult, language and temperament, although the Britons (like Caesar's Belgae) are fiercer in so far as they have had less enervating contact with Rome. After these three short chapters, Tacitus gently restarts up the historical movement. Britons are fierce, they once had kings (but no longer), like Herodotos' Thracians and Caesar's Gauls they are permanently at each others' throats. Discussion of the weather, the crops and the natural riches of Britain leads naturally into a short history of the Roman wars of conquest.

Tacitus' ethnography, at first apparently given a traditional segregated and disciplined place in the text, in fact colours the whole of it. Although the narrative direction is towards pacification, every opportunity is taken to stress the warlike nature of the Britons. The remoteness of Britain, its long axis extending away from the servitude of Rome and the province in the south of the island towards freedom on the shores of the wild ungovernable Ocean to the north, makes it the perfect stage on which to dramatize Tacitus' theses, that *eloquentia* and *libertas* now belong to Rome's enemies, and that heroism on the fringe of empire incriminates corruption at the centre.[3] That theme unites the ethnography with the speeches of both Calgacus the barbarian chieftain and Agricola before the final battle of Mons Graupius, and so provides a rationale for the prominence of Britain in the life story of Agricola. The grim conditions of Domitianic tyranny that frame the *Agricola* have turned the world upside down. Only at the edges of the earth can Agricola become a real Roman, and exhibit the virtues Romans had once claimed to be spreading across the world. Tacitus' ethnography is an inversion of that of Pliny the Elder. Pliny had presented the majesty of the Roman peace for driving magic (including the human sacrifice attributed to the Druids) to the margins of the world. Tacitus offers the image of Domitianic Rome as a cancer extinguishing freedom as it grows. The theme had been done before. Sallust's *Jugurtha* had presented the corruption of the Numidian prince as contagion from the corruption of the *nobiles* in Rome, making a foreign war into one episode in a narrative of domestic decline.[4] But where Sallust's ethnography, like Caesar's, had been allocated a more traditional place in the text, Tacitus breaks down the barriers between ethnographic and narrative modes and the set-piece speeches contained within the text.

Perhaps it is unnecessary to stress the fictional nature of Tacitus' account and the role ethnographic writing plays in it. The archaeology of southern Britain shows a precocious urbanism, the economy was running on Roman bronze coins at the time Tacitus wrote, the larger native farms were being transformed into villas. In some parts of the island the Latin alphabet and Roman iconography had been in use since before the Claudian invasion. Wine and olive oil, as Tacitus correctly points out, were not produced locally, but they were already imported in significant quantities in the late pre-Roman Iron Age.[5] The Agricolan advance was not the transformative event Tacitus presents it as, not militarily, not sociologically, nor in terms of Roman knowledge of the island and its inhabitants.[6]

Britain poses in an acute form the problem of the relationship between ethnographic writing and ethnographic knowledge. Remote as it may have been, the presence of three legions in the province for much of its history, and the repeated low-level conflicts that characterized the occupation, make it certain that actual conditions there were rather well known, perhaps especially to members of the ruling classes. Much must have been learned, even if it was never gathered together, about individual peoples and places. Yet the island never became domesticated in ethnographic writing. It remained irreducibly barbarian.

It is not difficult to explain the narrative pressures that drive Tacitus' emphasis on the enduring savagery of the Britons. The southerners had to wait for Agricola to initiate them into civilization. The northerners had to remain a threat for him to oppose. The needs of the argument, in other words, determined the kind of Britons portrayed. Perhaps the timelessness of ethnographic discourse avoided a blatant clash with actuality. The political marginalization of a province which, as far as we know, never produced any senators, meant there was no one to protest that the *Agricola* was composed (artfully enough) of tropes and stereotypes, that it too depended on eloquence, not faithfulness to the facts.

Tacitus was not alone in refusing to write realistic ethnography of the Britons under Roman rule. The remoteness of Britain was – like that of India or Ethiopia or the remotest parts of Germany – simply too useful in classical thought to be surrendered. These edges of the world and the empire were good to think with.[7] Pliny and Tacitus each needed Britain to help them describe Rome. So did others.

Consider for example Plutarch's dialogue *On the Decline of Oracles*, composed in Greek around the same time as the *Agricola*. The two central figures in the dialogue are Kleombrotos the Spartan, who is introduced as having travelled in Egypt, to the lands of the Troglodytes and even beyond the Persian Gulf, seeking material for a work of philosophy and theology, and the grammarian Demetrios of Tarsus, on his way back from a visit to Britain where he has been exploring the westernmost isles on the orders of the emperor. Plutarch emphasizes that these are the opposed margins of the world by introducing the dialogue with the legend of how either two eagles or two swans set out from the opposite ends of the earth and met at Delphi, thereby establishing its position as the true centre of the world. There is no reason to believe either voyage took place, of course. The dialogue assembles alien wisdom and testimony from the margins of the earth to establish the existence of *daimones*, Platonic demigods with immense lifetimes but who do, eventually, pass away, their deaths explaining why some oracles have stopped functioning. Both a fascination with oracles, and the belief that religious insights might be gained from distant foreign peoples were characteristic features of religious writing of the early Roman empire. Philostratos has Apollonios of Tyana travel around the margins of the world collecting wisdom before returning to enlighten the Roman emperor and the Greek world. Plutarch's dialogue *On Isis and Osiris* is motivated by similar interests, which would actually become stronger with the rise of Christianity.[8] It is in the context of this discussion that Demetrios describes how the islands off the west coast of Britain, named after heroes and demigods, were largely uninhabited except for holy men and how they interpreted one great storm for him as a sign that some great soul had perished. On one island, moreover, Cronos was imprisoned, guarded and attended by various monsters from classical myth.[9] Kleombrotos, naturally, had matching tales from the other end of the world.

A final example of the irreducible barbarity of Britain is provided by its treatment in the *Roman History* of Cassius Dio, composed in the early third century shortly after the emperor Severus had campaigned there.[10] Britain features in Dio's narratives of the Caesarian and Claudian invasions, reappears in that of the Boudiccan war, and seems to have been treated at length in Book 77, of which only an epitome survives, which related the Severan wars of Dio's own lifetime. Like the western provinces in all Roman period historiography, in other words, Britain is made visible only by conflict. The way Dio introduces the island will not be a surprise either.

> Caesar, then, was at this time the first of the Romans to cross the Rhine and also the first to cross over to Britain which he did a little time afterwards, in the consulship of Pompey and Crassus. This country is, by the shortest route, sixty miles away from the Belgic mainland where the Morini live. It extends alongside the rest of Gaul and nearly all of Spain, reaching out into the sea. The earliest Greek and Roman writers did not even know it existed, and their successors argued over whether it was a continent or an island. Accounts of it have been written from both points of view by many who knew nothing about it, because they had neither seen it with their own eyes nor heard about it from the natives with their own ears. These writers indulged in surmises determined by the scholarly sect [*schole*] or branch of learning [*philologia*] to which each belonged. But it has eventually been clearly proved to be an island, first under Agricola, the propraetor, and now under the emperor Severus.[11]

Dio's self-positioning in relation to his predecessors and his emphasis on the remoteness of Britain and the advances in knowledge brought about now by Severus' campaigns as well as Agricola's hardly need comment. And yet the knowledge of Britain has not been advanced.[12] Britain remains a distant land of horrors and marvels. The Boudiccan narrative in Book 62 is furnished with ghastly omens: the barbarian queen is portrayed vividly in her exotic appearance but her denunciation of Roman rule (like that of Calgacus in

the *Agricola* or the letter of Mithridates in Sallust's *Histories*) is full of praise
for liberty and allusions to the tropes of Greek and Roman geography. The
Britons are hardy barbarians opposed to the softness created by Roman
luxury in an antithesis that goes back to Herodotos.

Nothing has changed when Severus arrives, a century and a half and fifteen
books later.

> There are two principal races of Britons, the Caledonians and the Maeatae,
> and the names of the others have been merged in these two. The Maeatae live
> next to the cross-wall which cuts the island in half, and the Caledonians are
> beyond them. Both tribes inhabit wild and waterless mountains and desolate
> and swampy plains, and they possess neither walls, nor cities, nor cultivated
> fields. They live on their flocks, wild game, and certain fruits; for they do not
> touch the fish which are there found in immense and inexhaustible quantities.
> They dwell in tents, naked and unshod, possess their women in common, and in
> common rear all the offspring. Their form of rule is democratic for the most
> part, and they are very fond of plundering; consequently they choose their
> boldest men as rulers. They go into battle in chariots, and have small, swift
> horses; there are also foot-soldiers, very swift in running and very firm in
> standing their ground. For arms they have a shield and a short spear, with a
> bronze pommel attached to the end of the spear-shaft, so that when it is shaken
> it may clash and terrify the enemy; and they also have daggers. They can endure
> hunger and cold and any kind of hardship; for they plunge into the swamps and
> exist there for many days with only their heads above water, and in the forests
> they support themselves upon bark and roots, and for all emergencies they
> prepare a certain kind of food, the eating of a small portion of which, the size of
> a bean, prevents them from feeling either hunger or thirst.[13]

The most original feature of the account occurs at the end of the book, in an
imagined exchange between Julia Augusta and the captive wife of a Cale-
donian chief. When the empress criticizes the sexual freedom of the Britons,
the chieftain's wife replies that at least British women have sex in the open
with the best of men, whereas Roman women are enjoyed in secret by the
worst. How should we read this anecdote? The chronological distance
between Severus' invasion and Dio's account of it was very slight: he knew
Severus and Julia Domna personally. Did Romans really go to Britain
expecting to find Caesar's and Tacitus' savages still in possession? If so,
they had to pass the monuments of Roman London and the Wall to reach
them. Imperial women at least were more likely to banter with captive
princesses at the headquarters and palace in York than on the battlefield. Are
we hearing the wit of an educated provincial cast in the role of latter-day
Boudicca? a translator's invention? or Dio's? What licence was allowed to
those who described Rome's permanent barbarian theme park? Had ethnographic discourse become so well marked, that no disparities were felt
between fabulous text and lived experience?

Further Variations

Text versus experience is, indeed, the crux of the matter. But before pursuing that further I want to pause to emphasize the essential continuity of scholarly activities from the formative period of the late republic through to the third century CE and beyond. Much had clearly changed since Sallust and Caesar penned the first Latin ethnographies. The emperors had created great libraries in the capital: now it was their patronage, rather than that of great aristocrats like Lucullus, that gave access to scholarly works. The number of Italian and provincial towns with libraries of their own – some dedicated structures, some in *gymnasia* or bath-complexes – had increased. A modest increase in the book trade and private ownership of books is also probable.[14] But for those whose *magna opera* required the consultation of past scholarly works, only great centres such as Alexandria, Athens and Rome seem to have been adequate, presumably because there were never very many copies made of either local histories or vast compendia, as opposed to the small canons created in Greek and Latin of classic texts read in school and the more popular poetic genres. Among scholars, however, fascination with earlier writing of the obscurest kind was if anything even stronger in the second century CE, whether we consider the classicism of the so-called Second Sophistic or the parallel fascination with early Latin displayed by Gellius, Fronto and Hadrian.

Great works of compilation and large-scale histories, based on the rear-rangement of material excerpted from earlier works of all kinds, continued to be produced. Those engaged in such projects included senators such as Tacitus, Arrian and Dio and also others of slightly lower status, the equestrian successors of Pliny. Just as in the first century CE, there is more consistency in the components of ethnographic writing, than in the shapes into which it was arranged. I have already mentioned the work of Solinus, painstaking dismantling Pliny's great work to recombine elements from it into a history of marvels organized on a similar perigetic model to the *Chorographia* of Mela which he also used. That project was probably accomplished in the fourth century CE. Ethnographic writing continued to be employed across a wide range of texts and, as my discussion of the *Agricola* suggests, there seems to have been some interest in finding innovative uses for it.

One novel format was apparently invented by Appian of Alexandria, who compiled his history of Rome in the mid-second century CE, for his account of Roman republican history in Greek. It began with a short tour of the Mediterranean, framed as a mini-periegesis, and then organized its narrative through a series of books each devoted to Rome's conflicts with one particular enemy people, beginning with Rome's earliest opponents and progressing to the later ones. Inevitably each of these books tended to be divided into successive bouts of combat. Together with three books of civil wars, they culminated in an ethnographically ordered account of republican history that must – like Plutarch's Roman *Lives* – have been almost incomprehensible to those who did not already know the outline history of the period. Thucydides and Polybios had each resorted to juxtaposing, within each individual book, separate narratives dealing with events in different regions over the same year or years. Appian, on the other hand, constructed parallel histories of conflict from the first encounter of each people with Rome up until the principate of Augustus. How far Appian exploited the opportunity that this new structure gave him to make use of ethnographical information is unclear. The beginning of the *Iberike*, which narrates Rome's wars in Spain from the Hannibalic War to Augustus' campaigns, feigns (rather like Livy's *Preface*) a reluctance to incorporate legends of the earliest period. After describing, with more enthusiasm than accuracy, the shape and location of Iberia and the Pyrenees which he describes as the greatest mountains in Europe, Appian continues:

> What nations occupied it first, and who came after them, it is not very important for me to inquire, since my concern is only with the affairs of the Romans. However, it is my opinion that the Celts, passing over the Pyrenees at some former time, mingled with the natives, and that the name Celtiberia originated in that way. I think also that from an early time the Phoenicians came to the Iberian peninsula to trade and settled in part of it. In a similar way the Greeks visited Tartessos and its king Arganthonios, and some of them too settled in Iberia; for the kingdom of Arganthonios was located in Iberia. It is my opinion that Tartessos was then the city on the seashore which is now called Karpessos. It is also my opinion that it was the Phoenicians who built the temple of Herakles which stands at the straits. The rituals performed there are still of Phoenician type, and the god is considered by the worshippers to be the Tyrian, not the Theban, Herakles. But I will leave such matters to the antiquarians [*palaiologoi*].[15]

Despite the suspicion aroused by these formulaic disavowals of interest followed by learned conjectures, Appian really does seem uninterested in exploiting the rich ethnography of the Iberians. The whole of this book survives, and contains almost no further mention of the customs or peculiarities of the inhabitants of Spain and certainly makes no use of them. It is just possible that this limitation was imposed by his source material. Only an epitome and some fragments survive of the *Keltike* which narrated Roman conflict with Keltoi from the invasion of Italy, through the sack of Rome and the wars in the Po valley and the Marches, to Caesar's Gallic War, and here there is a little more ethnography. The epitome mentions the bellicosity and

great stature of the Gauls in relation to the Cimbric Wars and writes how
Caesar

> also overcame the Germans under Ariovistos, a people who excelled all others,
> even the largest men, in size; savage, the bravest of the brave, despising death
> because they believe they shall live hereafter, bearing heat and cold with equal
> patience, living on grass in time of scarcity, and their horses browsing on trees.
> But it seems that they were without patient endurance in their battles, and did
> not fight in a scientific way or in any regular order, but with a sort of high spirit
> simply made an onset like wild beasts, for which reason they were overcome by
> Roman science and endurance.[16]

The longer fragments of the *Keltike* mostly come from the tenth-century
Byzantine collection of excerpts *On Embassies*. These do include a few
colourful descriptions, including that of an embassy from Bituitus, king of the
Allobroges, to the Roman commander campaigning in southern Gaul in the
120s BCE, in which the ambassador and his train arrived magnificently clad
and accompanied by fighting dogs and a bard who sang praises of the king,
the tribe and the ambassador. Another pair of fragments, from the *Suda*,
describe how the invading Gauls were so uncontrolled in their appetites that
they gorged themselves on the unaccustomed plenty of Italy and their large
bodies became so flabby they were incapable of exercise: Camillus displayed
some of them (presumably captives) naked to his troops to encourage them.
These anecdotes perhaps suggest Appian was aware of how ethnography
might be made to serve explanatory ends of history, but there is no sign of the
dense engagement with predecessors' work that marked out Polybios,
Poseidonios and Strabo. The peculiar structure of his history also made
impossible the attempt to connect up barbarian histories across the wide span
of the Mediterranean world upon which they impinged.

Tacitus, Plutarch, Dio and Appian together illustrate some of the ways in
which tales of the barbarians continued to be of use, long after those societies
had been transformed by the experience of Roman rule. Not all of these uses
were equally original, but they suggest the currency of older stereotypes and
learned conjectures. For some purposes – their deployment in republican
history, in theological-cum-philosophical dialogue, in sophistical self-fash-
ioning or as background for the ancient novel – the gulf between these fictions
and the empire of experience posed no real problems. But not all imperial
writing was quite so disengaged from the real and the contemporary. Texts
like Dio's history of his own age purported to make truth claims, and claimed
to be informed by experience and recent information. When these texts
contained blatantly out-of-date characterizations, did they not undermine
the plausibility of other accounts? What protected the plausibility of Dio's
Severus from the fantastic setting in which he fought his last war and died?

The threat of dissonance of this kind is a key problem posed by the evident survival of ethnic stereotypes and myths created at the dawn of empire.

Getting to Know the Germans

Yet new information was being collected all the time. One obvious region in which more knowledge was accumulated during the first centuries of the principate was along the German frontier. Halfway through the reign of Augustus, most of the Roman forces were moved out of Gaul to take part in a great eastern movement across the Rhine, to be co-ordinated with a northern advance across the upper Danube. These advances first succeeded, and then failed with the Pannonian Revolt and the loss of 'Free Germany' after 9 CE. To simplify a long and complex military history, as much as a third of the total Roman legionary strength was for a couple of generations concentrated in the Rhineland. They shared this space with veteran soldiers, Gallic settlers and members of tribes brought across the Rhône by Roman generals. After the Flavian creation of the two German provinces and an advance to the Neckar, the frontier more or less became fixed. But what was created was not an iron curtain so much as a broad, polyglot zone within which members of provincial and external populations moved back and forth. Beyond the reach of law and taxation, the area under loose military control and surveillance shaded off into zones of exchange and interaction, in effect a new middle ground.[17]

Archaeologically this zone is visible as a great margin to the empire, extending up to 200 km from the now more or less fixed positions occupied by military camps. Within this region Roman ceramics, coins, bronze and glassware and even occasionally building materials are regularly recovered.[18] Roman narratives give us occasional tantalizing glimpses of frontiersmen of different kinds. Several of Tacitus' German leaders, among them Arminius and Segimundus, turn out to be former Roman auxiliaries returned to their peoples; one former soldier even shelters a detachment of legionaries surprised by the Frisian revolt of 28 CE.[19] Then there is the Roman knight whom Pliny says was sent north from Carnuntum on the Danube to find amber to make ornaments for Nero's gladiatorial games. The story is presumably true, since Pliny knows that amber originates as resin and describes how it was gathered on the shores of the Baltic by people who made great necklaces of it, and then traded it over 600 miles to the Danube. Wonderful amber necklaces of this kind can be seen today in the National Museum of Denmark in Copenhagen. Pliny also surmises, again correctly, that before Roman rule a longer route had brought it to the head of the Adriatic where classical authors first mentioned it in connection with the myth of Phaethon.[20] Other merchants presumably came in search of wild beasts for those games in which exotic European fauna were pitted against African ones in a pageant of world domination.[21] And there will have been less exotic and less glamorous commerce, including the trade in slaves.[22] The Hermundurii, apparently, had at one point the unique privilege of travelling freely within Raetia while all other peoples traded on the bank or in the camps.[23] The implication is that there was a real desire for contact, sufficient that Rome could ration it and needed to provide outlets for it. Similar pressure came from within the empire. On the rare occasions when the frontier did shift outwards during this period – with the absorption of the *Agri Decumates* in the Flavian period, and of Dacia in the reign of Trajan – the military advance was immediately followed by miners, settlers and other entrepreneurs. And with all these crossings and exchanges, came new information.

Tacitus' *Germania* offers a case study in how ethnographic discourse might respond to an increase in knowledge. The gap between Caesarian and Tacitean testimony is certainly significant and one major contrast is an increase in the amount of data presented. Caesar's Germania was in some senses a vacant space.[24] It was mostly wilderness, and mostly unknown, presented as a stark contrast to Gaul. No internal divisions of the Germani were mentioned (although some tribal names do appear in Caesar's narrative). Caesar's Germans worshipped only the sun, Vulcan and the moon and had not even heard of any other gods. They were defined by negatives: no Druids, no government, no permanent property, no laws, no imported luxuries, no pre-marital sex. Caesar's sociology fades out into geography and zoology. When the narrative resumes (ch. 29) he (and we) discover that the Suebi he had been pursuing had meantime melted away into the forests.

Tacitus' account, on the other hand, takes the form of a forty-six-chapter monograph.[25] The *Germania* begins with a definition of its subject. The first twenty-seven chapters discuss the Germans in general, their origins and physical appearance, the landscape, their styles of fighting and of government, German women, religion, their conduct of business and battle, their entertainment, residences and clothing, marriage, sexual habits and child-raising, their banquets and their attitudes to slavery, gambling and death. The remainder of the work consists of an account of the distinctive features of each tribe, organized in a sequence beginning from the frontiers of the empire and extending to the remotest part of Germania.

The tight organization of the *Germania* has persuaded some scholars that it was conforming to a generic blueprint for (otherwise vanished) ancient ethnographic treatises. I have already made clear why I do not think it helpful to think of a 'genre' of ethnography. But there are some similarities with longer discussions, for example the Scythian ethnography in *Airs, Waters, Places* that begins with a general account and moves to a geographically ordered differentiation of the various Scythian peoples and tribes. The significance of this can be over-estimated: it is a regular and unsurprising feature of ancient *ekphraseis* to begin with a characterization of the whole, followed by a minute description of the parts. The topics covered in the general description of the Germans are conventional, but there was no fixed list of subjects that had to be covered. The first part of the *Germania* has in any case a moral character all of its own, engaging with contemporary anxieties about Roman society, identity and history. That ethnographies of barbarian peoples were often mirrors of civilization is a cardinal principle of studies based on *alterité*.[26] But in this case the incriminating finger is pointed very clearly at the contemporary urban vices of the world inhabited by Tacitus and his readers. It has been well written that Tacitus' Germania is 'no place like Rome'.[27] Unlike the Britain of the *Agricola*, Germany resists conquest, its primitive virtues successfully keeping enfeebled Rome at bay.

How was Caesar's empty account expanded into such a detailed portrait of a people and a place? It is too easy to attribute this simply to the expansion of knowledge over the century and a half that separate the two texts. Caesar clearly omitted much he knew in order to give the Germans a certain uniform austerity and lack of definition. Pliny's Germans too display this quality. The short notice he gives to Germany within his geographical survey of the entire world emphasizes the vast extent of its Baltic shore and the complete disagreements on its length between authorities, before itemizing the major tribes and rivers and commenting on the great size of the Hercynian Mountains. At a later point he reports his own observations of the miserable lives of the Chauci, forced to live on low mounds in a landscape flooded twice daily by the tide and to live off nothing but fish and rainwater.[28] Pliny not only wrote from autopsy but had also composed a vast account of Rome's German Wars, now lost. Yet his ethnography marginalizes them in terms of both what is known of them and how they live.

Tacitus could easily have followed similar tactics had it suited its interests. But there is a deliberate compositional difference. Caesar obliterated all internal differentiation.[29] Even the generalizing first half of Tacitus' text seems, by contrast, to struggle against a mass of data. It is not unusual, of course, for successive classical prose texts on the same subject matter to become longer and longer as each attempts to outdo its predecessors. The introduction of increasingly elaborate differentiation is a common means by which this is done: this dynamic has been demonstrated in relation to treatises on agriculture, astrology and medicine.[30] Yet Tacitus is not in competition with Caesar to create a definitive didactic work or master a given genre: and his parade of detail must serve other ends. At times the amount of information he displays threatens the very unity of Germania and the Germans. His Germany is unseizable because it is so vast, not so empty. So where Caesar generalized about the Germans as a whole, and Pliny divides them into five great tribal groups with internal subdivisions, Tacitus offers the folk genealogy I have discussed already, that divides the Germans into three (three of Pliny's five divisions incidentally) but at once states that there are other genealogies which allow the Germans to be divided differently. Where Caesar is silent, and Pliny claims authoritative knowledge, Tacitus refuses to decide between the different versions.

Geography creates a similar impression. The *Germania* begins by establishing its subject as a territory defined by natural boundaries – rivers, mountain ranges and the Ocean – and at the same time as an ethnic province, the Germans bordered by other peoples – Gauls, Sarmatians and so on. The boundedness of Germania could hardly be greater. Yet already in chapter 2 we learn that the name *Germani* is itself new, a recent extension of the name of the Tungri (who now live west of the Rhine) to the rest of the Germans, and then that there are several variant traditions of ethnic genealogies. Tacitus then adds legends of classical founders, the wandering heroes Hercules and Ulixes (ch. 3), before disparaging these stories in favour of assertions of German autochthony creating a unified identity preserved by a refusal to marry their neighbours. That definition seems clear enough (although it will unwind presently) but even at this point the reader is left with an impression that the Germans are not easy to pin down. It is as if more information makes knowledge less rather than more secure. Hence the passive aggressive *aporia*:

> It is not my intention either to support these assertions with proofs or to refute them: each reader may withhold or bestow credence according to his own inclination. For myself, I agree with the views of those who think that the inhabitants of Germania have not been tainted by any intermarriage with other tribes, but have existed as a distinct and pure people, resembling only themselves.[31]

That stoicizing notion of integrity is immediately followed by a description of the Germans in terms of their bodies and temperament, linked conventionally to the climate and geography of their native land. But this turns out to be a false resolution of the problem of the integrity of the Germans. Tacitus has been making an *epideixis* of his knowledge of ethnographic theories and tropes; where in other texts these are deftly disciplined to avoid contradiction, here they seem to be deliberately set at odds to generate a sense of restless incoherence.

For Tacitus goes on to makes it clear that the apparently clear natural and cultural boundaries of Germania are in fact compromised. The Rhine, it emerges, was no kind of barrier (ch. 28). The Gallic Helvetii and Boii used to live east of it. Perhaps the Gauls once invaded Germany? Equally the Danube divides two peoples – the Osi and the Avarisci – who have the same speech, institutions and customs but it is not clear if one group are Pannonians who migrated into Germania, or the other are Germans who migrated into Pannonia. So much for an ethnography that equated common customs with common identity. West of the Rhine not just the Tungri but also the Ubii are said to be of German descent, as are the Vangiones, Triboci and Nemetes. The natural geographic boundedness of Germany collapses. Next the Treveri and Nervi are said to be very eager to claim descent from Germans ... but only in order to distance themselves from their Gallic neighbours. That sardonic comment hints at an awareness of the strategic content of origin myths. The destabilizing consequences for any ethnography based on peoples united by common descent should be obvious.

At the further limits of Germany the boundaries are just as blurred. The Cotini and Osi are not Germans, both on linguistic grounds and because they tolerate paying tribute to the Quadi and the Sarmatians (ch. 43). Tacitus hesitates (ch. 46) how to classify the Peucini, the Veneti and the Fenni, whether as Germans or Sarmatians. Each in different ways seems to combine German and Sarmatian traits of appearance, language, habit and custom. Intermarriage and the abandonment of ancestral custom are the culprits. Beyond the Fenni, Tacitus signals, we enter the territory of myth, the frontier between certain and uncertain knowledge. 'The rest is the stuff of tall tales: the Hellusii and Oxiones who have human faces and features, but the bodies and limbs of beasts. This, as something not yet ascertained, I shall leave open.'[32]

The *Germania* poses real questions about the stability and reality of ethnic boundaries and the possibility of ethnography. If even the Germans are not a real people, like unto themselves, of common descent, physiognomically distinct and living precisely as their climate dictates ... then who is? The modern ethnographer will sympathize too with the problem of accumulating knowledge: the better we know the Germans, the less knowable they seem.

I am not suggesting, of course, that there really was something mysterious about the populations of these regions. Boundary problems, issues of definition, contradictions between local testimony and examples that resist neat classificatory schemata and analytical frameworks are the bread and butter of all ethnographies. What is remarkable about the *Germania*, however, is the extent to which Tacitus deliberately foregrounds these difficulties and resists offering solutions. That refusal to adjudicate between rival accounts of distant peoples and places had been part of the ethnographer's toolkit since at least Herodotos. All the same there is a contrast with the authoritative voice of Caesarian ethnography. More information has only made the Germans seem less graspable.

This compositional tactic does not invalidate the actual items of information included within the text. Some at least of these sound highly plausible, and seem to cohere well with archaeological data. As well as the genealogical charters of descent from Mannus, there are a number of other data which sound rather plausible. Consider for example this piece of testimony.

some people are of the opinion that Ulysses as well, in his lengthy and storied wanderings, travelled into this part of the Ocean and visited the lands of Germania, and that the Asciburgium which stands on the banks of the Rhine and is to this day inhabited, was founded and named by him. Not only that but they also say that an altar consecrated by Ulysses, appending the name of his father Laertes, was once discovered in the same place, and that certain monuments and burial-mounds inscribed with Greek letters still exist in the borderland between Germania and Raetia.[33]

The combination of a story of Odysseus' wandering, backed up with toponymic evidence and reference to monuments, sounds very like the kind of investigation conducted by Asklepiades of Myrleia at the city of Odysseia in Turdetania. In other words, this looks very like another tradition invented on the middle ground. It perhaps brought together an awareness of the theories of Krates of Mallos on Odysseus' exploration of the Ocean, with a bogus etymology for a small town in the densely militarized zone of the Rhineland, perhaps bolstered by the discovery of genuine texts. Greek script was, after all, used in southern Germany and in Burgundy to write Celtic languages during the late Iron Age.[34]

A different kind of problem is posed by information about distant parts of Germania, especially when these notices are peppered with incidental detail that does not seem to contribute to any grander schematic or rhetorical aim. Consider the account of distant peoples given in chapter 44. We read that the Gotones live beyond the Lugii, that they have a monarchy but not of the kind that stifles freedom, and that they border the Rugii and the Lemovii who live on the Ocean. All these peoples have circular shields and short swords and are ruled by kings. Then we learn about islanders, the Suiones, their ships, the peculiarities of their oars and their political system and so on. What kinds of source should we imagine for this information? It would seem bizarre to suppose that these details were Tacitus' own invention: apart from the side swipe at the connection between autocracy and restrictions on freedom of speech, none of these details seems to have any special significance for Rome. Tacitus could conceivably have visited western regions of Germany – he has often been supposed to have served in Cologne – but it is unlikely he went as far as this, and besides he makes no claims to autopsy. It is possible that he was using a written source. If so, the most likely candidate is usually regarded as Pliny's *German Wars* (although there are other candidates and we have no reason to believe this contained more ethnographic detail than did the *Natural History*). But in any case, attributing this information to another Latin text – whether that of Pliny or another – simply defers the question of how information about the further reaches of Germany reached that author. Given the absence of a tradition of exploration, the most likely scenario is that Tacitus, or just possibly the author of texts he used, learned these details in conversation with one or more Germans. Most likely these conversation would have been conducted in Latin, since it is certain many Germans spoke the language from service in the Roman auxilia.[35] We have returned, in other words, to Clifford's 'Squanto effect' and to researches conducted on the middle ground.

Occasionally, it seems possible to reconstruct the broad lines of some of these conversations. Consider one of the most often discussed passages of Tacitus' *Germania*, the source of the notorious phrase *interpretatio romana*.[36]

> In the country of the Nahanarvali may be seen a grove, hallowed by rituals of great antiquity. A priest dressed in woman's clothing officiates. However the gods they worship there are, according to the Roman translation, Castor and Pollux. At least that is the nature of the deities [*vis numini*] but they call them the Alci. There are no images and no traces of foreign religious practices [*superstitio*], all the same they are venerated as brothers and as young men.[37]

The context is a discussion of some of the most distant German tribes, a series of peoples of the Suebi inhabiting regions north of the Hercynian Forest, on the borders of the territory of the Sarmatians. Nothing much is known of most of them but their names, and, in this case, one oddity of cult. The same chapter includes the information that the Cotini mine iron and the Harii paint themselves black. We are on the borders of the exotic, then, three chapters before the peoples said to be half-human, half-beast. No Roman army had ever fought in that territory. These can only be German stories, told about Germans by Germans to Roman enquirers. The enquirer is invisible, obscured by Tacitus' text, but the information that there are no images, and no trace of a foreign (i.e., non-German) origin for the cult, presupposes a process of interrogation. Who supplies the identification with the Dioscuri? Given that the *Germania* stresses the unique features of the cult, it is unlikely to be Tacitus. The translation looks like the work of Germans familiar with Roman deities.[38] It is not always noticed that the issue of translatability between German and Roman religion is on occasion deliberately problematized in the *Germania*.

> Of all the gods they worship Mercury most of all. They even think it is lawful [*fas est*] on certain days to perform human sacrifice to him. Herakles and Mars they propitiate with more conventional animal sacrifice. A part of the Suebi even perform rites for Isis. The cause and provenence of this alien ritual, I have not been able to discover. But the the fact that she is represented with the symbol of a galley [*liburna*] suggests that the religion came from abroad. It is their view that the majesty of gods means they should not be confined within the walls of a temple, nor portrayed anthropomorphically. For this reason they

dedicate woods and groves, and they give the names of the gods to hidden beings that only their reverence allows them to behold.[39]

What were the questions here? Why do you call her Isis? What does the cult image look like? Where did the cult come from?

If the enquirer is obscured, local informants in fact appear quite frequently. Between the account of the historical epics sung about the sons of Mannus, and the posited connection of Odysseus with Asciburgium, is the notice that they say Hercules visited them and that they hail him as the greatest of heroes when they go into battle. Who interpreted either German oral poetry or battle cries for the benefit of whoever first recorded these stories? Squanto again. The name of Hercules evokes the many legends of his travels and marriages across the vast swathe of territory from the Straits of Gibraltar to Scythia, leaving behind a string of founding heroes. Tacitus treats this in a different way from Diodoros. His insistence that this is a native story distances himself from it, and raises other questions. How reliable are German cultural mediators? And can Germany ever make sense in Roman terms? The ferocity of Ocean frustrated Roman attempts to test for themselves stories about a set of Pillars of Hercules north of the Rhine mouth.[40] Tacitus offers us not so much an authoritative account of Germany and the Germans as an image of his attempts to make sense of it, attempts that were often inconclusive. Expressions of uncertainty and even frustration are common. Sometimes native testimony was the best that could be got, yet their translations were unreliable. Despite all this new information, all these frontiersmen, all the opportunities for enquiry across the vast contact zone, sometimes there were no answers.

The cultural gap is not reduced by ethnographical exertion. Understanding the other seems to involve characterization more than familiarization. Writing peoples enshrines a moment of miscomprehension or wonder into texts from which tropes emerge that have their own currency. Neither conquest nor cultural change completely effaced the tales first told of barbarians in the last generations of the republic.

A Stratified Ethnography of Gaul

To show how this happens I want to discuss in detail just one more ethnography, a much later account of the Gauls offered by Ammianus Marcellinus in Book 15 of his *Res Gestae* composed at the end of the fourth century CE.[41] It will be no surprise to find that the 'excursus' is inserted in the narrative at the most dramatic moment possible.[42] Not only has Julian just been elevated to the rank of Caesar, married to Constantius' sister and sent by the emperor to defend the Gallic provinces, but the moment has been surrounded by an air of prophesy ... and also of epic. Julian supplies both when – at the moment of his elevation – he mutters *ex Homerice carmine* the line 'purple death and mighty fate seized him'.[43] As he heads north, encountering en route the terrifying news of the fall of Cologne to the barbarians – news Constantius had known but not revealed, in the first sign of bad faith between them – Julian is greeted by a blind woman who prophesies that he has come to restore the temples of the gods. It is at this point that Ammianus invokes Virgil (*Mantuanus vates*) and declares that he too now begins a greater work.[44] The citation is from the so-called second preface of the *Aeneid* that marks the arrival of Aeneas in Italy and (for modern scholars) the transition from Odyssean to Iliadic modes. Julian and Ammianus collude, that is, in proclaiming the epic nature of what is to follow. Like Achilles, Julian will quarrel with his king; like Aeneas, he will re-establish the cult of the ancestral gods. Gaul will make Julian an emperor, as Italy made Aeneas a king. It is for this reason – that he is taking up a greater theme – declares Ammianus, that he should now make clear the regions and situation of the Gallic provinces,[45] especially to avoid having to stop to explain unfamiliar matters in the midst of his narrative of fiery attacks and fierce battles that will follow.[46]

Ammianus launches into a virtuoso display of his erudition, and incidentally of the materials available to a late antique ethnographer:

Uncertain about the earliest origin of the Gauls, the older writers left our knowledge of the truth very imperfect. But then Timagenes, a Greek in his scholarly diligence as well as in language, collected from a great mass of books facts which had been long unknown. Guided by his faithful statements, and avoiding all obscurity, I will now give a plain and intelligible account. Some claim that the first inhabitants ever seen in these regions were called Celtae, after the name of a much loved king, and sometimes also Galatae, after the name of his mother. For Galatae is the Greek named for the Galli. Others state that they are Dorians who followed the older Hercules and then chose to settle the districts bordering on the ocean. The Druids affirm that a portion of the people really was indigenous, but that other inhabitants poured in from the islands on the coast, and from the districts across the Rhine, driven from their former homes by frequent wars, and the inroads of a tempestuous sea. Some again maintain that, after the destruction of Troy, a few Trojans fleeing from the Greeks, who were then scattered over the whole world, occupied these districts, which at that time had no inhabitants at all. But the natives of these countries affirm more positively than any other fact (and, indeed, I myself have seen it engraved on their monuments), that when Hercules, the son of Amphitryon, marched to the destruction of those cruel tyrants, Geryon and Tauriscus, one of whom was oppressing the Gauls, and the other Spain, after he had conquered both of them, took as wives some women of noble birth in those countries, and became the father of many children; and that his sons called the districts of which they became the kings after their own names. And then again an Asiatic people coming from Phocaea to escape the cruelty of Harpalus, the lieutenant of Cyrus the king, sought to sail to Italy. A part of them founded Velia, in Lucania, others settled a colony at Marseilles, in the territory of Vienne; and then, in subsequent ages, these towns increasing in strength and importance, founded other cities. But I should cut short this discussion of different versions, since they can often seems excessive.[47]

This passage might easily seem almost parodically over-authorized. Timagenes is preferred, in part for his authority as a Greek, the same identity Ammianus notoriously claims for himself, despite the fact that, unlike Timagenes, Ammianus writes in Latin. Also unlike Timagenes, Ammianus writes in an historiographical tradition that repeatedly alludes to Latin predecessors.[48] Ammianus implies too that he has selected Timagenes only after a careful perusal of the alternatives. It is far from clear at what point Timagenes begins to be supplemented by others.[49] It sounds as if the various accounts of Herculean wanderings and Trojan *nostoi* and the discussion of nomenclature are from Timagenes – I have already discussed the similar accounts in Diodoros and Strabo – and perhaps Druidical testimony was also in his account. Ammianus is quick to supplement this with his own autopsy of monuments in Gaul. Are the wanderings of the Phocaeans part of Timagenes' testimony too, or does this relate to their prominence in Trogus? Or is Ammianus just showing off? The final clause – *evectus sum longius* – surely hammers it home that Ammianus is putting on a show. Whatever else this ethnography is doing, it demands *not* to be read at face value.

Ammianus continues with an account of Druids, bards and other natural philosophers. A geographical sketch leads into a longer discussion of the Alps, King Cottius and Susa, the various passes and how they are crossed, the legends attached to each – more about Hercules – then the dramatic tale of Scipio versus Hannibal, and the latter's bold carving out of a new route into Italy. Then we return to the ancient accounts of Gaul divided into three parts, the ferocity of the Belgae and the effeminacy of the Aquitani, related, as in Caesar, to their relative distance from and contact with Rome. At this point, ancient history is replaced by an account of the late antique provincial organization, and especially the mighty cities of Roman Gaul, some with their very recent histories. Trier is celebrated as a tetrarchic capital, the ruin of Avenches is lamented, the barbarian disasters of the cities of the middle Rhine are recalled. After the account of Aquitania, the Rhône is presented as a great waterway and following this, Ammianus offers an account of the 'appearance and habits of the inhabitants'.[50] What follows is mostly familiar stuff. Gauls are tall, fair, ferocious and the women are fiercer than the men; Gauls are militaristic and brave but cannot resist wine. Drawing to a close with a short account of their pacification, Ammianus cites in rapid succession

Cato, Cicero, Sallust and Caesar. And then suddenly he claims he has gone on too long and must return to his subject.[51]

This passage has often been discussed. First of all, a distinguished line of scholars, Mommsen among them, have debated the extent of Ammianus' debt to different predecessors, and the sources, direct and indirect, of each part of this description.[52] This is a particularly complex passage, to be sure, as it is far from clear that Ammianus does know and use at first hand some of the authorities he cites, rather than knowing them only second hand, for example through Livy to whom there is no explicit reference but whose accounts of the period he almost certainly used. Ammianus has in a sense deliberately set a puzzle in the number of authorities cited. All the same, *Quellenforschung* may have distracted some readers from Ammianus' rhetorical aims, from what effects he was trying to achieve.[53]

Second, there is the location of this passage within the larger narrative. I mentioned already the general function of digressions of this sort in ancient historical texts. These passages always do more than simply arouse the expectations of expert readers and create tension through separating a momentous action from its consequences: they also colour the narrative that follows.[54] I have already suggested some particular resonances for this passage that not only emphasize the significance of Julian's elevation, but also associate him with epic heroes and perhaps invite us to think of the sort of fates that awaited him and them.[55] Ammianus, too, takes the opportunity to build his authority as an historian: the *diligentia* of Timagenes his fellow 'Greek', the allusions to and quotations from Latin historians, and the implicit claim to play Virgil to Julian's Aeneas/Augustus are supplemented by the conventional display of the historian sifting rival accounts and importing his own knowledge based on his travels through and observations within the region.[56]

Yet even if we could be sure about Ammianus' sources and reach a satisfactory account of the literary function of this passage within Ammianus' history of Julian's reign, the same question remains. How was Ammianus able to ethnologize Gaul as it had been at the time of the first Greek accounts and Roman interventions in its history, given the enormous space of time that separates him from those accounts, and given his *own* experience and knowledge of the region? What kind of significance did all these tales of Druids and savage Belgae have, so long afterwards? And how did he, and at least some of his readers, manage the cognitive dissonance between the barbarized world of texts like these, and the utterly different landscapes and societies of the Roman provinces they knew half a millennium later?

A good starting point is to examine a little more closely the place occupied by anachronistic elements within Ammianus' account, and ask more precisely what kinds of outdated material he deploys, and where and why he does so. The summary of Ammianus' Gallic ethnography offered above illustrates a sometimes abrupt alternation between time periods. Ammianus' account deals at various points with (a) the mythic past of wandering Trojans and the Herakles legend; (b) conditions at the time of the Roman conquests, mostly Caesarian, but perhaps containing older strata; and (c) conditions in Ammianus' own day. During his account of the Alps, he also deals with other historical episodes, specifically the second Punic War – ostensibly as part of an explanation of the name Alpes Poeninae – and the Augustan period, again in relation to the reign of King Cottius after whom the Alpes Cottii were named. I shall say less about those two aetiological-cum-etymological interventions.

As we read, our attention is shifted backwards and forwards between the three main periodizations. Sometimes the juxtaposition of past and present seems to emphasize the transformative effects of Roman rule. So the classic characterization of the Gauls as drunks and fighters in 15.12.1–4 is followed by a chapter on their pacification.[57] This sort of effect – a leading narrative set in one period, periodically interrupted by statements that call into question its currency – is something of a leitmotif of Strabo's *Geography*. But this theme seems less appropriate for Julian's story and in any case, the contrast, borrowed directly or indirectly from Caesar, between the savagery of the Belgae and the effeminacy of the Aquitani, is not very obviously picked up in the account of the cities, administrations and rivers of the two areas. Other passages – such as the differentiation of Druids, bards and *euhages* – sandwiched between legendary origins and the description of the natural limits of Gaul – seem to have no clear relation to the rest of the account. The problem is that of the relationship between experience and stereotype, between Things Seen and Things Read.[58]

Perhaps it is not surprising that Ammianus includes material from period (c) relating to his own service in Gaul. After all, autopsy is repeatedly validated, explicitly in relation to the Herakles monuments, more generally in the *persona* Ammianus develops for himself throughout the work. It is a fair inference that he passed through Susa when travelling from Milan to the Rhineland with Ursicinus in 354, saw the tomb of Cottius and was impressed by the other monuments of the city. During the following three years, he may well have visited a number of the northern Gallic cities he mentions. Perhaps he did see there monuments relating to local traditions and foundation myths. All this builds his reputation as a well-travelled witness, often at the centre of events, a *persona* that is developed across the whole of his work.

More puzzling is the inclusion of ethnographic material relating to the condition of the Gauls at the time of the first Roman encounters. Ammianus is careful to situate his account of Druidism in the past, and also introduces the account of the threefold division of Gaul with *temporibus priscis*, 'in former times'. But his account of the manners of the Gauls, their ferocity and fondness of drink, and of their wives, more formidable than the men, is set in the present tense, and Cato the Elder and Cicero are recruited as additional witnesses to the drunkenness of the Gauls. Does Ammianus mean to imply that in terms of character, the Gauls have not really changed? This seems unlikely, and if so the theme is not developed. On the other hand the rapid movement back and forth between the three principal time periods of his account might well confuse the unwary reader, offering a sense of Gaul as a province 'out of time', part of a world the difference of which was marked by its essential immunity to history.[59] Is Ammianus preparing for Julian a Gaul more wild and formidable than it really was? Tacitus might be suspected of using his ethnographic passages in the *Agricola* to prepare a primitive Britain within which his protagonist could exercise those ancient virtues that no longer could be accommodated in the capital. But this suits Julian's story less well, since his enemies will be Germans not Gauls and he will exercise a different kind of virtue there. Besides, if the period (b) material is intended to make Gaul seem more primitive, is not the aim undermined by the inclusion of material from period (c), especially the reference to the grand cities of Gaul which, to a modern reader, recalls Ausonius' *Ranking of Noble Cities*? The learned Roman reader, however – more familiar with classical texts than with contemporary realities – may have found Ammianus' Gauls reassuringly exotic. The role reversals between men and women; the ignorant abuse of wine, itself one of the key products of civilization; even the mystic wisdom of the Druids, find dozens of parallels in other writing on northern barbarians. Ammianus' Gauls have the conventional physical strength combined with moral and intellectual weakness, characteristics that making them quasi-bestial.[60] Rather than asking why Ammianus has not brought his ethnography up to date by correcting what he had read from his personal observation, the proper question to ask is: What work did these archaizing stereotypes do in his text?

The shape of my answer to these questions will, I suspect, by now be no surprise. Ammianus' own passage through the Gallic provinces generated certain information – what the ruins of Aventicum looked like, what it was like to cross the Alps – but not the same kind of ethnographic knowledge as that created in the original middle ground, where dense intercultural contacts provided the necessary data and informants for *historie*. For that category of knowledge his own experience was largely useless, and he had to rely on others – on Things Read rather than Things Seen. For all *generalizing* accounts of the local customs (the *mores Gallorum*) and form of the provinces (the *Galliarum tractus et situm*) Ammianus referred to existing texts. These texts were out of date, indeed it is quite probable that no more recent ethnographies of the region had been written, since the Latin tradition in this field seems to have been confined within a relatively short period of time.[61] He could supplement this material with his own anecdotal knowledge, maybe with a little culled from official documents. But his own role in the province limited his vision. The kind of knowledge he could contribute would neither replicate nor falsify existing ethnography. What his learned sources could do, however, was add *colour*, mood music, a sense of place and with it of occasion.

The corollary of my argument is that we must imagine his intended readers to have understood the implicit distinctions made between different kinds of knowledge, and also that although different kinds might be artfully inter- woven and juxtaposed, as they are here in Ammianus' account of the Gauls, they could not be combined. This segregation of knowledge into different realms, different spheres of exchange, is not unusual. Folk ethnography, personal experience and what one read in books could equally well be com- partmentalized, since they would rarely be needed on the same occasion. Balkanized ethnographic knowledge of this kind, and similarly fragmented views of other peoples are probably fairly common today as they were in antiquity.[62] Ammianus' description cannot have been incomprehensible to his contemporary readers. As well as recognizing particular tropes of representation, they must have been able to recognize the clues that signified a shift in the category of information. Long experience of reading texts in which ethnography was tightly disciplined ought to have developed appro- priate reading practices. Given that part of its intended effect must have come precisely from the shifting juxtaposition of time-frames, it would be sensible to begin with the assumption that the abrupt contrasts in his account between different kinds of ethnographic knowledge would have attracted the atten- tion of his readers, rather than have struck them as confusing. Readers able to navigate the conventional juxtaposition of myths of the *nostoi* with more recent history should in principle have been able to tolerate a third category of knowledge without experiencing a disorienting sense of dissonance.[63] Given readers of this kind, there was no obstacle if an historian wished to people the Roman provinces with ethnographic ghosts. Maybe the very blandness and homogeneity of the imperial provinces invited the resuscita- tion of ancient colour, whether simply to differentiate one region from another or to briefly give an emperor a suitable stage on which to play his role. Perhaps, in other words, it was the very diversity of barbarian stereo- types that gave them such staying power in an increasingly Roman world.

The Fate of Myth

I have been considering ethnic stereotypes. Stereotypes tend to emerge in quite particular contexts, and to reflect the interests and world views of those who employ them.[64] This is implicit in all recent studies of classical barba- rism. Most of the original uses of barbarism are inaccessible to us now. Either they were formed in encounters on Greek colonial grounds and have left little trace, or else they first gained currency orally, then in conversation and oratory, before developing into ideologies and discourses we can study only at second hand. It is an irony that the history of barbarism has had to be written in relation to the most literary of texts, which themselves often challenged the common opinions of their day.[65]

Roman notions of the barbarian, at first appropriated from Greek models, underwent their own transformations: first through a process of universalization, one to which not all Greek writers objected, and then through a new domestication in Italy, and then a fresh universalization at the heart of a world empire which had recruited older civilizing myths in framing its own claims to a divine mandate and cosmological centrality.[66] Barbarians, silent partners in this complex dance, shifted their identities to match the evolution of each new species of civilization. That familiar thematic is the background against which new barbarian histories were created in the Roman West, and also against which later texts made their own appropriations of the ethnographic voice.

Stereotypes in common use have no inertia; they change constantly to suit the communicative and persuasive strategies of those who to employ them. At the very largest scale, this seems true of ancient constructions of the barbarian. So the ends of the earth may recede in the face of exploration; noble savages may become vicious barbarians (or vice versa) as relations in the contact zone change; and the normalized centre of the world may shift in relation to political change. Since Thucydides, ancient writers had been prepared to assert that particular groups might become civilized, or indeed be barbarized, changing their institutions, habits and customs, as a consequence of various kinds of intercourse with their neighbours, the debilitating effects of luxury and the like.

Yet one part of the ethnography of the Roman West seems oddly resistant to change. Archaeology and epigraphy show how western societies underwent cataclysmic changes around the turn of the millennium, and slower but persistant and wide-ranging transformations thereafter.[67] The introduction of new ritual systems and cosmologies, the impact of urbanization and monetarization, major shifts in consumption and in production, the creation of new built and farmed environments, are merely the most evident signs of processes that erased most traces of the world that had been observed by Polybios, Artemidoros and Poseidonios. The most traumatic stages of this process coincided chronologically with the period in which myth-making seems to have been most energetic.[68] Yet the stereotypes that emerged from the earliest classical ethnographies evidently had a good deal of staying power. How should we explain this?

One approach would be to treat the world of texts as essentially insulated from social and historical processes. This might seem attractive to anyone who sees imperial literature as obsessively classicizing and introverted, a game played by a very small number of hyper-educated *littérateurs*, within a universe defined by strict canons and a complicated rules of allusion. But few today hold such an austere position. A central argument of this book has been that these stories and descriptions make most sense when set in the contexts of their creation and retelling. Hence my zigzagging back and forth between the middle ground or contact zone where they were created, and the great libraries at the core of the empire. As it happens, the authors of the texts considered in this final chapter were neither ivory tower scholars, nor pampered court poets. Tacitus and Dio were consular senators and both served as provincial governors; Pliny the Elder and Appian were lesser functionaries; Ammianus self-identified as a soldier, although he was more than that. It is just conceivable that all these individuals employed mental reservations to segregate life from work, Things Seen from Things Read, but this seems an unnecessarily extreme solution. Besides, we are familiar today with many other examples of the tenacity of ethnic stereotypes, even in the face of the increased knowledge and familiarity brought by travel and communication. On the face of it, this apparent inertia poses problems for historicizing and contextualizing explanations. The only way of rescuing the argument that ancient stereotyping was essentially a matter of social strategy, is to ask what functions enduring stereotypes continued to serve in the lifetimes of those who redeployed them with varying degrees of originality.

Stereotypes of barbarism and civilization had a variety of uses in classical culture. They might provide frames of reference against which historical events or political actions acquired significance. They offered philosophers imaginative spaces, in the past, in the future and at the edges of the world, whether to envisage utopias or else to mark those points at which men and beasts became almost indistinguishable. Poets and historians drew on them for exotic settings. Panegyrics in prose and verse set up barbarians as anti-types of emperors, as did sculptors. Tropes of the barbarian had ancient rhetorical and dramatic applications for humour and invective. The shifting images of the Gauls, formed first in the context of wars in central Italy, modified during the Roman conquest of Cisalpina, and again when Romans first fought north of the Alps, provide many examples.[69] Cicero's Gauls were not Cato's, and Caesar's were different again. Nor were these stereotypes necessarily simple. Cicero's negative characterization of the Allobroges in the *pro Fonteio* contrasts with his emphasis on their trustworthiness as vital witnesses to Catiline's plotting. Caesar offers images of faithful Roman allies as well as cannibalistic savages.

Just as with other peoples – Greeks most obviously – a variety of stereo-types were available for use. When gathered together in modern collections and sourcebooks,[70] these formulations can seem contradictory, and might easily give the impression that Roman images of aliens were either incoherent or else so various as to resist analysis. In fact, a relatively small range of types was all that was required by orators, philosophers and poets. Druids were *either* natural philosophers who taught the transmigration of souls, mediators in their own communities and respected beyond it for their great reserves of orally transmitted wisdom, *or else* they were terrifying barbarian priests who conducted savage human sacrifices.[71] Gallic warriors were *either* symbols of the strength that came from a simple life and diet *or* illustrations of the limits of that strength and passion without discipline and intelligence. Intermediate positions were needed much more rarely. Little contradiction was felt since different contexts and rhetorical purposes called for different stereotypes to be deployed. The essential conservatism of Latin and Greek literatures under the Roman empire did help to keep these stories in circulation. Yet another consequence of that conservatism was to incite and permit subtly original recombinations or re-evaluations of established tropes. Dio's Keltoi and Ammianus' Druids were sustained by this intertextual play, as well as by their general utility. Good to think with, carriers of particular resonances, evocative tokens in a complicated but well-loved set of rhetorical games, these stories had a life all of their own. Ethnography had become a new species of myth.

The utility of these myths set limits on their revisability. Ammianus' Gaul could not become unrecognizably un-Gallic. As with other kinds of myth, new twists and variants might be added, but Medea in the end could not spare her children, and Troy had to fall to the Greeks. We might think of this as the gulf between the generalizing knowledge encoded in ethnographic passages, and the detail produced by eye-witnesses, which emerges in Tacitus' ethnography of Britain and Caesar's of the Gauls. The kind of details which a Roman soldier or general might add to an account from his own experience would never be enough to challenge its grand lines. Holding incommensurate elements together required a disciplining of the ethnographic text. The cost of this short-term rhetorical gain was the loss not only of a developing ethnographic science, but also of a properly historical account of the civilizing process. As the historian's gaze turned to habits and customs, so the narrative mode was set aside for the ethnographic. As a result we have no native social history to set alongside what can be reconstructed from documents and artefacts. Roman Gauls would always remain belligerent flies caught in rhetorical amber.

The implications are wide ranging. For a start, it means we can make little or no use of these authors as witnesses to the way barbarians really lived. Fragments of information, – Caesar's aurochs, Sallust's *mapalia* and Ammianus' vivid account of the Alps – remain reliable. But almost all generalizing claims have to be treated as potentially cultural fossils, an afterglow of patterns first discerned on those middle grounds where Mediterranean visitors and local populations got to know each other better than we can now hope to know either group.

What was it like to live among these reverberating echoes from the contact period? Educated Africans, Spaniards and Gauls were aware, naturally enough, of the semantic resonances of their ethnonyms. Perhaps that is why they were rarely used, as opposed to tribal ethnics, on epigraphic self-representation. Those orators who did emerge from conquered provinces seem to have been just as likely to stress the barbarity of their origins as anyone else.[72] The sophist Favorinus allegedly summarized his unique achievement in a series of self-characterizing paradoxes. The first was that although a Gaul he could perform as a Greek.[73] Gauls and Greeks were occasional polar opposites in Roman throught, representatives of barbarism and decadence, and of different kinds of enemies. Favorinus, from the Roman colony of Arles, was hardly a trousered and moustachioed barbarian. But what better means than this of appropriating the civilizing myth into a story of personal triumph. Did stereotype turn into prejudice in the capital? It is hard to find examples later than the jibes apparently made against the Gallic senators admitted from Cisalpina by Caesar and Comatan Gaul by Claudius. The accelerating recruitment of provincial senators may have put a stop to that. Pretty soon any senators who threw stones of that kind would find out that they were living in a glasshouse.

So much for stereotypes of barbarism. What of those other barbarian tales, the genealogies and foundation stories first told in that formative age on the middle ground to make precious connections between local knowledge and the global wisdom of the Greeks and their Roman masters? How long did Spaniards and Gauls remember Antenor and Diomedes? Here things are less clear. One of the most striking features of the culture of the cities of the Roman East is a fascination with both ancient myths and the new ones created in the Hellenistic and Roman periods. Founding figures and foundation legends appeared on coinage and monumental art, were celebrated in civic festivals, were commemorated by inscriptions, and were the subject of orations and poetry. Local experts are a feature of the period, either writing accounts of their city's myths and history or ready to inform visitors about the same. Civic centres were turned into virtual memory theatres.[74]

Nothing quite like this is visible in the Roman West. Did it ever exist? Most of what we know of Eastern festivals comes from great monumental inscriptions, of the kind that were probably never created in western cities. Hardly any western cities created coinages that may be compared to the hundreds minted in parts of the East, coinages on which local heroes and deities were often depicted. Monumental sculpture rarely compared to that of the East, whether for economic reasons, because of an absence of the proper stone or simply a different aesthetic. Our ignorance of the value placed on local traditions in the early imperial West might be simply a product of the absence of evidence. On the other hand, the absence of that evidence might reflect a general lack of interest in the media through which collective memory and tradition might be memorialized. It is fairly clear that pre-Roman traditions were not maintained. When provincial Latin literatures appeared in late antiquity, the past they remember is largely one based on Latin texts.[75] Pre-Roman sites sometimes show signs of continuing cult on a small scale, but most were abandoned or else obliterated by subsequent building. Did western communities voluntarily live with no history beyond the collective history of Rome? It seems scarcely conceivable that they showed no interest in what was, in effect, a mythic *lingua franca* across the Mediterranean world.[76] Who would voluntarily live mythless in such a world?

There are tantalizing hints of local traditions. Consider Herakles, so prominent in the invented traditions of Spain, Africa and Gaul.[77] The Phoenician temple of Melqart at Cadiz laid the foundations of cult in many Mediterranean cities, and Herodotos offered Greek ethnographers with models of how to insert local episodes into the common narrative. Tacitus and Ammianus suggest that legends of Herakles' travels remained important in northern Europe too, and there are the occasional references to Pillars of Hercules at the mouth of the Baltic. Lucian's short introduction *Herakles* offers an account of a peculiar local iconography for the hero in Gaul, interpreted to the narrator by a local expert knowledgeable in Greek literature and myth. No image has ever been found that resembles the strange figure described by Lucian: perhaps he invented it, although it is a bizarre fiction, and in his other ethnographic writings he preferred to exercise his art on interpretation rather than falsification of the bizarre. Either way Herakles really was among the most widely worshipped deities of the lower Rhineland and of Gaul more generally. A long dossier of temples, inscriptions and images of all kinds has been compiled.[78] Connections have been proposed between his cult and the creation of new identities on the northernmost edge of the empire.[79] How long were the marriages of Herakles remembered in the West?

Then there is the Trojan myth and the stories of the *nostoi* of Greek heroes. There is less evidence here of cult to set alongside the ubiquitous references in ethnographic writing. Local traditions evidently snowballed for a while. What were the sources for the mass of local legends on which Silius seems to have drawn to characterize the many Spanish components of Hannibal's army?[80] Then there are a few puzzling references to claims of Trojan descent made by the Arverni in Gaul and perhaps the Aedui too, if that is what lies behind the tradition of their brotherhood with Rome.[81] Were myths of this kind still being elaborated and rehearsed and retold in the western provinces during the early empire? Our first source for an alleged Arvernian claim to Trojan ancestry is two lines of Lucan. The second is included in a letter of Sidonius Apollinaris, bishop in the fifth century of Clermont-Ferrand, the capital of the Roman period Arverni. It has sometimes been suggested that Sidonius is recounting a local tradition, transmitted orally for half a millennium, but in fact his lines are echoes of Lucan's.[82] Maybe other stories, known only in late sources, were drawn not from oral tradition but from revisiting texts created in the age of Diodoros and Dionysius, Parthenios and Strabo.

Some of these stories had a strange afterlife. The *Liber Historiae Francorum*, composed in northern France in the eighth century CE, told the story of the Trojan origins of the Franks.[83] Priam and Antenor had escaped from the wreck of Troy and took refuge in the Crimea at the same time as Aeneas fled to Italy. From there their descendants moved up the Danube and eventually formed an alliance with the Roman emperor Valentinian. A different story of Trojan origins was told in the slightly earlier chronicle of Fredegar. The story of the Trojan origins of the Franks had a long afterlife, and many imitations. Nennius' ninth-century *Historia Britonum* etymologizes Britain from Brutus of Troy, a descendant of Aeneas. The story was picked up and elaborated by Geoffrey of Monmouth. Many other works from the twelfth century in both English and French were devoted to the Trojan myth.[84] Elaborated by Renaissance mythographers, these stories enjoyed a wide popularity well into the early modern period. Perhaps first formed to assert alliances with (or claims to be the heirs of) Rome or else invented to give new peoples some connection with antiquity, these myths would link the great works of the classical canon to late mediaeval scholarship. Eventually Trojan descent became important to the kings of France for the evidence it provided that they, and the Franks, were in no way German.[85] Did this later generation of barbarians find in genealogy and myth the same sort of ways of reconstituting the world that had appealed to Iron Age communities? Or when they entered the empire did they find themselves in a world still reciting the wanderings of Herakes and Odysseus and Aeneas? It would be wonderful to hear provincial voices passing these stories on from generation to generation, all the way from Caesar's conquests to the world of Charlemagne. Perhaps they did. But however hard we listen, we cannot quite hear them telling tales.

Notes

Introduction

1 Catharine Edwards, ed., *Roman Presences. Receptions of Rome in European culture, 1789–1945* (Cambridge: Cambridge University Press, 1999). For the converse impact of empire on the study of archaeology, Richard Hingley, *Roman Officers and English Gentlemen. The imperial origins of Roman archaeology* (London: Routledge, 2000).

2 Christopher Stray, '"Patriots and professors." A century of Roman studies 1910–2010', *Journal of Roman Studies* 100 (2010), 1–31.

3 Yvon Thébert, 'Romanisation et déromanisation en Afrique: histoire décolonisée ou histoire inversée?' *Annales ESC* 33, 1 (1978), 64–82; David Mattingly, *An Imperial Possession. Britain in the Roman Empire 54 BC–AD 409* (London: Allen Lane, 2006).

4 Eric R. Wolf, *Europe and the People without History* (Berkeley: University of California Press, 1982), for the observation as well as the phrase.

5 For a clear statement of the distance (and connections) between ancient and modern anthropologies see Wilfried Nippel, 'Anthropology', in *Brill's New Pauly* (2008). The same themes are treated more discursively in Nippel, *Griechen, Barbaren und 'Wilde'. Alte Geschichte und Sozialanthropologie* (Frankfurt-am-Main: Fischer Taschenbuch Verlag, 1990).

6 Among others, Nicholas Thomas, *Out of Time. History and evolution in anthropological discourse* (Ann Arbor: University of Michigan Press, 1989); James Clifford and George Marcus, eds, *Writing Culture. The poetics and politics of ethnography* (Berkeley: University of California Press, 1986); John Comaroff and Jean Comaroff, *Ethnography and the Historical Imagination* (Boulder, CO: Westview Press, 1992); George E. Marcus, *Ethnography Through Thick and Thin* (Princeton, NJ: Princeton University Press, 1998); James Clifford, *Routes. Travel and translation in the late twentieth century* (Cambridge: Cambridge University Press, 1999).

7   Of many accounts, I recommend Claude Nicolet, ed., *Rome et la conquête du monde méditerranéen. 264–27 avant J.C.* (Paris: Presses Universitaires de France, 1977).

8   On the characterization and limits of the Mediterranean, Peregrine Horden and Nicholas Purcell, *The Corrupting Sea. A study of Mediterranean history* (Oxford: Blackwell Publishers, 2000), with the discussions collected in William Vernon Harris, ed., *Rethinking the Mediterranean* (Oxford: Oxford University Press, 2005); Irad Malkin, ed., *Mediterranean Paradigms and Classical Antiquity* (London and New York: Routledge, 2005).

9   These three peoples were already contrasted as different in kind and requiring a different style of rule to Greek subjects by Cicero, *ad Quintum fratrem* 1.1.27.

10 Most recently Susan E. Alcock, John F. Cherry, and Jas Elsner, eds, *Pausanias. Travel and memory in Roman Greece* (New York: Oxford University Press, 2001); Christina T. Kuhn, 'Mythos und Historie in kaiserzeitlichen Smyrna. Kollektive Identitätsstiftung im Kontext der Romanisierung', *Scripta Classica Israelica* 28 (2009), 93–111; Simon Price, 'Local mythologies in the Greek East', in *Coinage and Identity in the Roman Provinces*, ed. Christopher Howgego, Volker Heuchert and Andrew Burnett (Oxford: Oxford University Press, 2005), 115–24.

11 For a wide-ranging exploration of this idea see Chris Gosden, *Archaeology and Colonialism. Cultural contact from 5000 BC to the present* (Cambridge: Cambridge University Press, 2004), chapter 6.

12 Eric Hobsbawm and Terence Ranger, eds, *The Invention of Tradition* (Cambridge: Cambridge University Press, 1983) is the classical treatment of the theme. For recent applications to Rome see Andrew Wallace-Hadrill, *Rome's Cultural Revolution* (New York: Cambridge University Press, 2008); Emma Dench, *Romulus' Asylum. Roman identities from the age of Alexander to the age of Hadrian* (Oxford: Oxford University Press, 2005).

13 Edward Said, *Orientalism* (London: Routledge and Kegan Paul, 1978). The subsequent bibliography is enormous, but see for instance the responses of John M. MacKenzie, *Orientalism. History, theory and the arts* (Manchester: Manchester University Press, 1995); D.A. Washbrook, 'Orients and occidents. Colonial discourse theory and the historiography of the British empire', in *The Oxford History of the British Empire*, ed. R.R. Winks (Oxford: Oxford University Press, 1999), 596–611; Christopher A. Bayly, *Empire and Information. Intelligence gathering and social communication in India, 1780–1870* (Cambridge: Cambridge University Press, 1996).

14 For example, Jason König and Tim Whitmarsh, eds, *Ordering Knowledge in the Roman Empire* (Cambridge: Cambridge University Press, 2007); Trevor Murphy, *Pliny the Elder's Natural History. The empire in the encyclopaedia* (Oxford: Oxford University Press, 2004), Claude Nicolet, *Space, Geography and Politics in the Early Roman Empire*, trans. Hélène Leclerc (Ann Arbor, MI: University of Michigan Press, 1991).

15 For a helpful summary, Phillip B. Wagoner, 'Precolonial intellectuals and the production of colonial knowledge', *Comparative Studies in Society and History* 45, 4 (2003), 783–814.

16   Some idea of the range of these enquiries is given by the nearly forty contributions to Patrick Petitjean, Catherine Jami and Anne Marie Moulin, eds, *Science and Empire. Historical studies about scientific development and European expansion* (Dordrecht, Boston and London: Kluwer Academic Publishers, 1992).

17   Above all Klaus E. Müller, *Geschichte der antiken Ethnographie und ethnologischen Theoriebildung. Von den Anfängen bis auf die Byzantinischen Historiographen*, 2 vols. (Wiesbaden: F. Steiner Verlag GMBH, 1972, 1980); Felix Jacoby, *Die Fragmente der griechischen Historiker*, 15 vols (Berlin and Leiden: Weidemann and Brill, 1923–58).

18   I shall cite it here as Nicolet, *Space, Geography and Politics*.

1   Telling Tales on the Middle Ground

1   Pliny *Natural History* 5.1 (author's translation).

2   On Rome's growing fascination with grotesques and marvels especially in Africa see Rhiannon Evans, 'Ethnography's freak show. The grotesques at the edges of the Roman earth', *Ramus* 28, 1 (1999), 54–73.

3   Pliny *Natural History* 5.5: *per quam iter est ad montem Africae vel fabulosissimum Atlantem.*

4   Pliny *Natural History* 5.7 (author's translation).

5   The term *periplus* describes travel accounts, or accounts organized in a linear way that invite readers to make an imaginary tour of the world.

6   Pliny *Natural History* 5.12 (author's translation).

7   Pliny *Natural History* 5.22.

8   On Pliny as the culmination of a trend widely exemplified among members of his own social world, Mary Beagon, *Roman Nature. The thought of Pliny the Elder* (Oxford: Clarendon Press, 1992), chapter 1.

9   Mela I.25–38. On their relationship, Rhiannon Evans, 'Geography without people. Mapping in Pliny's *Historia Naturalis* Books 3–6', *Ramus* 34, 1 (2005), 47–74. I am grateful to Dr Evans for discussion of this.

10   Brent D. Shaw, 'The Elder Pliny's African geography', *Historia. Zeitschrift für Alte Geschichte* 30, 4 (1981), 421–71.

11   On Sallust's ethnography of the same region see Renato Oniga, *Sallustio e l'etnografia*, ed. Maurizio Bettini and Gian Biagio Conte (Pisa: Giardini, 1995); Robert Morstein-Marx, 'The myth of Numidian origins in Sallust's African excursus (*Iugurtha* 17.7–18.12)', *American Journal of Philology* 122, 2 (2001), 179–200; C.M.C. Green, '*De Africa et eius incolis*. The function of geography and ethnography in Sallust's history of the Jugurthine War (*J* 17–19)', *The Ancient World* 24, 2 (1993), 185–97. On Africa in ancient ethnographic discourse see C.R. Whittaker, 'Ethnic discourses on the frontiers of Roman Africa', in *Ethnic Constructs in Antiquity. The role of power and tradition*, ed. Ton Derks and N. Roymans (Amsterdam: Amsterdam University Press, 2009), 189–206.

12   Among them Valérie Naas, *Le projet encyclopédique de Pline l'ancien* (Rome: École française de Rome, 2002); Murphy, *Pliny the Elder's Natural History*;

Andrew Wallace-Hadrill, 'Pliny the Elder and man's unnatural history', *Greece and Rome* 37, 1 (1990), 80–96; Beagon, *Roman Nature*; Sorcha Carey, *Pliny's Catalogue of Culture. Art and empire in the Natural History* (Oxford: Oxford University Press, 2003); Gian Biagio Conte, 'The inventory of the world. Form of nature and encyclopedic project in the work of Pliny the Elder', in *Genres and Readers. Lucretius, love elegy, Pliny's Encyclopedia* (Baltimore, MD, and London: Johns Hopkins University Press, 1994), 67–104.

13   For the opening see most recently Aude Doody, 'Finding facts in Pliny's encyclopaedia. The *Summarium* of the *Natural History*', *Ramus* 30 (2001), 1–22. For exploration of some of these themes in relation to ethnography see Murphy, *Pliny the Elder's Natural History*, chapters 3–5; Evans, 'Geography without people'.

14   Umberto Eco, 'Portrait of the Elder as a Young Pliny. How to build fame', in *On Signs*, ed. Marshall Blonsky (Baltimore, MD, and London: Johns Hopkins University Press, 1985), 289–302.

15   On the respective places of myth and history in these accounts see chapter 2 below and Paul Veyne, *Les grecs ont-ils cru à leurs mythes? Essai sur l'imagination constituante* (Paris: Editions du Seuil, 1983), chapter 4.

16   On the variety of ways authors of long prose works might choose to combine geographical and historical material, focused on an earlier period, see Katherine Clarke, *Between Geography and History. Hellenistic constructions of the Roman world* (Oxford: Oxford University Press, 1999). See too John Marincola, *Authority and Tradition in Ancient Historiography* (Cambridge: Cambridge University Press, 1997), 83–5.

17   Roger Batty, 'Mela's Phoenician geography', *Journal of Roman Studies* 90 (2000), 70–95.

18   Diodoros *Library* 1.3.6–8.

19   For a marvellous characterization see Nicholas Thomas, *Colonialism's Culture. Anthropology, travel and government* (Oxford: Polity Press, 1994).

20   Thomas, *Out of Time*.

21   Clifford and Marcus, *Writing Culture*.

22   From a vast bibliography, Karl Trüdinger, *Studien zur Geschichte der griechisch-römischen Ethnographie. Dissertation* (Basel: Emil Birkhäuser, 1918); Müller, *Geschichte der antiken Ethnographie und ethnologischen Theoriebildung*; Alfredus Schroeder, *De Ethnographiae Antiquae locis quibusdam communibus observationes. Dissertation* (Halle, 1921); Albrecht Dihle, 'Zur Hellenistischen Ethnographie', in *Grecs et barbares* (Vandoeuvres and Geneva: Fondation Hardt, 1962), 205–39; Allan A. Lund, *Zum Germanenbild der Römer. Eine Einführung in der antike Ethnographie* (Heidelberg: Carl Winter Universitätsverlag, 1990); James B. Rives, *Tacitus. Germania translated with introduction and commentary*, Clarendon Ancient History Series (Oxford and New York: Clarendon Press, 1999), 11–21. There has been more agreement on the enduring elements of the tradition than on how it developed.

23   Jacoby, *Die Fragmente der griechischen Historiker*. Biography has been added as a fourth major division by Jacoby's continuators.

24   On the relation between taxonomy and evolutionary schema in Jacoby see Katherine Clarke, *Making Time for the Past. Local history and the polis* (Oxford: Oxford University Press, 2008); Robert L. Fowler, 'Herodotos and his contemporaries', *Journal of Hellenic Studies* 116 (1996), 62–87.

25   Examples of this approach include Simon Hornblower, 'Introduction: summary of the papers; the story of Greek historiography; intertextuality and the Greek historians', in *Greek Historiography*, ed. Simon Hornblower (Oxford: Clarendon Press, 1994), 7–54; Oswyn Murray, 'Herodotus and Hellenistic culture', *Classical Quarterly* 22, 2 (1972), 161–82; Rosalind Thomas, *Herodotus in Context. Ethnography, science and the art of persuasion* (Cambridge: Cambridge University Press, 2000).

26   For a succinct account, Klaus E. Müller, *Geschichte der antiken Ethnologie*, Rowohlts Enzyklopädie (Reinbeck bei Hamburg: Rowohlt Taschenbuch Verlag, 1997). A number of fascinating episodes in this story are illuminated in the essays collected in Kurt Raaflaub and Richard J.A. Talbert, eds, *Geography and Ethnography. Perceptions of the world in pre-modern societies* (Malden, MA, and Oxford: Wiley-Blackwell, 2010).

27   Nippel, 'Anthropology'.

28   For thoughtful discussion and suggestive analogies see Ian Rutherford, '*Theoria* and *Darsan*. Pilgrimage and vision in Greece and India', *Classical Quarterly* 50, 1 (2000), 133–46. Part of the theme has been followed up by Jas Elsner and Ian Rutherford, eds, *Pilgrimage in Graeco-Roman and Early Christian Antiquity. Seeing the gods* (Oxford: Oxford University Press, 2005).

29   The theme of James S. Romm, *The Edges of the Earth in Ancient Thought. Geography, exploration, and fiction* (Princeton, NJ: Princeton University Press, 1992), chapter 2.

30   On which see Carol Dougherty, *The Raft of Odysseus. The ethnographic imagination of Homer's Odyssey* (New York: Oxford University Press, 2001).

31   A basic knowledge of geography, as of astronomy or music, was naturally part of a general education. Cicero knew enough to deploy appropriate stereotypes about the Gauls in *pro Fonteio* and could presume they would be recognized, and he even contemplated writing a geography on the model of Eratosthenes (*ad Atticum* 2.6.1).

32   This is the technique used by Richard F. Thomas, *Lands and Peoples in Roman Poetry: The ethnographical tradition* (Cambridge: Cambridge Philological Society, 1982), following Eduard Norden, *Die germanische Urgeschichte in Tacitus* Germania (Leipzig and Berlin: B.G. Teubner, 1920). On the ethnographic nature of the latter see Rives, *Tacitus, Germania*.

33   On ancient Indology, Grant Parker, *The Making of Roman India* (Cambridge: Cambridge University Press, 2008); Romm, *The Edges of the Earth in Ancient Thought*, chapter 3.

34   Strabo 8.1.1 (translation Hamilton and Falconer, adapted).

35   Thomas, *Lands and Peoples in Roman Poetry*.

36   This is the theme, for example, of the final chapter of Nigel Barley, *The Innocent Anthropologist. Notes from a mud hut* (London: Penguin Books, 1983).

37   E.g. Yves-Albert Dauge, *Le barbare. Recherches sur la conception romaine de la barbarie et de la civilisation* (Brussels: Latomus, 1981); François Hartog, *Le miroir d' Hérodote: essai sur la représentation de l'autre* (Paris: Gallimard, 1980); Edith Hall, *Inventing the Barbarian. Greek self-definition through tragedy* (Oxford: Oxford University Press, 1989); Dench, *Romulus' Asylum*; Paul Veyne, '*Humanitas*: Romans and non-Romans', in *The Romans*, ed. Andrea Giardina (Chicago: University of Chicago Press, 1993), 342–70.

38   See the remarks of Thomas, *Herodotus in Context*, 42–5.

39   E.g. Brent D. Shaw, '"Eaters of flesh, drinkers of milk". The ancient Mediterranean ideology of the pastoral nomad', *Ancient Society* 13 (1982), 5–31; Thomas Wiedemann, 'Between men and beasts. Barbarians in Ammianus Marcellinus', in *Past Perspectives. Studies in Greek and Roman historical writing*, ed. I.S. Moxon, J.D. Smart and A.J. Woodman (Cambridge: Cambridge University Press, 1986), 189–201; Ellen O'Gorman, 'No place like Rome. Identity and difference in the *Germania* of Tacitus', *Ramus* 22 (1993), 135–54.

40   See for example discussion in Murphy, *Pliny the Elder's Natural History*, 77–83.

41   Marincola, *Authority and Tradition in Ancient Historiography*, chapter 2.

42   Ronald Mellor, *The Roman Historians* (London: Routledge, 1999), 185–7.

43   Romm, *The Edges of the Earth in Ancient Thought*.

44   For a careful demonstration of how many *Realien* may be extracted from texts of this kind see T.C. Champion, 'Written sources and the study of the European Iron Age', in *Settlement and Society. Aspects of West European prehistory in the first century* BC, ed. T.C. Champion and J.V.S. Megaw (Leicester: Leicester University Press, 1985), 9–22.

45   R. White, *The Middle Ground. Indians, empires, and republics in the Great Lakes region, 1650–1815* (Cambridge: Cambridge University Press, 1991).

46   For my earlier attempt to tell this story in relation to Gaul see chapter 2 of Greg Woolf, *Becoming Roman. The origins of provincial civilization in Gaul* (Cambridge: Cambridge University Press, 1998). For the wider picture Stephen L. Dyson, *The Creation of the Roman Frontier* (Princeton, NJ: Princeton University Press, 1985).

47   Hainz. E. Herzig, '*Novum genus hominum*: Phänomene der Migratione im römischen Heer', in '*Troianer sind wir gewesen' Migrationen in der antiken Welt. Stuttgarter Kolloquium zur Historischen Geographie des Altertums, 8 2002* ed. Eckart Olshausen and Holger Sonnabend, *Geographica Historica* (Stuttgart: F. Steiner, 2006), 325–8.

48   Greg Woolf, 'Cruptorix and his kind. Talking ethnicity on the middle ground', in *Ethnic Constructs in Antiquity. The role of power and tradition*, ed. Ton Derks and N. Roymans (Amsterdam: Amsterdam University Press, 2009), 207–17.

49   The phrase is that of Murphy, *Pliny the Elder's Natural History*, 77.

50   For the formulation 'invention of tradition', still inspirational, see Hobsbawm and Ranger, *The Invention of Tradition*.

51   Diodoros 4.19.1–2 (author's translation).

52   Diodoros 5.24 (author's translation). Timagenes, another contemporary, is probably behind what seems to be an allusion to a similar story in Ammianus 15.9.6. Parthenios *Erotica* 30 names the princess as Keltine and her son Keltos,

while Dionysius 14.1.3 reports that Celtus was one of two sons Herakles had with Asterope the daughter of Atlas, the other being Iberos. Discussion of all these variants, and more, in Jane. L. Lightfoot, *Parthenius of Nicaea. The poetical fragments and the 'Ερωτικὰ παθήματα*. (Oxford: Clarendon Press, 1999), 531–5. That myths of this kind often originated in local traditions is a thesis of Alan Cameron, *Greek Mythography in the Roman World* (New York: Oxford University Press, 2004), ix, 224–8. For similar arguments about the sources of Pausanias' local knowledge and myths see Christian Habicht, *Pausanias' Guide to Ancient Greece* (Berkeley: University of California Press, 1985); Christopher P. Jones, 'Pausanias and his guides', in *Pausanias. Travel and memory in ancient Greece*, ed. Susan E. Alcock, John F. Cherry and Jas Elsner (New York: Oxford University Press, 2001), 33–9. The latter piece argues that Pausanias and similar travellers learned about sites from respectable local antiquarians with a certain level of education.

53   Corinne Bonnet and Colette Jourdain-Annequin, eds, *Héraclès. D'une rive à l'autre de la Mediterranée* (Brussels and Rome: Institut Historique Belge de Rome, 1992); Attilio Mastrocinque, ed., *Ercole in Occidente* (Trento: Dipartimento di Scienze Filologiche e Storiche, Università degli Studi di Trento, 1993); Colette Jourdain-Annequin, *Héracles aux Portes du Soir. Mythe et histoire* (Besançon: Centre de Recherches d'Histoire Ancienne, 1989). On Herakles' role as the ancestor of ethnic groups see Hans-Joachim Gehrke, 'Heroen als Grenzgänger zwischen Griechen und Barbaren', in *Cultural Borrowings and Ethnic Appropriations in Antiquity*, ed. Erich Gruen (Stuttgart: Franz Steiner Verlag, 2005), 50–67. On Herakles' love life see T. Peter Wiseman, '*Domi nobiles* and the Roman cultural elite', in *Les bourgeoisies municipales italiennes aux IIe et Ier siècles av. J.-C.* (Naples: Editions du CNRS and Bibliothèque de l'Institut Français de Naples, 1981).

54   Diodoros *Library* 5.32 has Keltoi to the south, Galatai to the north; Strabo *Geography* 4.1.14 distinguishes Keltae as the original name for peoples of the south, on the basis of which the Greeks use the name Keltoi for Galatai. Dio 39.49 has the Rhine divide Galatia from the Keltoi, and states that all were once called Keltoi. For similar usage by Crinagoras (*Anthologia Palatina* 9.283) and Josephos (*Jewish Antiquities* 19.119) see discussion on p. 23 of Rives, *Tacitus, Germania*.

55   Jourdain-Annequin, *Héracles aux Portes du Soir*, 242–6.

56   Jerome's *Chronikon* records the height of Diodoros' fame under the entry for 49 BCE. By his own account, Diodoros was in Egypt in the 180th Olympiad (60–56 BCE). The notional terminal date of the history is 59 BCE.

57   What follows is deeply endebted to the discussion in chapter 2 of Jonathon H.C. Williams, *Beyond the Rubicon. Romans and Gauls in northern Italy* (Oxford: Oxford University Press, 2001).

58   Polybios *Histories* 2.17.9–12 (translation Loeb, adapted).

59   Cato *Origines* 2.2: *pleraque Gallia duas res industrissime persequitur, rem militare et argute loqui*.

60   Williams, *Beyond the Rubicon*, 22–35.

61   Daphne Nash, 'Reconstructing Poseidonius' Celtic ethnography: some considerations', *Britannia* 7 (1976), 111–26. A sense of the full range of anecdotes and characteristics that eventually emerged is provided by H.D. Rankin, *Celts and the Classical World* (London and Sydney: Croom Helm, 1987).

62   On the migrations G. Nachtergael, *Les Galates en Grèce et les Sôteria de Delphes. Recherches d'histoire et d'épigraphie hellénistiques* (Brussels: Académie Royale de Belgique, 1977). For the formative nature of these experiences see Antti Lampinen, 'Narratives of impiety and epiphany. Delphic Galatomachy and Roman traditions of the Gallic sack', *Studia Celtica Fennica* 5 (2008), 38–53; Christian Peyre, 'Tite-Live et la "férocité" gauloise', *Revue des Etudes Latines* 48 (1970), 277–96.

63   Something similar is observed by White, *The Middle Ground*. Noting that the period of co-existence and accommodation in the region was bracketed by periods of greater hostility before and afterwards, White writes (p. xv) 'Europeans met the other, invented a long-lasting and significant common world, but in the end reinvented the Indian as other.'

64   Polybios 2.17.5–6 notes how much the tragic poets have written on the Veneti, similar to the Keltoi in all but language, while the earlier portion of Cato's *Origines* seems to have consisted largely of genealogies.

65   For an exhaustive account of representations drawn mainly from Livy, Cicero and Caesar see Bernhard Kremer, *Das Bild der Kelten bis in augusteische Zeit. Studien zur Instrumentalisierung eines antiken Feindbildes bei griechischen und romischen Autoren* (Stuttgart: Steiner, 1994).

66   Malcolm Chapman, '"Semantics" and "the Celt"', in *Semantic Anthropology*, ed. David Parkin (London: Association of Social Anthropology, 1982), 123–43; Malcolm Chapman, *The Celts. The construction of a myth* (Basingstoke: Macmillan, 1992); Joep Leerssen, 'Celts', in *Imagology. The cultural construction and literary representation of national characters. A critical survey*, ed. Manfred Beller and Joep Leerssen (Amsterdam and New York: Editions Rodopi, 2007). On the problems this history has created for interpretation of Iron Age societies see Simon James, *The Atlantic Celts. Ancient people or modern invention?* (London: British Museum Press, 1999); Nick Merriman, 'Value and motivation in prehistory. The evidence for "Celtic spirit"', in *The Archaeology of Contextual Meaning*, ed. Ian Hodder (Cambridge: Cambridge University Press, 1987), 111–16; John R. Collis, *The Celts. Origins, myths and inventions* (Stroud: Tempus, 2003). For philologists' attempts to establish ethnic histories of all these groups see chapter 5 of Lund, *Zum Germanenbild der Römer*.

67   Parthenius *Erotica* 30, translation Lightfoot.

68   Herodotos *Histories* 4.8–9. The place name Erythaia features in both versions.

69   Strabo *Geography* 3.4.3–4 (translation Hamilton and Falconer, adapted). The anecdote was regarded as paradigmatic by Elias Bickermann, 'Origines gentium', *Classical Philology* 47 (1952), 65–81.

70   Elizabeth Rawson, *Intellectual Life in the Late Roman Republic* (London: Duckworth, 1985); Daniela Dueck, *Strabo of Amasia. A Greek man of letters in Augustan Rome* (London and New York: Routledge, 2000).

71   On the complex development of these geographies see now Gonzalo Cruz Andreotti, 'Acerca de las identidades meridionales en época prerromana. Alguno planteamientos geográficos', in *Identidades, Culturas y Territorios en la Andalucia Prerromana*, ed. Fernando Wulff Alonso and Manuel Álvarez Marti-Aguilar (Malaga and Seville: Universidades de Malaga and Sevilla, 2009).

72   On priests as informants Marincola, *Authority and Tradition in Ancient Historiography*, 108–12.

73   Kai Brodersen and Jas Elsner, eds, *Images and Texts on the 'Artemidorus Papyrus'. Working papers on P. Artemid. (St John's College Oxford, 2008)* (Stuttgart: Franz Steiner Verlag, 2009).

74   Although the entry confuses more than one Asklepiades, this chronology for Asklepiades of Myrleia seems secure in the most recent study, that of Roberto Polito, 'On the life of Asclepiades of Bithynia', *Journal of Hellenic Studies* 119 (1999) 48–66.

75   On the evolutions of geographical understandings of Spain see now Gonzalo Cruz Andreotti, Patrick Le Roux, and Pierre Moret, eds, *La invención de una geografía de la península ibérica. I. La época republicana* (Málaga and Madrid: Centro de Ediciones de la Disputación de Málaga and Casa de Velázquez, 2006), and *La invención de una geografía de la Península Ibérica. II. La época imperial* (Málaga and Madrid: Centro de Ediciones de la Disputación de Málaga and Casa de Velázquez, 2007).

76   Clifford, *Routes*.

77   Diodoros *Library* 1.96 with Oswyn Murray, 'Hecataeus of Abdera and Pharaonic kingship', *Journal of Egyptian Archaeology* 56 (1970), 141–71.

78   On all this Irad Malkin, *Myth and Territory in the Spartan Mediterranean* (Cambridge: Cambridge University Press, 1994) and Malkin, *The Returns of Odysseus. Colonization and ethnicity* (Berkeley, Los Angeles and London: University of California Press, 1998).

79   Strabo *Geography* 3.2.12–14.

80   Morstein-Marx, 'The myth of Numidian origins in Sallust's African excursus'.

81   Compare, in relation to Pomponius Mela, Batty, 'Mela's Phoenician geography', 73. As Batty puts it 'many educated provincials in the West must have been searching for a new model of geography – a new model for the world of the West'.

82   On the challenge posed to European knowledge regimes by the discovery of America see among much else, John H. Elliott, *The Old World and the New 1492–1650* (Cambridge: Cambridge University Press, 1970); Anthony Pagden, *European Encounters with the New World. From renaissance to romanticism* (New Haven, CT, and London: Yale University Press, 1993).

83   There is a clear parallel here with the case of Strabo, see Katherine Clarke, 'In search of the author of Strabo's *Geography*', *Journal of Roman Studies* 87 (1997), 92–110.

84   Justin *Epitome* 43.5.11–12 (translation Watson, adapted).

85   For characterizations, Liv Mariah Yarrow, *Historiography at the End of the Republic. Provincial perspectives on Roman rule* (Oxford and New York: Oxford University Press, 2006); José Miguel Alonso-Nuñez, 'An Augustan

world history: The *Historiae Philippicae* of Pompeius Trogus', *Greece & Rome* 34, 1 (1987), 56–72.

86 Katherine Clarke, 'Universal perspectives in historiography', in *The Limits of Historiography. Genre and narrative in ancient historical texts*, ed. Christina Shuttleworth Kraus, (Leiden, Boston and Cologne: Brill, 1999), 249–79.

87 For the term, and its application to tradition building, see Emma Dench, 'Ethnography and history', in *A Companion to Greek and Roman Historiography*, ed. John Marincola (Malden, MA and Oxford: Blackwell, 2007), 493–503.

88 Carol Dougherty, *The Poetics of Colonization. From city to text in archaic Greece* (New York and Oxford: Oxford University Press, 1993).

2   Explaining the Barbarians

1   Ammianus 15.12.1 (author's translation).

2   Kremer, *Das Bild der Kelten bis in augusteische Zeit*; Rankin, *Celts and the Classical World*, chapter 2; Andrew Riggsby, *War in Words. Caesar in Gaul and Rome* (Austin, TX: University of Texas Press, 2006), 47–50.

3   Peter Garnsey, *Food and Society in Classical Antiquity* (Cambridge: Cambridge University Press, 1999).

4   On Agatharchides, Jacoby, *FGrH* 86 and Stanley Burnstein, *Agatharchides of Cnidus, On the Erythraean Sea* (London: Hakluyt Society, 1989). For discussion of the dietary ethnography of early Rome see Nicholas Purcell, 'The way we used to eat. Diet, community, and history at Rome', *American Journal of Philology* 124, 3 (2003), 329–58.

5   On the limitations of that formulation see Steven Shapin, *The Scientific Revolution* (Chicago: University of Chicago Press, 1996).

6   Strabo 4.1.1 (translation Hamilton and Falconer, adapted).

7   Strabo 4.4.2 (translation Hamilton and Falconer, adapted).

8   Strabo 4.4.2 (translation Hamilton and Falconer, adapted).

9   This set of idea has been dubbed 'Borealism' in Christopher B. Krebs, 'Borealism. Caesar, Seneca, Tacitus and the Roman concept of the North', in *Cultural Identity in the Ancient Mediterranean*, ed. Erich Gruen (Los Angeles: Getty Publications, forthcoming), 202–21.

10 Strabo *Geography* 2.2.1–2.3.2.

11 Monique Clavel-Lévêque, 'Les gaules et les gauloises. Pour une analyse du fonctionnement de la *Géographie* de Strabon', *Dialogues d'Histoire Ancienne* 1 (1974), 75–93; Patrick Thollard, ed., *Barbarie et civilisation chez Strabon. Étude critique des livres III et IV de la* Géographie, (Paris: Belles Lettres, 1987). On Strabo's idea of civilization see L.A. Thomson, 'Strabo on civilisation', *Platon* 31 (1979), 213–30; Edward C.H.L. van der Vliet, 'The Romans and us. Strabo's *Geography* and the construction of ethnicity', *Mnemosyne* 56, 3 (2003), 257–72.

12 On this, in all its complexity, Romm, *The Edges of the Earth in Ancient Thought*.

13 On the tension between the two, Conte, 'The inventory of the world'; Evans, 'Geography without people'.

14   Robert Bartlett, *The Natural and the Supernatural in the Middle Ages* (Cambridge and New York: Cambridge University Press, 2008).

15   For a lucid discussion of the priority of theory over observation in the construction of ethnographies, see Edmund Leach, *Political Systems of Highland Burma. A study of Kachin social structure* (London: G. Bell & Son Ltd, 1954).

16   The connected tension between ordering by time and ordering by space is a theme of Clarke, *Between Geography and History*.

17   Not only in Clifford and Marcus, *Writing Culture* but already in the notion of ethnography as 'thick description' at the heart of Clifford Geertz, *The Interpretation of Cultures. Selected essays* (New York: Basic Books, 1973).

18   Veyne, *Les grecs ont-ils cru à leurs mythes?* Compare the argument for the co-existence of different modes of logic in Dan Sperber, *Le symbolisme en général* (Paris: Herman, 1974).

19   Jack R. Goody and Ian Watt, 'The consequences of literacy', *Comparative Studies in Society and History* 5 (1963), 304–45; Walter J. Ong, *Orality and Literacy. The technologising of the word* (London: Methuen, 1982).

20   For a case in point Mary Beard, 'Cicero and divination. The formation of a Latin discourse', *Journal of Roman Studies* 76 (1986), 33–46.

21   On this use of allusion in different contexts see Stephen Hinds, *Allusion and Intertext. Dynamics of appropriation in Roman poetry* (Cambridge: Cambridge University Press, 1998).

22   For some points of similarity see Clarke, 'Universal perspectives in historiography'.

23   Bickermann, '*Origines gentium*', 78.

24   Livy 5.34 (translation Foster, adapted).

25   R.M. Ogilvie, *A Commentary on Livy Books 1–5* (Oxford: Clarendon Press, 1965). to which this discussion is much endebted. Williams, *Beyond the Rubicon*, 117–27 very plausibly sets the creation of the story within the context of the intellectual activity of Transpadane intellectuals in the 40s BCE.

26   On the creation of legendary origins for Italian towns in this period, Wiseman, '*Domi nobiles* and the Roman cultural elite'.

27   Plutarch *Comparison of Dion and Brutus* 5 with discussion by G.E.F. Chilver, *Cisalpine Gaul. Social and economic history from 49 BC to the death of Trajan* (Oxford: Clarendon Press, 1941), 80–1.

28   The classic study is Laura Bohannan, 'A genealogical charter', *Africa* 22 (1952), 301–15.

29   For discussion of all this, see Jonathon M. Hall, *Ethnic Identity in Greek Antiquity* (Cambridge: Cambridge University Press, 1997), 40–4.

30   Herodotos *Histories* 1.94.

31   Tacitus *Germania* 2.2 (translation Rives).

32   For discussion see Emma Dench, *From Barbarians to New Men. Greek, Roman and modern perceptions of peoples of the central Apennines* (Oxford: Oxford University Press, 1995).

33   So Bickermann, '*Origines gentium*', 71–2; Williams, *Beyond the Rubicon*, 118–22; Andrew Erskine, *Troy between Greece and Rome, Local tradition and imperial power* (Oxford: Oxford University Press, 2001), 37–43.

34   Robert L. Fowler, 'Genealogical thinking, Hesiod's *Catalogue*, and the creation of the Hellenes', *Proceedings of the Cambridge Philological Society* 44 (1998), 1–19.
35   Dougherty, *The Poetics of Colonization*, chapter 4.
36   For other legendary genealogies see T. Peter Wiseman, 'Legendary genealogies in late-republican Rome', *Greece & Rome* 21, 1 (1974), 153–64. For other Trojan myths, Erskine, *Troy between Greece and Rome*.
37   For the early mediaeval model see Reinhard Wenskus, *Stammesbildung und Verfassung. Das Werden der frühmittelalterlichen Gentes* (Cologne: Böhlau, 1961). Closer to my argument here is the thesis of Peter Heather, 'Cassiodorus and the rise of the Amals. Genealogy and the Goths under Hun domination', *Journal of Roman Studies* 79 (1989), 103–28, which sees the manipulation of genealogies as an instrument for creating and legitimizing political confederation and the dominance of particular families in the present. For the application of Wenskus' ideas to Iron Age Europe, see most recently Nico Roymans, *Ethnic Identity and Imperial Power. The Batavians in the Roman Empire* (Amsterdam: Amsterdam University Press, 2004).
38   For discussion of one possible example see Greg Woolf, 'Urbanization and its discontents in early Roman Gaul', in *Romanization and the City. Creations, transformations and failures*, ed. Elizabeth Fentress (Portsmouth, RI: Journal of Roman Archaeology, 2000).
39   A good introduction to his Eastern analogues is provided by John Dillery, 'Greek historians of the Near East. Clio's "other" sons', in *A Companion to Greek and Roman Historiography*, ed. John Marincola (Malden, MA and Oxford: Blackwell Publishers, 2007). Alongside Berossos' *Babyloniaka* and Manetho's *Aegyptiaca*, both produced in the early Hellenistic period, can be set the rather earlier account of Lydia composed by Xanthus, and the later researches of Josephus and Philo of Byblos on Jewish and Phoenician antiquities respectively. On the fascinating synthesis of Greek and biblical world views produced by the author of the Book of Jubilees see now James M. Scott, 'On earth as in heaven. The apocalyptic vision of world geography from Urzeit to Endzeit according to the Book of Jubilees', in *Geography and Ethnography. Perceptions of the world in pre-modern societies*, ed. Kurt Raaflaub and Richard J.A. Talbert (Malden, MA and Oxford: Wiley-Blackwell, 2010).
40   The connections can be traced by Jacoby *FGrH* 273 (Polyhistor) and 680 (Berossos).
41   On Juba see Duane W. Roller, 'Juba II of Mauretania (275)', in *Brill's New Jacoby* (online), Editor in Chief Ian Worthington (Leiden: Brill, 2010) and Duane W. Roller, *The World of Juba II and Kleopatra Selene. Royal scholarship on Rome's Africa frontier* (London and New York: Routledge, 2003).
42   For the story see Plutarch *Sertorius* 9.8.
43   Most recently, Thomas, *Herodotus in Context*; Hartog, *Le miroir d' Hérodote*. The relevance of this passage was noticed already by Trüdinger, *Studien zur Geschichte der griechisch-römischen Ethnographie*.
44   *Airs, Waters, Places* 16 (trans. Jones adapted).

45   Thomas S. Kuhn, *The Structure of Scientific Revolutions* (Chicago: University of Chicago Press, 1962).

46   Pliny *Natural History* 2.189–90 (author's translation). On this passage see Mary Beagon, 'Situating nature's wonders in Pliny's *Natural History*', in *Vita Vigilia Est. Essays in honour of Barbara Levick*, ed. Edward Bispham, Greg Rowe, and Elaine Matthews (London: Institute of Classical Studies, 2007), 19–40.

47   Compare Isidore *Etymologies* 14.4.25: 'Gaul is so called from the pallor of its inhabitants for milk is called *gala* in Greek. or the mountains and the harsh climate shut out the sun's warmth from this part of the earth, with the result that the whiteness of their bodies acquires no colour.'

48   Vitruvius *On Architecture* 6.1.3–4 (translation Granger, adapted).

49   For the centrality of diplomatic claims based on kinship throughout antiquity see Christopher P. Jones, *Kinship Diplomacy in the Ancient World*, ed. Glen Warren Bowersock (Cambridge, MA: Harvard University Press, 1999).

50   For a short account of the variety of versions of this see M.R. Wright, *Cosmology in Antiquity*, ed. Roger French (London: Routledge, 1995). Some of the same themes are explored in Gordon Lindsay Campbell, *Strange Creatures. Anthropology in antiquity* (London: Duckworth, 2006).

51   Romm, *The Edges of the Earth in Ancient Thought*, chapter 4.

52   Bartlett, *The Natural and the Supernatural in the Middle Ages*.

53   For what follows, and especially for encouragement to look at Manilius' ethnography, I am very grateful to Duncan Kennedy. On Manilius' context see now Katharina Volk, *Manilius and his Intellectual Background* (New York: Oxford University Press, 2009).

54   Tamsyn Barton, *Power and Knowledge. Astrology, physiognomics and medicine under the Roman Empire* (Ann Arbor: Michigan University Press, 1994).

55   For microcosm/macrocosm relations in Manilius see Volk, *Manilius and his Intellectual Background*, 102–3. For the term 'zodiacal geography', and further discussion of its origins, see Godefroid de Callataÿ, 'La géographie de Manilius (*Astr.* 4, 744–817), avec une note sur *l'Énéide* virgilienne', *Latomus* 60, 1 (2001), 35–66. For a brief overview, Tamsyn Barton, *Ancient Astrology*, ed. Roger French, (London: Routledge, 1994), 179–85.

56   Manilius *Astronomica* 4.585–695.

57   Manilius *Astronomica* 4.711–21 (trans. Goold).

58   Josèphe-Henriette Abry, 'Une carte du monde à l'époque d'Auguste. Manilius *Astronomiques* IV, 585–817', in *L'espace et ses représentations*, ed. Annie Bonnafé, Jean-Claude Decourt and Bruno Helly (Lyon: Maison de l'Orient Méditerranéen, 2000).

59   On the difficulties in tracing the sources of Ptolemy's astrological thought, however, see Liba Taub, *Ptolemy's Universe. The natural philosophical and ethical foundations of Ptolemy's astronomy* (Chicago and LaSalle, IL: Open Court, 1993), 13–17.

60   Ptolemy *Tetrabiblos* 2.2–3.

61   Strabo 2.3.7 (translation Hamilton and Falconer, adapted).

62   Caesar *Gallic War* 1.1 (author's translation).

63   Most recently by Riggsby, *War in Words*, 59–60.

64 On which Catharine Edwards, *The Politics of Immorality in Ancient Rome* (Cambridge: Cambridge University Press, 1993). Parallel deployments of the theme in an ethnographic context are offered by the *Jugurtha* on which see D.S. Levene, 'Sallust's *Jugurtha*. An "historical fragment"', *Journal of Roman Studies* 82 (1992), 53–70. On the *Germania* see O'Gorman, 'No place like Rome'. See also on the *Agricola* Greg Woolf, 'A distant mirror. Britain and Rome in the representation of empire', in *Laudes Provinciarum, Rétorica y política en la representación del imperio romano*, ed. Juan Santos Yanguas and Elena Torregaray Pagola, (Vitoria: Universidad del Pais Vasco, 2007), 135–47.

65 Reviel Netz, 'Greek mathematicians. A group picture', in *Science and Mathematics in Ancient Greek Culture*, ed. C.J. Tuplin and T.E. Rihll (New York: Oxford University Press, 2002), 196–216.

66 Vivian Nutton, *Ancient Medicine*, ed. Liba Taub (London: Routledge, 2004).

67 For what follows I am endebted to Oniga, *Sallustio e l'etnografia*; Morstein-Marx, 'The myth of Numidian origins in Sallust's African excursus'.

68 Green, '*De Africa et eius incolis*'.

69 Sallust *Jugurtha* 16.5–6 (author's translation).

70 Sallust *Jugurtha* 16.7 (author's translation).

71 For discussion Shaw, '"Eaters of flesh, drinkers of milk"'; Wiedemann, 'Between men and beasts'.

72 Sallust *Catiline* 6.1–3.

73 The suggestion is that of Morstein-Marx, 'The myth of Numidian origins in Sallust's African excursus'.

3   Ethnography and Empire

1 Pliny *Natural History* 5.9 (author's translation).

2 The fundamental starting point for this enquiry is Arnaldo Momigliano, *Alien Wisdom. The limits of Hellenisation* (Cambridge: Cambridge University Press, 1975).

3 An exhaustive survey of Pliny's sources of information finds as examples of reports from military expeditions, only those from Paulinus' campaigns in Africa and from Gallus' into Arabia with Polybios's journey the only voyage of exploration. See chapter 4 of John F. Healy, *Pliny the Elder on Science and Technology* (Oxford and New York: Oxford University Press, 1999).

4 For Alexander Polyhistor, Jacoby *FGrH* 273, for Timagenes, *FGrH* 88 with Marta Sordi, 'Timagene di Alessandria. Un storico hellenocentrico e filobarbaro', in *Aufstieg und Niedergang der römischen Welt II.30.1*, ed. Hildegard Temporini and Wolfgang Haase (Berlin and New York: De Gruyter, 1982), 775–97.

5 For a wider investigation of the ethnographic dimensions of Roman identity formation over this long period, see Dench, *Romulus' Asylum*, chapter 1.

6 E.g. in Nicolet, *Space, Geography and Politics* and Murphy, *Pliny the Elder's Natural History*.

7 On all this, Rawson, *Intellectual Life in the Late Roman Republic*. See the thoughtful comments of Andrew Wallace-Hadrill, 'Greek knowledge, Roman

power' (review article), *Classical Philology* 83, 3 (1988), 224–33. On the latter phases, Glen Warren Bowersock, *Augustus and the Greek World* (Oxford: Clarendon Press, 1965).

8   For Philodemus in social context, Marcello Gigante, *Philodemus in Italy. The books from Herculaneum*, trans. Dirk Obbink (Ann Arbor: University of Michigan Press, 1995); Oswyn Murray, 'Philodemus on the Good King according to Homer', *Journal of Roman Studies* 55, 1/2 (1965), 161–82. On literary patronage in Rome, and its evolution, Barbara K. Gold, ed., *Literary and Artistic Patronage in Ancient Rome* (Austin, TX: University of Texas Press, 1982).

9   Andrew Wallace-Hadrill, '*Mutatas formas*. The Augustan transformation of Roman knowledge', in *The Cambridge Companion to the Age of Augustus*, ed. Karl Galinsky (New York: Cambridge University Press, 2005), 55–84; Thomas Habinek and Alessandro Schiesaro, eds, *The Roman Cultural Revolution* (Cambridge: Cambridge University Press, 1997); Woolf, *Becoming Roman*; Wallace-Hadrill, *Rome's Cultural Revolution*.

10   For the Roman reception of Greek thought in this period see Jonathon Barnes and Miriam Griffin, eds, *Philosophia Togata II. Plato and Aristotle in Rome* (Oxford: Oxford University Press, 1997); David Sedley, *Lucretius and the Transformation of Greek Wisdom* (Cambridge: Cambridge University Press, 1998); Ingo Gildenhard, *Paideia Romana. Cicero's Tusculan Disputations*, ed. Tim Whitmarsh and James Warren (Cambridge: Cambridge Philological Society, 2007); Miriam Griffin and Jonathon Barnes, eds, *Philosophia Togata I. Essays on philosophy and Roman society* (Oxford: Oxford University Press, 1989).

11   Nicolet, *Space, Geography and Politics*. But note also the remarks of Nicholas Purcell, 'Maps, lists, money, order and power', *Journal of Roman Studies* 80 (1990), 178–82.

12   Momigliano, *Alien Wisdom*, 25.

13   Polybios 34.4.8 *apud* Athenaios 7.302E.

14   Polybios 34.9.14–15 *apud* Athenaios 1.16C.

15   Polybios 34.10.8 *apud* Strabo 4.6.10.

16   Strabo 3.2.15 (translation Hamilton and Falconer, adapted).

17   Polybios 34.8.4–9 *apud* Athenaios 8.330C.

18   Polybios 34.9.8–11 *apud* Strabo 3.2.10.

19   Nicolet, *Space, Geography and Politics*, 73–4.

20   Murray, 'Herodotus and Hellenistic culture'.

21   José Miguel Alonso-Nuñez, 'Herodotus' conceptions of historical space and the beginnings of Universal History', in *Herodotus and his World. Essays from a conference in memory of George Forrest*, ed. Peter Derow and Robert Parker (Oxford and New York: Oxford University Press, 2003), 145–52.

22   Parker, *The Making of Roman India*. Chapter 5 considers the impact of Alexander on later imperial understandings of India.

23   Romm, *The Edges of the Earth in Ancient Thought*.

24   Polybios *Histories* 3.57.2–3 (translation Paton adapted).

25   Polybios *Histories* 3.59.3–8 (translation Paton, adapted).

26   For later elaborations on the theme see Livy 9.16–17 and Plutarch *On the Fortune of the Romans* with Simon Swain, 'Plutarch's *De Fortuna Romanorum*', *Classical Quarterly* 39, 2 (1989), 504–16, who also gathers other Plutarchian comments on the comparison.

27   Polybios 34.10.6–7 *apud* Strabo 4.2.1.

28   Pliny *Natural History* 8.47.

29   For Polybios' interest in foregrounding the visual in other parts of his history see James Davidson, 'The gaze in Polybius' histories', *Journal of Roman Studies* 81 (1991), 10–24.

30   Elliott, *The Old World and the New*; Pagden, *European Encounters with the New World*.

31   Rawson, *Intellectual Life in the Late Roman Republic*, 257 puts it very well: 'the Romans did not organize anything to compare with the exploratory expeditions dispatched by a number of states during the Renaissance' going on to explain this in terms of the absence of mercantile motivations, Rome's dependence on land-power, and the different situation of a world of competing nations whose expansion was fueled by religion and powered by technological advantage.

32   On Poseidonios, see the suggestions in Hermann Strasburger, 'Poseidonios on problems of the Roman empire', *Journal of Roman Studies* 55, 1/2 (1965), 40–53. The best short account is on pp. 3–28 of I.G. Kidd, *Posidonius III, The translation of the fragments* (Cambridge: Cambridge University Press, 1999).

33   Rawson, *Intellectual Life in the Late Roman Republic*, 62–4, refuting these suggestions made by Momigliano, *Alien Wisdom*.

34   Giuseppe Nenci, 'L'occidente "barbarico"', in *Hérodote et les peuples non grecs* (Vandoeuvres and Geneva: Fondation Hardt, 1988), 308

35   An earlier version of this discussion was given at a conference in Seville and owes a great deal to the participants there. It will appear as Greg Woolf, 'Greek archaeologists in Rome', in *Ruling through Greek Eyes. Interactions between Rome and the Greeks in imperial times*, ed. Elena Muñiz Grivalvo, Juan Manual Cortés Copete and Fernando Lozano (Leiden and Boston: Brill, forthcoming).

36   Miriam Griffin, 'Philosophy, politics and politicians at Rome', in *Philosophia Togata I. Essays on philosophy and Roman society*, ed. Miriam Griffin and Jonathon Barnes (Oxford: Oxford University Press, 1989), 1–37.

37   Arnaldo Momigliano, 'Athens in the third century BC and the discovery of Rome in the *Histories* of Timaeus of Tauromenium', in *Essays in Ancient and Modern Historiography*, ed. Arnaldo Momigliano (Oxford: Blackwell, 1977).

38   What follows is deeply endebted to the account provided by Rawson, *Intellectual Life in the Late Roman Republic*. See also Michael H. Crawford, 'Greek intellectuals and the Roman aristocracy in the first century BC.', in *Imperialism in the Ancient World*, ed. Peter Garnsey and C.R. Whittaker (Cambridge: Cambridge University Press, 1978), 193–207.

39   For trenchant comments on our continued tendency to downplay the intellectual life of mid-republican Rome see Nicholas Purcell, 'Becoming historical. The Roman case', in *Myth, History and Culture in Republican Rome. Studies in honour of T.P. Wiseman*, ed. David Braund and Christopher Gill (Exeter: Exeter University Press, 2003), 12–40.

40   Diodoros Siculus 1.4.2–5 (translation Oldfather, adapted).

41   On his self-effacement in the text, Clarke, 'In search of the author of Strabo's *Geography.*' For what can be reconstructed of his life, Dueck, *Strabo of Amasia*; Daniela Dueck, Hugh Lindsay, and Sarah Pothecary, eds, *Strabo's Cultural Geography. The making of a kolossourgia* (Cambridge: Cambridge University Press, 2005).

42   Dionysios *Roman Antiquities* 1.7.2–3 (translation Cary and Spelman, adapted).

43   Dionysios *Roman Antiquities* 1.73.1 (translation Cary and Spelman, adapted).

44   See for example T. Peter Wiseman, *Remus. A Roman myth* (Cambridge and New York: Cambridge University Press, 1995).

45   For discussion of the limitations of public records see Phyllis Culham, 'Archives and alternatives in republican Rome', *Classical Philology* 84, 2 (1989), 100–15.

46   For Lucullus' library, with wide discussion of its use, contents and parallels, see T. Keith Dix, 'The Library of Lucullus', *Athenaeum* 88, 2 (2000), 441–64. For more general discussion, see Lionel Casson, *Libraries in the Ancient World* (New Haven, CT, and London: Yale University Press, 2001).

47   Plutarch *Life of Lucullus* 42. 1–2 in *Plutarch's Lives*, vol. 2: *Themistocles and Camillus; Aristides and Cato Major; Cimon and Lucullus*, with an English translation by Bernadotte Perrin. Loeb Classical Library. London: Heinemann, 1914.

48   On the way philosophically inclined Romans differentiated themselves by philosophical allegiance see David Sedley, 'Philosophical allegiance in the Greco-Roman world', in *Philosophia Togata I. Essays on philosophy and Roman society*, ed. Miriam Griffin and Jonathon Barnes (Oxford: Oxford University Press, 1989), 97–119.

49   Wallace-Hadrill, *Rome's Cultural Revolution*, 169–208.

50   On the care taken to elaborate this setting see Miranda Marvin, 'Copying in Roman sculpture. The replica series', in *Retaining the Original. Multiple originals, copies and reproductions*, ed. Kathleen Preciado (Washington, DC: National Gallery of Art, 1989), 29–46.

51   The phrase is that of Denis Feeney, *Literature and Religion at Rome. Culture, contexts and beliefs* (Cambridge: Cambridge University Press, 1998). Two alternative ways of imagining this segregation are offered by Wallace-Hadrill, 'Greek knowledge, Roman power' and his 'To be Roman, Go Greek. Thoughts on hellenization at Rome', in *Modus Operandi. Essays in honour of Geoffrey Rickman*, ed. Michel Austin, Jill Harries, and Christopher Smith (London: Institute of Classical Studies, 1998), 79–91.

52   Polybios 5.33.2, Diodoros 11.37.6.

53   For a definition so narrow that even Polybios fails it, see Clarke, 'Universal perspectives in historiography'. Slightly more flexible is Alonso-Nuñez, 'Herodotus' conceptions of historical space'.

54   Nicholas Purcell, 'Romans in the Roman world', in *The Cambridge Companion to the Age of Augustus*, ed. Karl Galinsky (New York: Cambridge University Press, 2005), 85–105.

55   Catharine Edwards and Greg Woolf, eds, *Rome the Cosmopolis* (Cambridge: Cambridge University Press, 2003).

56   On the stereotyping of the nomad, Shaw, '"Eaters of flesh, drinkers of milk"';
Brent D. Shaw, 'Rebels and outsiders', in *Cambridge Ancient History*, vol. XI:
The High Empire, AD 70–192, ed. Alan Bowman, Peter Garnsey, and Dominic
Rathbone (Cambridge: Cambridge University Press, 2000), 361–403. On the
local rooting of the city, see most recently Clarke, *Making Time for the Past*.

57   Roymans, *Ethnic Identity and Imperial Power*.

58   One of the best examples is offered by the numerous stories generated by the
great Gallic raid on Delphi in the early third century BCE and its sequels in Asia
Minor. For an exhaustive study see Nachtergael, *Les Galates en Grèce*.

59   For the political context and consequences see Erich S. Gruen, 'Political
Prosecutions in the 90s BC', *Historia. Zeitschrift für Alte Geschichte* 15, 1
(1966), 32–64.

60   Strabo 4.1.13 (translation Kidd, as Fragment 274 of Poseidonios).

61   Susan E. Alcock, *Graecia Capta. The landscapes of Roman Greece* (Cambridge
and New York: Cambridge University Press, 1993), 175–80 for discussion.

62   *I Lamp*. 4, an honorific degree issued in 196/5 BCE for an ambassador who had
visited Massalia to seek support for a Lampsakene embassy to Rome, mentions
that he also persuaded the Massiliots to give him a letter to the Galatian
Tolistoagioi. The circumstances are unclear but this seems to suggest an early
interest in connecting up the Gauls of the east with their supposed western kin.

63   Strabo 7.2.1–3.

64   Strabo 7.2.2 (translation Hamilton and Falconer, adapted).

65   Stephen L. Dyson, 'Caepio, Tacitus and Lucan's sacred grove', *Classical
Philology* 65, 1 (1970), 36–8.

66   Justin 32.3.2 (translation Watson, adapted).

67   Strabo 1.2.1 (translation Hamilton and Falconer, adapted).

68   Alonso-Nuñez, 'An Augustan world history'.

69   This has been slightly obscured by the juxtaposition of the excellent studies of
imperial propaganda, of geography and of Roman government in Nicolet,
Space, Geography and Politics. Compare the same tactic in Murphy, *Pliny the
Elder's Natural History*.

70   On the problems of its wide use see Michael F. Brown, 'On resisting resistance',
American Anthropologist 98, 4 (1996), 729–35. Also Shelley Ortner,
'Resistance and the problem of ethnographic refusal', *Comparative Studies in
Society and History* 37, 1 (1995), 173–93.

71   David Braund, 'Greek geography and Roman empire. The transformation of
tradition in Strabo's Euxine', in *Strabo's Cultural Geography. The making of a
kolossourgia*, ed. Daniela Dueck, Hugh Lindsay, and Sarah Pothecary
(Cambridge: Cambridge University Press, 2005), 216–34; Rawson, *Intellectual
Life in the Late Roman Republic*, 258–66.

72   On which Gildenhard, *Paideia Romana*.

73   Cicero *ad Atticum* 2.4, 2.6, 2.7.

74   Cicero *de Divinatione* 1.90. The context is the speech of Quintus which gathers
a vast number of testimonies to the practice of divination among them that of
Divitiacus the Aeduan, described as *hospitem tuum laudatoremque*, and his
claim that he (as a Druid) possessed a knowledge of nature (*naturae rationem*)

equivalent to what the Greeks call φυσιολογίαν. There was a later tradition that Divitiacus had visited Rome as an ambassador, which might explain why he might be a guest friend of Cicero's.

75   On Trogus, Yarrow, *Historiography at the End of the Republic.* On Mela, Batty, 'Mela's Phoenician geography'.

76   On the wonders of the Euxine as related by Arrian and others, Stephanie West, '"The most marvellous of all seas". The Greek encounter with the Euxine', *Greece & Rome* 50, 2 (2003), 151–67. On Dio's Britons, described mainly in Book 62 in the context of the Boudiccan war, see Giovanna Martinelli, *Roma e i barbari. Dai Giulio Claudii agli Antonini*, I (Lecce: Edizioni Pensa Multimedia, 2005).

77   On Pliny's ethnographies Murphy, *Pliny the Elder's Natural History*; Evans, 'Ethnography's freak show'.

78   Beagon, *Roman Nature*, 1–18.

79   Pliny *Letters* 3.5.6: *opus diffusum eruditum, nex minus varium quam ipsa natura.*

80   Gellius *Attic Nights* 9.4.13–16 (on Book 7).

81   On Isidore's ordering, A.H. Merrills, *History and Geography in Late Antiquity*, ed. Rosamund McKitterick (Cambridge: Cambridge University Press, 2005); John Henderson, *The Mediaeval World of Isidore of Seville. Truth from words* (Cambridge: Cambridge University Press, 2007).

82   The phrase is Trevor Murphy's to whose work what follows owes a considerable debt, even where our analysis differs in emphasis.

83   On the character, and limits, of Pliny's Romanocentrism see chapter 2 of Carey, *Pliny's Catalogue of Culture*.

84   On this double structure see Conte, 'The inventory of the world'.

85   On Pliny's anthropocentrism, see Naas, *Le projet encyclopédique de Pline l'ancien*. For the moralizing frame, Beagon, *Roman Nature*; Wallace-Hadrill, 'Pliny the Elder and man's unnatural history'.

86   Evans, 'Geography without people'. On the Chauci see chapter 5 of Murphy, *Pliny the Elder's Natural History*.

87   Edwards, *Politics of Immorality in Ancient Rome*; Barbara Levick, 'Morals, politics and the fall of the Roman republic', *Greece & Rome* 29 (1982), 53–62; Andrew Lintott, 'Imperial expansion and moral decline in the Roman Republic', *Historia. Zeitschrift für Alte Geschichte* 21 (1972), 626–38.

88   Pliny *Natural History* Preface 17. The discussion of possible titles at 24–6 makes it clear that Pliny positions himself in some respects to stand in a tradition started by Hellenistic miscellanies (although one that also includes Diodoros' *Bibliotheke*), in others in succession to Cato and Varro.

89   For characterization of this literature see Christian Jacob, 'De l'art de compiler à la fabrication du merveilleux. Sur la paradoxographie grecque', *Lalies* 2 (1980), 121–40. For the surviving Greek examples, Alexander Giannini, *Paradoxographorum graecorum reliquae* (Milan: Istituto Editoriale Italiano, 1966). A wide-ranging collection of studies is published in Olivier Bianchi and Olivier Thévenaz, eds, *Mirabilia. Conceptions et représentations de l'extraordinaire dans le monde antique. Actes du colloque international, Lausanne 20–22 mars 2003* (Bern: Peter Lang, 2004).

90   On Pliny's concept of *mirabilia*, and the language he uses to designate them, see especially chapter 5 of Naas, *Le projet encyclopédique de Pline l'ancien*. Also chapter 5 of Healy, *Pliny the Elder on Science and Technology*; Philippe Mudry, '"Mirabilia" et "Magica."' Essai de définition dans l'*Histoire Naturelle* de Pline l'Ancien', in *Mirabilia*, ed. Bianchi and Thévenaz, 239–52.

91   Gellius 9.4.1–16 is the *locus classicus* and a typically artful portrayal of the fascination for marvels with its peculiar blend of triviality and erudition.

92   Rhiannon Ash, 'The wonderful world of Mucianus', in *Vita Vigilia Est. Essays in honour of Barbara Levick*, ed. Edward Bispham, Greg Rowe and Elaine Matthews (London: Institute of Classical Studies, 2007), 1–17.

93   Mary Beagon, *The Elder Pliny on the Human Animal. Natural History Book 7 translated with commentary* (New York: Clarendon Press, 2005).

94   Beagon, 'Situating nature's wonders in Pliny's *Natural History*'. The concentration of marvels in Book 7 (humans) and Book 36 (the city of Rome) are the subjects of chapters 6 and 7 of Naas, *Le projet encyclopédique de Pline l'ancien*.

95   On the reality of marvels deliberately accumulated at Rome and its representation see Catharine Edwards, 'Incorporating the alien. The art of conquest', in *Rome the Cosmopolis*, ed. Catharine Edwards and Greg Woolf (Cambridge: Cambridge University Press, 2003), 44–70; Catharine Edwards, *Writing Rome. Textual approaches to the city*, ed. Denis Feeney and Stephen Hinds (Cambridge: Cambridge University Press, 1996), chapter 4.

96   The classic discussion is Emilio Gabba, 'True history and false history in classical antiquity', *Journal of Roman Studies* 71 (1981), 50–62.

97   Nicolet, *Space, Geography and Politics*, chapters 1 and 2; Mary Beard, *The Roman Triumph* (Cambridge, MA: Harvard University Press, 2007), chapter 4. On monumental representations, P. Holliday, *The Origins of Roman Historical Commemoration in the Visual Arts* (Cambridge: Cambridge University Press, 2002), chapter 2. Key examples are provided by R.R.R. Smith, '*Simulacra Gentium*: The Ethne from the Sebasteion at Aphrodisias', *Journal of Roman Studies* 78 (1988), 55–77; M. Sapelli, ed., Provinciae Fideles. *Il fregio del templo di Adriano in Campo Marzio* (Milan: Electa, 1999).

98   For the phrase see chapter 4 of Murphy, *Pliny the Elder's Natural History*. In fact much of this chapter is a subtle exposition of how similar modes of representing geographical space in text recur across Roman and Greek culture.

99   Illustrations in Rolf Michael Schneider, *Bunte Barbaren. Orientalenstatuen aus farbigem Marmor in der römischen Repräsentationskunst* (Worms: Wernersche Verlagsgeselschaft, 1986); Paul Zanker, *Augustus und die Macht der Bilder* (Munich: Beck, 1987).

100   For explorations of different relationships I have found especially helpful Bayly, *Empire and Information*; Laura Hostetler, *Qing Colonial Enterprise. Ethnography and cartography in early modern China* (Chicago: University of Chicago Press, 2001).

101   Edwards, *Roman Presences*.

102   On the practical needs of the military in the early empire see Susan P. Mattern, *Rome and the Enemy. Imperial strategy in the principate* (Berkeley, Los Angeles and London: University of California Press, 1999). Compare, on late

antiquity, A.D. Lee, *Information and Frontiers. Roman foreign relations in late antiquity* (Cambridge: Cambridge University Press, 1993), 81–90. On the debate over what cartography meant in ancient conditions see O.A.W. Dilke, *Greek and Roman Maps* (London: Thames and Hudson, 1985); Kai Brodersen, *Terra cognita. Studien zur römischen Raumerfassung* (Hildersheim: Olms, 1995). The general direction of the discussion has tended to mark the distinction between devices needed for practical purposes (such as itineraries and cadastral maps) and whatever larger-scale representations of space were used for propagandistic purposes.

103 For a clear introduction see Brian Campbell, 'Shaping the rural environment. Surveyors in ancient Rome', *Journal of Roman Studies* 86 (1996), 74–99.

104 Caesar *Gallic War* 6.11–20 on the Gauls, 21–8 on the Germans.

105 On Caesarian ethnography in Gaul see Brenda M. Bell, 'The contribution of Julius Caesar to the vocabulary of ethnography', *Latomus* 54 (1995), 753–67; Riggsby, *War in Words*, 59–71.

106 See most recently, with guides to the vast bibliography, Lund, *Zum Germanenbild der* Römer; Christopher B. Krebs, '"Imaginary geography" in Caesar's *Bellum Gallicum*', *American Journal of Philology* 127, 1 (2006), 111–36. On the more general issue of the politicization of Caesar's narrative, see the essays collected in Kathryn Welch and Anton Powell, eds, *Julius Caesar as Artful Reporter. The war commentaries as political instruments* (Swansea: Classical Press of Wales and London: Duckworth, 1998).

4 Enduring Fictions?

1 Tacitus *Agricola* 10 (author's translation).

2 Tacitus *Agricola* 11.2 (author's translation).

3 On the characterization of the ends of the earth see Romm, *The Edges of the Earth in Ancient Thought*. For recent discussions of the moral valency of Britain in Roman writing see Katherine Clarke, 'An island nation. Re-reading Tacitus' *Agricola*', *Journal of Roman Studies* 91 (2001), 94–112; Woolf, 'A distant mirror'; Peter C.N. Stewart, 'Inventing Britain. The Roman creation and adaptation of an image', *Britannia*, 26 (1995), 1–10.

4 Levene, 'Sallust's *Jugurtha*'.

5 On early assimilation of Roman imagery and ideas, John Creighton, *Coins and Power in Late Iron Age Britain* (Cambridge: Cambridge University Press, 2000). On the late pre-Roman Iron Age see Martin Millett, *The Romanization of Britain. An archaeological essay* (Cambridge: Cambridge University Press, 1990).

6 For the archaeological traces W.S. Hanson, *Agricola and the Conquest of the North* (London: Batsford, 1987). For the historical outline Mattingly, *An Imperial Possession*.

7 Romm, *The Edges of the Earth in Ancient Thought*.

8 For Apollonius, see Jas Elsner, 'Hagiographic geography. Travel and allegory in the *Life of Apollonius of Tyana*', *Journal of Hellenic Studies* 117 (1997), 22–37. For the growing interest in religious wisdom from the east see Glen

Bowersock, *Hellenism in Late Antiquity*, (Cambridge: Cambridge University Press, 1990), Momigliano, *Alien Wisdom*.

9   Plutarch *On the Decline of Oracles* 18.

10   Martinelli, *Roma e i barbari. Dai Giulio Claudii agli Antonini.*

11   Dio 39.50 (translation Cary and Foster, adapted).

12   Peter Garnsey and Richard P. Saller, *The Roman Empire. Economy, society and culture* (London: Duckworth, 1987), 16–17.

13   *Epitome* of Dio Book 77 12.1–4 (translation Cary and Foster, adapted).

14   For these developments, T. Keith Dix and George W. Houston, 'Public libraries in the city of Rome. From the Augustan age to the time of Diocletian', *Melanges de l'École française à Rome* 118, 2 (2006), 671–717; T. Keith Dix, '"Public libraries" in ancient Rome. Ideology and reality', *Libraries and Culture* 29, 3 (1994), 282–96.

15   Appian *Iberike* 1.2 (translation White, adapted).

16   Appian *Keltike* Epitome chapter 3 (translation White, adapted).

17   This conceptions of the frontier zone owes everything to C.R. Whittaker, *Frontiers of the Roman Empire. A social and economic study* (Baltimore, MD, and London: Johns Hopkins University Press, 1994).

18   Lynn F. Pitts, 'Relations between Rome and the German "kings" on the Middle Danube in the first to fourth centuries AD', *Journal of Roman Studies* 79 (1989), 45–58; Michael G. Fulford, 'Roman material in barbarian society. *c.* 200 BC–AD 400', in *Settlement and Society. Aspects of West European prehistory in the first millenium BC,* ed. T.C. Champion and J.V.S. Megaw (Leicester: Leicester University Press, 1985), 91–108; Michael G. Fulford, 'Roman and barbarian. The economy of Roman frontier systems', in *Barbarians and Romans in North-West Europe from the Later Republic to Late Antiquity,* ed. J.C. Barrett (Oxford: British Archaeological Reports, 1989), 81–95; L. Hedeager, 'Empire, frontier and the barbarian hinterland. Rome and northern Europe from AD 1–400', in *Centre and Periphery in the Ancient World,* ed. Michael Rowlands, Møgens Trolle Larsen and Kristian Kristiansen (Cambridge: Cambridge University Press, 1987), 125–40; Jürgen Kunow, *Der römische Import in der Germania libera bis zu den Markomannenkrieg. Studien zu Bronze- und Glasgefässen* (Neumunster: K. Wachholtz, 1983).

19   Tacitus *Annales* 1.57, 2.9, 4.72–4. Compare the bilingual Pannonian auxiliaries discussed by A Mócsy, 'The civilized Pannonians of Velleius', in *Rome and her Northern Provinces. Papers presented to Sheppard Frere,* ed. Brian Hartley and John Wacher (Gloucester: Alan Sutton, 1983), 169–78. Similar effects just within the frontier were experienced by groups such as the Batavians and Tungri, on which see Roymans, *Ethnic Identity and Imperial Power*; Franz Schön, 'Germanen sind wir gewesen? Bemerkungen zu den Tungri und Germani Cisrhenani und zum sogennanten taciteischen Namensatz (Tac. *Germ.* 2.2f.)', in *'Troianer sind wir gewesen'. Migrationen in der antiken Welt. Stuttgarter Kolloquium zur Historischen Geographie des Altertums, 8 2002,* ed. Eckart Olshausen and Holger Sonnabend (Stuttgart: F. Steiner, 2006), 167–83.

20   Pliny *Natural History* 37.45. On trade routes and their relation to geographical knowledge of Germany see Rives, *Tacitus, Germania*, 38–41.

21   E.g. Dio *Roman History* Epitome of Book 77 chapter 1 on Severus' decennalian games. I owe this observation to Nicholas Purcell.

22   For recent comment on the significance of transfrontier slaving in the early empire see William Vernon Harris, 'Demography, geography and the sources of Roman slaves', *Journal of Roman Studies* 89 (1999), 62–75.

23   Tacitus *Germania* 41.

24   Caesar *Gallic War* 6.21–4, anticipated in 4.1–3. For the pathless undifferentiated nature of Caesar's Germania see the discussion in chapter 3 above. The best short characterization is Krebs, '"Imaginary geography" in Caesar's *Bellum Gallicum*'.

25   For much of what follows Rives, *Tacitus*, Germania.

26   Among them Hartog, *Le miroir d' Hérodote*; Paul Cartledge, *The Greeks. A portrait of self and others* (Oxford and New York: Oxford University Press, 1993); Dench, *From Barbarians to New Men*.

27   O'Gorman, 'No place like Rome'.

28   Pliny *Natural History* 4.28–29. Notably the Chauci, described in Pliny *Natural History* 16.2–3, well discussed in chapter 5 of Murphy, *Pliny the Elder's Natural History*. On pre-Tacitean accounts of the Germans see Rives, *Tacitus, Germania*, 35–41.

29   Riggsby, *War in Words*, 67–8 on the contrast between the information conveyed in the ethnographic passages and that in the rest of the text.

30   Barton, *Power and Knowledge*. Barton labels the process 'involution'. For a different approach to the issue, John Henderson, 'Columella's living hedge. The Roman gardening book', *Journal of Roman Studies* 92 (2002), 110–33.

31   Tacitus *Germania* 3.3–4.1 (translation Rives).

32   Tacitus *Germania* 46.4 (translation Rives). *Quod ego ut incompertum in medio relinquam* is the ultimate refusal of closure.

33   Tacitus *Germania* 3.2 (translation Rives whose commentary on this passage is extremely helpful).

34   Greg Woolf, 'Power and the spread of writing in the west', in *Literacy and Power in the Ancient World*, ed. Alan Bowman and Greg Woolf (Cambridge: Cambridge University Press, 1994), 84–98.

35   I first explored some of these ideas in Woolf, 'Cruptorix and his kind'. On interpretors and cross-border contact, mostly in the late empire, see Lee, *Information and Frontiers*, 66–78.

36   The starting point is Georg Wissowa, '*Interpretatio Romana*. Römische Götter im Barbarenlande', *Archiv für Religionswissenschaft* 19 (1916–19), 1–49. For different recent views see Jane Webster, 'Translation and subjection. *Interpretatio* and the Celtic gods', in *Different Iron Ages. Studies on the Iron Age in temperate Europe*, ed. J.D. Hill and C. Cumberpatch (Oxford: British Archaeological Reports, 1995), 175–83; Clifford Ando, '*Interpretatio romana*', *Classical Philology* 100 (2005), 41–51.

37   Tacitus *Germania* 43.3 (author's translation).

38   For a parallel argument that *interpretationes* among the Treveri presuppose locals expert in Roman religion see John Scheid, 'Sanctuaires et territoire dans la

Colonia Augusta Treverorum', in *Les sanctuaires celtiques et le monde méditerranéen*, ed. Jean-Louis Brunaux (Paris: Errance, 1991), 42–57.

39   Tacitus *Germania* 9 (author's translation).

40   Tacitus *Germania* 34.

41   An earlier version of this section was presented at the Getty Villa at the invitation of Erich Gruen and will appear as 'Saving the barbarian', in *Cultural Identity in the Ancient Mediterranean*, ed. Erich Gruen (Los Angeles: Getty Publications, forthcoming), 255–71.

42   On the conventional aspects of Ammianus' ethnography see Gavin A Sundwall, 'Ammianus Geographicus', *American Journal of Philology* 117, 4 (1996), 619–43.

43   ἔλλαβε πορφύρεος θάνατος καὶ μοῖρα κραταιή (Iliad 5.83).

44   *maius opus moveo* (*Aeneid* 7.44).

45   *Galliarum tractus et situm ostendere puto* (Ammianus 15.9.1).

46   Erich Gruen points out to me the very similar reason Diodoros gives, at 1.9.5 for presenting his barbarian histories in a single place: 'The first peoples which we shall discuss will be the barbarians, not that we consider them to be earlier than the Greeks, as Ephorus has said, but because we wish to set forth most of the facts about them at the outset, in order that we may not, by beginning with the various accounts given by the Greeks, have to interpolate in the different narrations of their early history any event connected with another people' (translation Oldfather).

47   Ammianus Marcellinus 15.9.2–7 (translation Yonge, adapted).

48   For a demonstration of the intensity of Ammianus' engagement with his predecessors see Gavin Kelly, *Ammianus Marcellinus. The allusive historian* (Cambridge and New York: Cambridge University Press, 2008).

49   For discussion see Sordi, 'Timagene di Alessandria', 778–80.

50   *Nunc figuras et mores hominum designabo* (Ammianus 15.11.18).

51   *Evectus sum longius; sed remeabo tandem ad coepta* (Ammianus 15.12.6).

52   For full discussion see T.D. Barnes, *Ammianus Marcellinus and the Representation of Historical Reality* (Ithaca, NY: Cornell University Press, 1998). Pages 95–100 discuss the passage, arguing that relatively little was owed to Sallust or direct use of Caesar's commentaries, and emphasizing the contribution of autopsy.

53   P. De Jonge, *Philological and Historical Commentary on Ammianus Marcellinus XV 6–13* (Groningen: Wolters-Noordhoff, 1953). *ad loc.* for this point.

54   Thomas, *Lands and Peoples in Roman Poetry*.

55   So John F. Matthews, *The Roman Empire of Ammianus* (London: Duckworth, 1989), 463–4, on the digressions more generally, and noting that 'the description of the mythology, history and cities of Gaul goes far beyond what would be needed to understand in any strictly military sense the Gallic campaigns of Julian' and explaining it in terms of Ammianus' desire to elevate the tone of the Julian section of his history.

56   On all this see Marincola, *Authority and Tradition in Ancient Historiography*.

57   Although Barnes, *Ammianus Marcellinus and the Representation of Historical Reality*, suggests the description of belligerent Gallic women as reflecting a

personal reminiscence. The time reference of some other passages is equally uncertain.

58   This nice formulation is that of Barnes.

59   Thomas, *Out of Time*.

60   Wiedemann, 'Between men and beasts'.

61   On the origins of ethnographic writing in Latin see Rawson, *Intellectual Life in the Late Roman Republic*, chapter 7, esp. pp. 256 ff. and Braund, 'Greek geography and Roman empire'.

62   I am endebted in this part of the argument to Paul Veyne, *Did the Greeks Believe in Their Myths? An essay in the constitutive imagination*, trans. Paula Wissing (Chicago: University of Chicago Press, 1988), 54–7.

63   On the mythological literacy of ancient Roman readers, see chapter 9 of Cameron, *Greek Mythography in the Roman World*.

64   D.H. Miller and W.W. Savage, 'Ethnic stereotypes and the frontier. A comparative study of Roman and American experience', in *The Frontier I. Comparative Studies*, ed. D.H. Miller and J.O. Steffen (Norman: University of Oklahoma Press, 1977), 109–37. For antiquity, Wilfried Nippel, 'Ethnic images in classical antiquity', in *Imagology. The cultural construction and literary representation of national characters. A critical survey*, ed. Manfred Beller and Joep Leerssen (Amsterdam and New York: Editions Rodopi, 2007), 33–44.

65   For the historical emergence of barbarism see Hall, *Inventing the Barbarian*. See also N.T. Croally, *Euripidean Polemic. The Trojan Women and the function of tragedy* (Cambridge: Cambridge University Press, 1994), 103–15, Thomas Harrison, ed., *Greeks and Barbarians* (Edinburgh: Edinburgh University Press, 2002). The notion of a civilizing process in the course of which Greeks and barbarians became differentiated is a theme of Thucydides' archaeology, especially Book 1.3–6, showing the barbarous nature of ancient Greeks. Strabo 1.4.9 shows that from at least Eratosthenes' day, a debate was open on whether barbarians were to be opposed to Greeks alone or more generally to peoples who had political institutions and civilized behaviour. The best discussion of the uses and significance of the concept remains that of Shaw, '"Eaters of flesh, drinkers of milk"'.

66   On Roman barbarism, Dauge, *Le barbare*; Dench, *From Barbarians to New Men*; Martina Jantz, *Das Fremdenbild in der Literatur der Römischen Republik und der Augustische Zeit. Vorstellungen und Sichtweisen am Beispiel von Hispanien und Gallien* (Frankfurt-am-Main: Peter Lang, 1995); Woolf, *Becoming Roman*, chapter 3; Shaw, 'Rebels and outsiders'; Dench, *Romulus' Asylum*, chapter 1.

67   The case for this two stage transformation is made in Woolf, *Becoming Roman*.

68   For the wider context Greg Woolf, 'The Roman cultural revolution in Gaul', in *Italy and the West. Comparative issues in Romanization*, ed. Simon Keay and Nicola Terrenato (Oxford: Oxbow Books, 2001), 173–86.

69   Williams, *Beyond the Rubicon*; Kremer, *Das Bild der Kelten bis in augusteische Zeit*.

70   Such as, for example, J.P.V.D. Balsdon, *Romans and Aliens* (London: Duckworth, 1979).

71 For documentation of these views, a sane guide is provided by Stuart Piggott, *The Druids* (London: Thames and Hudson, 1968). The idea that the two images represent two different traditions no longer seems necessary.

72 No British sophists are known, but on Favorinus' exploitation of his Gallic origins see Maud Gleason, *Making Men. Sophists and self-presentation in ancient Rome* (Princeton, NJ: Princeton University Press, 1995). Lucian's use of his Assyrian identity offers an Eastern parallel, on which see Christopher P. Jones, *Culture and Society in Lucian* (Cambridge, MA: Harvard University Press, 1986). On these issues see Tim Whitmarsh, ed., *Local Knowledge and Microidentities in the Imperial Greek World* (Cambridge: Cambridge University Press, 2010).

73 Philostratus *Lives of the Sophists* 489.

74 For overviews see Price, 'Local mythologies in the Greek East', Simon Price, 'Memory and ancient Greece', in *Religion and Society. Rituals, resources and identity in the ancient Graeco-Roman world. The BOMOS conferences 2002–5*, ed. Anders Holm Rasmussen and Suzanne William Rasmussen (Rome: Edizioni Quasar, 2008), 167–78; Susan E. Alcock, *Archaeologies of the Greek Past. Landscape, monuments and memories* (Cambridge: Cambridge University Press, 2002). For festival culture, Michael Wörrle, *Stadt und Fest in kaiserzeitlichen Kleinasien. Studien zu einer agonistischen Stiftung aus Oinoanda* (Munich: C.H. Beck, 1988); Guy M. Rogers, *The Sacred Identity of Ephesos. Foundation myths of a Roman city* (London: Routledge, 1991).

75 Greg Woolf, 'The uses of forgetfulness in Roman Gaul', in *Vergangenheit und Lebenswelt. Soziale Kommunikation, Traditionsbildung und historisches Bewußtsein*, ed. Hans-Joachim Gehrke and Astrid Möller (Tübingen: Gunter Narr Verlag, 1996), 361–81. Compare Graeme Clarke, Brian Croke, Raoul Mortley and Alana Emmett Nobbs, eds, *Reading the Past in Late Antiquity* (Sydney: Australian National University Press, 1990).

76 See the papers gathered in Valérie Fromentin and Sophie Gotteland, eds, *Origines Gentium* (Paris and Bordeaux: De Boccard, 2001); Erich Gruen, ed., *Cultural Borrowings and Ethnic Appropriations in Antiquity* (Stuttgart: Franz Steiner Verlag, 2005).

77 On Herakles in the West see Corinne Bonnet, *Melqart. Cultes et mythes de l' Héraclès Tyrien en Méditerranée* (Leuven: Presses Universitaires de Namur, 1988); Bonnet and Jourdain-Annequin, *Héraclès*; Irad Malkin, 'Herakles and Melqart: Greeks and Phoenicians in the middle ground', in Gruen, ed., *Cultural Borrowings*, 238–58. More generally see Gehrke, 'Heroen als Grenzgänger zwischen Griechen und Barbaren'.

78 On the distribution of the Herakles cult in the far north, Ton Derks, *Gods, Temples and Ritual Practices. The transformation of religious ideas and values in Roman Gaul* (Amsterdam: Amsterdam University Press, 1998). On Herakles in Gaul, Gérard Moitrieux, *Hercules in Gallia. Recherches sur la personnalité et le culte d'Hercule en Gaule* (Paris: De Boccard, 2002); Gerhard Bauchhenß, 'Hercules in Gallien – facts and fiction', in *Continuity and Innovation in Religion in the Roman West*, ed. Ralph Haeussler and Anthony C. King (Providence, RI: Journal of Roman Archaeology, 2008), 91–102. Debate

continues over the contribution of native deities to various Herakles cults, but the iconography is generally thoroughly classical.

79   For a careful discussion of one well-documented case. see Roymans, *Ethnic Identity and Imperial Power*. See also Ton Derks and N. Roymans, eds, *Ethnic Constructs in Antiquity. The role of power and tradition* (Amsterdam: Amsterdam University Press, 2009).

80   John Nicol, *The Historical and Geographical Sources used by Silius Italicus* (Oxford: Basil Blackwell, 1936).

81   David Braund, 'The Aedui, Troy and the *Apocolocyntosis*', *Classical Review* 30, 2 (1980), 402–25; Gerhard Dobesch, 'Zu zwei Daten der Geschichte Galliens: (1) Der Gastfreundschaftvertrag zwischen Haeduern und Romern, (2) Der Principat der Celtillus', in Dobesch, *Ausgewählten Schriften* (Cologne, Weimar and Vienna: Böhlau, 2001); Gerhard Dobesch, 'Arverner aus Troja (Lucan b.c.1, 427–428)? Kleine Überlegungen zur gallo-römischen Kultur', in *Italo-Tusco-Romana. Festschrift für Luciana Aigner-Foresti zum 70. Geburtstag am 30, Juli 2006*, ed. Petra Amann, Marco Pedrazzi, and Hans Taeuber (Vienna: Holzhausen Verlag, 2006), 143–84. On the Trojan myth more widely, Erskine, *Troy between Greece and Rome*; Andrew Erskine, 'Unity and identity. Shaping the past in the Greek Mediterranean', in Gruen, ed., *Cultural Borrowings*, 121–36.

82   Sidonius 7.7.2 begins *Arvernorum, pro dolor, servitus, qui, si prisca replicarentur, audebant se quondam fratres Latio dicere et sanguine ab Iliaco populos computare.* Lucan's line at *Pharsalia* 1.427–8 is *Arvernique, ausi Latio se fingere fratres | sanguine ab Iliaco populi.*

83   For this, Ian Wood, 'Defining the Franks. Frankish origins in early mediaeval historiography', in *Concepts of National Identity in the Middle Ages*, ed. Simon Forde, Lesley Johnson and Alan V. Murray (Leeds: Leeds University Press, 1995), 47–57. Wood also points out that this story competed with several others, including the descent of the Merovingians from a seamonster's union with a princess. For the broader context within which these myths were formed and related see Karl J. Leyser, 'Concepts of Europe in the early and high Middle Ages', *Past & Present* 137 (1992), 25–47.

84   Francis Ingledew, 'The *Book of Troy* and the genealogical construction of history. The case of Geoffrey of Monmouth's *Historia regum Britannae*', *Speculum* 69, 3 (1994), 665–704.

85   Robert E. Hallowell, 'Ronsard and the Gallic Hercules myth', *Studies in the Renaissance* 6 (1962), 242–55; George Huppert, 'The Trojan Franks and their critics', *Studies in the Renaissance* 12 (1965), 227–41.

References

Abry, Josèphe-Henriette. 'Une carte du monde à l'époque d'Auguste. Manilius *Astronomiques* IV, 585–817.' In *L'espace et ses représentations*, ed. Annie Bonnafé, Jean-Claude Decourt and Bruno Helly, 83–112. Lyon: Maison de l'Orient Méditerranéen, 2000.

Alcock, Susan E. *Archaeologies of the Greek Past. Landscape, monuments and memories.* Cambridge: Cambridge University Press, 2002.

Alcock, Susan E. *Graecia Capta. The landscapes of Roman Greece.* Cambridge and New York: Cambridge University Press, 1993.

Alcock, Susan E., John F. Cherry and Jas Elsner, eds. *Pausanias. Travel and memory in Roman Greece.* New York: Oxford University Press, 2001.

Alonso-Nuñez, José Miguel. 'An Augustan world history: The *Historiae Philippicae* of Pompeius Trogus.' *Greece & Rome* 34, 1 (1987): 56–72.

Alonso-Nuñez, José Miguel. 'Herodotus' conceptions of historical space and the beginnings of Universal History.' In *Herodotus and His World. Essays from a conference in memory of George Forrest*, ed. Peter Derow and Robert Parker, 145–52. Oxford and New York: Oxford University Press, 2003.

Ando, Clifford. 'Interpretatio romana.' *Classical Philology* 100 (2005): 41–51.

Ash, Rhiannon. 'The wonderful world of Mucianus.' In *Vita Vigilia Est. Essays in honour of Barbara Levick*, ed. Edward Bispham, Greg Rowe and Elaine Matthews, 1–17. Bulletin of the Institute of Classical Studies Supplement 100. London: Institute of Classical Studies, 2007.

Balsdon, J.P.V.D. *Romans and Aliens.* London: Duckworth, 1979.

Barley, Nigel. *The Innocent Anthropologist. Notes from a mud hut.* London: Penguin Books, 1983.

Barnes, Jonathon, and Miriam Griffin, eds. *Philosophia Togata II. Plato and Aristotle in Rome.* Oxford: Oxford University Press, 1997.

Barnes, T.D. *Ammianus Marcellinus and the Representation of Historical Reality.* Cornell Studies in Classical Philology. Ithaca, NY: Cornell University Press, 1998.

Bartlett, Robert. *The Natural and the Supernatural in the Middle Ages.* Cambridge and New York: Cambridge University Press, 2008.

Barton, Tamsyn. *Ancient Astrology.* Sciences of Antiquity. London: Routledge, 1994.

Barton, Tamsyn. *Power and Knowledge. Astrology, physiognomics and medicine under the Roman Empire.* The Body, in Theory. Histories of Cultural Materialism. Ann Arbor: Michigan University Press, 1994.

Batty, Roger. 'Mela's Phoenecian geography.' *Journal of Roman Studies* 90 (2000): 70–95.

Bauchhenß, Gerhard. 'Hercules in Gallien – facts and fiction.' In *Continuity and Innovation in Religion in the Roman West*, ed. Ralph Haeussler and Anthony C. King, 91–102. Journal of Roman Archaeology Supplementary Series 67.2 Providence, RI: Journal of Roman Archaeology, 2008.

Bayly, Christopher A. *Empire and Information. Intelligence gathering and social communication in India, 1780–1870.* Cambridge: Cambridge University Press, 1996.

Beagon, Mary. *Roman Nature. The thought of Pliny the Elder.* Oxford Classical Monographs. Oxford: Clarendon Press, 1992.

Beagon, Mary. *The Elder Pliny on the Human Animal. Natural History Book 7 translated with commentary.* Clarendon Ancient History Series. New York: Clarendon Press, 2005.

Beagon, Mary. 'Situating nature's wonders in Pliny's *Natural History.*' In *Vita Vigilia Est. Essays in honour of Barbara Levick*, ed. Edward Bispham, Greg Rowe and Elaine Matthews, 19–40. Bulletin of the Institute of Classical Studies Supplement 100. London: Institute of Classical Studies, 2007.

Beard, Mary. 'Cicero and divination. The formation of a Latin discourse.' *Journal of Roman Studies* 76 (1986): 33–46.

Beard, Mary. *The Roman Triumph.* Cambridge, MA: Harvard University Press, 2007.

Bell, Brenda M. 'The contribution of Julius Caesar to the vocabulary of ethnography.' *Latomus* 54 (1995): 753–67.

Bianchi, Olivier, and Olivier Thévenaz, eds. *Mirabilia. Conceptions et représentations de l'extraordinaire dans le monde antique. Actes du colloque international, Lausanne 20–22 mars 2003.* Echo. Collection de l'Institut d'Archéologie et des Sciences de l'Antiquité de l'Université de Lausanne. Bern: Peter Lang, 2004.

Bickermann, Elias. '*Origines gentium.*' *Classical Philology* 47 (1952): 65–81.

Bohannan, Laura. 'A genealogical charter.' *Africa* 22 (1952): 301–15.

Bonnet, Corinne. *Melqart. Cultes et mythes de l'Héraclès Tyrien en Méditerranée*, Studia Phoenecia. Leuven: Presses Universitaires de Namur,1988.

Bonnet, Corinne, and Colette Jourdain-Annequin, eds. *Héraclès. D'une rive à l'autre de la Mediterranée.* Brussels and Rome: Institut Historique Belge de Rome, 1992.

Bowersock, Glen W. *Augustus and the Greek World.* Oxford: Clarendon Press, 1965.

Bowersock, Glen W. *Hellenism in Late Antiquity.* Thomas Spenser Jerome Lectures. Cambridge: Cambridge University Press, 1990.

Braund, David. 'The Aedui, Troy and the *Apocolocyntosis.*' *Classical Review* 30, 2 (1980): 402–25.

Braund, David. 'Greek geography and Roman empire. The transformation of tradition in Strabo's Euxine.' In *Strabo's Cultural Geography. The making of a kolossourgia*, ed. Daniela Dueck, Hugh Lindsay and Sarah Pothecary, 216–34. Cambridge: Cambridge University Press, 2005.

Brill's New Pauly: encyclopaedia of the ancient world, ed. Hubert Cancik and Helmuth Schneider. Leiden and Boston: Brill, 2002–8.

Brodersen, Kai. *Terra cognita. Studien zur römischen Raumerfassung. Spudasmata* 59. Hildersheim: Olms, 1995.

Brodersen, Kai, and Jas Elsner, eds. *Images and Texts on the 'Artemidorus Papyrus'. Working papers on P. Artemid. (St John's College Oxford, 2008), Historia* Einzelschriften. Stuttgart: Franz Steiner Verlag, 2009.

Brown, Michael F. 'On resisting resistance.' *American Anthropologist* 98, 4 (1996): 729–35.

Burnstein, Stanley. *Agatharchides of Cnidus, On the Erythraean Sea.* London: Hakluyt Society, 1989.

de Callataÿ, Godefroid. 'La géographie de Manilius (*Astr.* 4, 744–817), avec une note sur *l'Énéide* virgilienne.' *Latomus* 60, 1 (2001): 35–66.

Cameron, Alan. *Greek Mythography in the Roman World.* American Classical Studies. New York: Oxford University Press, 2004.

Campbell, Brian. 'Shaping the rural environment. Surveyors in ancient Rome.' *Journal of Roman Studies* 86 (1996): 74–99.

Campbell, Gordon Lindsay. *Strange Creatures. Anthropology in antiquity.* London: Duckworth, 2006.

Carey, Sorcha. *Pliny's Catalogue of Culture. Art and empire in the Natural History*, Oxford Studies in Ancient Culture and Representation. Oxford: Oxford University Press, 2003.

Cartledge, Paul. *The Greeks. A portrait of self and others.* Oxford and New York: Oxford University Press, 1993.

Casson, Lionel. *Libraries in the Ancient World.* New Haven, CT, and London: Yale University Press, 2001.

Champion, T.C. 'Written sources and the study of the European Iron Age.' In *Settlement and Society. Aspects of West European prehistory in the first century* BC, ed. T.C. Champion and J.V.S. Megaw, 9–22. Leicester: Leicester University Press, 1985.

Chapman, Malcolm. '"Semantics" and "the Celt".' In *Semantic Anthropology*, ed. David Parkin, 123–43. ASA monographs 22. London: Association of Social Anthropology, 1982.

Chapman, Malcolm. *The Celts. The construction of a myth.* Basingstoke: Macmillan, 1992.

Chilver, G.E.F. *Cisalpine Gaul. Social and economic history from 49* BC *to the death of Trajan.* Oxford: Clarendon Press, 1941.

Clarke, Graeme, Brian Croke, Raoul Mortley and Alana Emmett Nobbs, eds. *Reading the Past in Late Antiquity.* Sydney: Australian National University Press, 1990.

Clarke, Katherine. 'In search of the author of Strabo's *Geography*.' *Journal of Roman Studies* 87 (1997): 92–110.

Clarke, Katherine. *Between Geography and History. Hellenistic constructions of the Roman world.* Oxford: Oxford University Press, 1999.

Clarke, Katherine. 'Universal perspectives in historiography.' In *The Limits of Historiography. Genre and narrative in ancient historical texts*, ed. Christina Shuttleworth Kraus, 249–79. Leiden, Boston and Cologne: Brill, 1999.

Clarke, Katherine. 'An island nation. Re-reading Tacitus' *Agricola.*' *Journal of Roman Studies* 91 (2001): 94–112.

Clarke, Katherine. *Making Time for the Past. Local history and the polis.* Oxford: Oxford University Press, 2008.

Clavel-Lévêque, Monique. 'Les gaules et les gauloises. Pour une analyse du fonctionnement de la *Géographie* de Strabon.' *Dialogues d'Histoire Ancienne* 1 (1974): 75–93.

Clifford, James. *Routes. Travel and translation in the late twentieth century.* Cambridge: Cambridge University Press, 1999.

Clifford, James, and George Marcus, eds. *Writing Culture. The poetics and politics of ethnography.* Berkeley: University of California Press, 1986.

Collis, John R. *The Celts. Origins, myths and inventions.* Stroud: Tempus, 2003.

Comaroff, John, and Jean Comaroff. *Ethnography and the Historical Imagination*, Studies in the Ethnographic Imagination. Boulder, CO: Westview Press, 1992.

Conte, Gian Biagio. 'The inventory of the world. Form of nature and encyclopedic project in the work of Pliny the Elder.' In *Genres and Readers. Lucretius, love elegy, Pliny's encyclopedia*, 67–104. Baltimore, MD, and London: Johns Hopkins University Press, 1994.

Crawford, Michael H. 'Greek intellectuals and the Roman aristocracy in the first century BC.' In *Imperialism in the Ancient World*, ed. Peter Garnsey and C.R. Whittaker, 193–207. Cambridge: Cambridge University Press, 1978.

Creighton, John. *Coins and Power in Late Iron Age Britain*, New Studies in Archaeology. Cambridge: Cambridge University Press, 2000.

Croally, N.T. *Euripidean Polemic. The Trojan Women and the function of tragedy*, Cambridge Classical Studies. Cambridge: Cambridge University Press, 1994.

Cruz Andreotti, Gonzalo. 'Acerca de las identidades meridionales en época prerromana. Algunos planteamientos geográficos.' In *Identidades, Culturas y Territorios en la Andalucia Prerromana*, ed. Fernando Wulff Alonso and Manuel Álvarez Marti-Aguilar, 297–316. Malaga and Seville: Universidades de Malaga and Sevilla, 2009.

Cruz Andreotti, Gonzalo, Patrick Le Roux, and Pierre Moret, eds. *La invención de una geografía de la península ibérica. I. La época republicana.* Málaga and Madrid: Centro de Ediciones de la Disputación de Málaga and Casa de Velázquez, 2006.

Cruz Andreotti, Gonzalo, Patrick Le Roux, and Pierre Moret, eds. *La invención de una geografía de la Península Ibérica. II. La época imperial.* Málaga and Madrid: Centro de Ediciones de la Disputación de Málaga and Casa de Velázquez, 2007.

Culham, Phyllis. 'Archives and alternatives in republican Rome.' *Classical Philology* 84, 2 (1989): 100–15.

Dauge, Yves-Albert. *Le barbare. Recherches sur la conception romaine de la barbarie et de la civilisation.* Collection Latomus. Brussels: Latomus, 1981.

Davidson, James. 'The gaze in Polybius' histories.' *Journal of Roman Studies* 81 (1991): 10–24.

De Jonge, P. *Philological and Historical Commentary on Ammianus Marcellinus XV 6–13.* Groningen: Wolters-Noordhoff, 1953.

Dench, Emma. *From Barbarians to New Men. Greek, Roman and modern perceptions of peoples of the central Apennines.* Oxford: Oxford University Press, 1995.

Dench, Emma. *Romulus' Asylum. Roman identities from the age of Alexander to the age of Hadrian.* Oxford: Oxford University Press, 2005.

Dench, Emma. 'Ethnography and history.' In *A Companion to Greek and Roman Historiography*, ed. John Marincola, 493–503. Malden, MA and Oxford: Blackwell Publishers, 2007.

Derks, Ton. *Gods, Temples and Ritual Practices. The transformation of religious ideas and values in Roman Gaul.* Amsterdam Archaeological Studies. Amsterdam: Amsterdam University Press, 1998.

Derks, Ton, and N. Roymans, eds. *Ethnic Constructs in Antiquity. The role of power and tradition.* Amsterdam Archaeological Studies 2. Amsterdam: Amsterdam University Press, 2009.

Dihle, Albrecht. 'Zur Hellenistischen Ethnographie.' In *Grecs et barbares*, Fondation Hardt Entretiens sur l'antiquité classique, vol. 8, 205–39. Vandoeuvres and Geneva: Fondation Hardt, 1962.

Dilke, O.A.W. *Greek and Roman Maps.* Aspects of Greek and Roman Life. London: Thames and Hudson, 1985.

Dillery, John. 'Greek historians of the Near East. Clio's "other" sons.' In *A Companion to Greek and Roman Historiography*, ed. John Marincola, 221–30. Malden, MA and Oxford: Blackwell Publishers, 2007.

Dix, T. Keith. '"Public libraries" in ancient Rome. Ideology and reality.' *Libraries and Culture* 29, 3 (1994): 282–96.

Dix, T. Keith. 'The library of Lucullus.' *Athenaeum* 88, 2 (2000): 441–64.

Dix, T. Keith, and George W. Houston. 'Public libraries in the city of Rome. From the Augustan age to the time of Diocletian.' *Melanges de l'École française à Rome* 118, 2 (2006): 671–717.

Dobesch, Gerhard. 'Zu zwei Daten der Geschichte Galliens: (1) Der Gastfreundschaftvertrag zwischen Haeduern und Romern, (2) Der Principat der Celtillus.' In *Gerhard Dobesch, Ausgewählten Schriften*, 755–80. Cologne, Weimar and Vienna: Böhlau, 2001.

Dobesch, Gerhard. 'Arverner aus Troja (Lucan b.c.1, 427–428)? Kleine Überlegungen zur gallo-römischen Kultur.' In *Italo-Tusco-Romana. Festschrift für Luciana Aigner-Foresti zum 70. Geburtstag am 30, Juli 2006*, ed. Petra Amann, Marco Pedrazzi and Hans Taeuber, 143–84. Vienna: Holzhausen Verlag, 2006.

Doody, Aude. 'Finding facts in Pliny's encyclopaedia. The *Summarium* of the *Natural History*.' *Ramus. Critical studies in Greek and Roman literature* 30 (2001): 1–22.

Dougherty, Carol. *The Poetics of Colonization. From city to text in archaic Greece.* New York and Oxford: Oxford University Press, 1993.

Dougherty, Carol. *The Raft of Odysseus. The ethnographic imagination of Homer's Odyssey.* New York: Oxford University Press, 2001.

Dueck, Daniela. *Strabo of Amasia. A Greek man of letters in Augustan Rome.* London and New York: Routledge, 2000.

Dueck, Daniela, Hugh Lindsay, and Sarah Pothecary, eds. *Strabo's Cultural Geography. The making of a kolossourgia.* Cambridge: Cambridge University Press, 2005.

Dyson, Stephen L. 'Caepio,Tacitus and Lucan's sacred grove.' *Classical Philology 65*, 1 (1970): 36–8.

Dyson, Stephen L. *The Creation of the Roman Frontier*. Princeton, NJ: Princeton University Press, 1985.

Eco, Umberto. 'Portrait of the Elder as a Young Pliny. How to build fame.' In *On Signs*, ed. Marshall Blonsky, 289–302. Baltimore, MD, and London: Johns Hopkins University Press, 1985.

Edwards, Catharine. *The Politics of Immorality in Ancient Rome*. Cambridge: Cambridge University Press, 1993.

Edwards, Catharine. *Writing Rome. Textual approaches to the city*, ed. Denis Feeney and Stephen Hinds. Roman Literature and Its Contexts. Cambridge: Cambridge University Press, 1996.

Edwards, Catharine, ed., *Roman Presences. Receptions of Rome in European culture, 1789–1945*. Cambridge: Cambridge University Press, 1999.

Edwards, Catharine. 'Incorporating the alien. The art of conquest.' In *Rome the Cosmopolis*, ed. Catharine Edwards and Greg Woolf, 44–70. Cambridge: Cambridge University Press, 2003.

Edwards, Catharine, and Greg Woolf, eds. *Rome the Cosmopolis*. Cambridge: Cambridge University Press, 2003.

Elliott, John H. *The Old World and the New 1492–1650*. Cambridge: Cambridge University Press, 1970.

Elsner, Jas. 'Hagiographic geography. Travel and allegory in the *Life of Apollonius of Tyana*.' *Journal of Hellenic Studies* 117 (1997): 22–37.

Elsner, Jas, and Ian Rutherford, eds. *Pilgrimage in Graeco-Roman and Early Christian Antiquity. Seeing the gods*. Oxford: Oxford University Press, 2005.

Erskine, Andrew. *Troy between Greece and Rome, Local tradition and imperial power*. Oxford: Oxford University Press, 2001.

Erskine, Andrew. 'Unity and identity. Shaping the past in the Greek Mediterranean.' In *Cultural Borrowings and Ethnic Appropriations in Antiquity*, ed. Erich Gruen, 121–36. Stuttgart: Franz Steiner Verlag, 2005.

Evans, Rhiannon. 'Ethnography's freak show. The grotesques at the edges of the Roman earth.' *Ramus. Critical studies in Greek and Roman literature* 28, 1 (1999): 54–73.

Evans, Rhiannon. 'Geography without people. Mapping in Pliny's *Historia Naturalis* Books 3–6.' *Ramus. Critical studies in Greek and Roman literature* 34, 1 (2005): 47–74.

Feeney, Denis. *Literature and Religion at Rome. Culture, contexts and beliefs*. Latin Literature in Context. Cambridge: Cambridge University Press, 1998.

Fowler, Robert L. 'Herodotos and his contemporaries.' *Journal of Hellenic Studies* 116 (1996): 62–87.

Fowler, Robert L. 'Genealogical thinking, Hesiod's *Catalogue*, and the creation of the Hellenes.' *Proceedings of the Cambridge Philological Society* 44 (1998): 1–19.

Fromentin, Valérie, and Sophie Gotteland, eds. *Origines Gentium*. Ausonius Publications. Paris and Bordeaux: De Boccard, 2001.

Fulford, Michael G. 'Roman material in barbarian society. *c.* 200 BC–AD 400.' In *Settlement and Society. Aspects of West European prehistory in the first millenium* BC, ed. T.C. Champion and J.V.S. Megaw, 91–108. Leicester: Leicester University Press, 1985.

Fulford, Michael G. 'Roman and barbarian. The economy of Roman frontier systems.' In *Barbarians and Romans in North-West Europe from the Later Republic to Late Antiquity*, ed. J.C. Barrett, 81–95. International Series 471. Oxford: British Archaeological Reports, 1989.

Gabba, Emilio. 'True history and false history in classical antiquity.' *Journal of Roman Studies* 71 (1981): 50–62.

Garnsey, Peter. *Food and Society in Classical Antiquity*. Key Themes in Ancient History. Cambridge: Cambridge University Press, 1999.

Garnsey, Peter, and Richard P. Saller. *The Roman Empire. Economy, society and culture*. London: Duckworth, 1987.

Geertz, Clifford. *The Interpretation of Cultures. Selected essays*. New York: Basic Books, 1973.

Gehrke, Hans-Joachim. 'Heroen als Grenzgänger zwischen Griechen und Barbaren.' In *Cultural Borrowings and Ethnic Appropriations in Antiquity*, ed. Erich Gruen, 50–67. Stuttgart: Franz Steiner Verlag, 2005.

Giannini, Alexander. *Paradoxographorum graecorum reliquae*. Classici Greci e Latini. Milan: Istituto Editoriale Italiano, 1966.

Gigante, Marcello. *Philodemus in Italy. The books from Herculaneum*. Trans. Dirk Obbink. The Body, in Theory. Histories of Cultural Materialism. Ann Arbor: University of Michigan Press, 1995.

Gildenhard, Ingo. *Paideia Romana. Cicero's Tusculan Disputations*. Ed. Tim Whitmarsh and James Warren. Proceedings of the Cambridge Philological Society Supplements. Cambridge: Cambridge Philological Society, 2007.

Gleason, Maud. *Making Men. Sophists and self-presentation in ancient Rome*. Princeton, NJ: Princeton University Press, 1995.

Gold, Barbara K., ed. *Literary and Artistic Patronage in Ancient Rome*. Austin, TX: University of Texas Press, 1982.

Goody, Jack R., and Ian Watt. 'The consequences of literacy.' *Comparative Studies in Society and History* 5 (1963): 304–45.

Gosden, Chris. *Archaeology and Colonialism. Cultural contact from 5000 BC to the present*. Topics in Contemporary Archaeology. Cambridge: Cambridge University Press, 2004.

Green, C.M.C. 'De Africa et eius incolis. The function of geography and ethnography in Sallust's history of the Jugurthine War (J 17–19).' *The Ancient World* 24, 2 (1993): 185–97.

Griffin, Miriam. 'Philosophy, politics and politicians at Rome.' C In *Philosophia Togata I. Essays on philosophy and Roman society*, ed. Miriam Griffin and Jonathon Barnes, 1–37. Oxford: Oxford University Press, 1989.

Griffin, Miriam, and Jonathon Barnes, eds. *Philosophia Togata I. Essays on philosophy and Roman society*. Oxford: Oxford University Press, 1989.

Gruen, Erich. 'Political Prosecutions in the 90s BC.' *Historia. Zeitschrift für Alte Geschichte* 15, 1 (1966): 32–64.

Gruen, Erich, ed. *Cultural Borrowings and Ethnic Appropriations in Antiquity*. Oriens et Occidens: Studien zu antiken Kulturkontakten und ihren Nachleben. Stuttgart: Franz Steiner Verlag, 2005.

Gruen, Erich, ed. *Cultural Identity in the Ancient Mediterranean*. Los Angeles: Getty Publications, forthcoming.

Habicht, Christian. *Pausanias' Guide to Ancient Greece*. Sather Classical Lectures, vol. 50. Berkeley: University of California Press, 1985.

Habinek, Thomas, and Alessandro Schiesaro, eds. *The Roman Cultural Revolution*. Cambridge: Cambridge University Press, 1997.

Hall, Edith. *Inventing the Barbarian. Greek self-definition through tragedy*. Oxford Classical Monographs. Oxford: Oxford University Press, 1989.

Hall, Jonathon M. *Ethnic Identity in Greek Antiquity*. Cambridge: Cambridge University Press, 1997.

Hallowell, Robert E. 'Ronsard and the Gallic Hercules myth.' *Studies in the Renaissance* 6 (1962): 242–55.

Hanson, W.S. *Agricola and the Conquest of the North*. London: Batsford, 1987.

Harris, William Vernon. 'Demography, geography and the sources of Roman slaves.' *Journal of Roman Studies* 89 (1999): 62–75.

Harris, William Vernon, ed. *Rethinking the Mediterranean*. Oxford: Oxford University Press, 2005.

Harrison, Thomas, ed. *Greeks and Barbarians*. Edinburgh Readings on the Ancient World. Edinburgh: Edinburgh University Press, 2002.

Hartog, François. *Le miroir d' Hérodote. Essai sur la représentation de l'autre*. Paris: Gallimard, 1980.

Healy, John F. *Pliny the Elder on Science and Technology*. Oxford and New York: Oxford University Press, 1999.

Heather, Peter. 'Cassiodorus and the rise of the Amals. Genealogy and the Goths under Hun domination.' *Journal of Roman Studies* 79 (1989): 103–28.

Hedeager, L. 'Empire, frontier and the barbarian hinterland. Rome and northern Europe from AD 1–400.' In *Centre and Periphery in the Ancient World*, ed. Michael Rowlands, Møgens Trolle Larsen and Kristian Kristiansen, 125–40. Cambridge: Cambridge University Press, 1987.

Henderson, John. 'Columella's living hedge. The Roman gardening book.' *Journal of Roman Studies* 92 (2002): 110–33.

Henderson, John. *The Mediaeval World of Isidore of Seville. Truth from words*. Cambridge: Cambridge University Press, 2007.

Herzig, Hainz. E. 'Novum genus hominum: Phänomene der Migratione im römischen Heer.' In *'Troianer sind wir gewesen' Migrationen in der antiken Welt. Stuttgarter Kolloquium zur Historischen Geographie des Altertums, 8 2002* ed. Eckart Olshausen and Holger Sonnabend, 325–8. Stuttgart: F. Steiner, 2006.

Hinds, Stephen. *Allusion and Intertext. Dynamics of appropriation in Roman poetry*. Latin Literature in Context. Cambridge: Cambridge University Press, 1998.

Hingley, Richard. *Roman Officers and English Gentlemen. The imperial origins of Roman archaeology*. London: Routledge, 2000.

Hobsbawm, Eric, and Terence Ranger, eds. *The Invention of Tradition*. Past and Present Publications. Cambridge: Cambridge University Press, 1983.

Holliday, P. *The Origins of Roman Historical Commemoration in the Visual Arts*. Cambridge: Cambridge University Press, 2002.

Horden, Peregrine, and Nicholas Purcell. *The Corrupting Sea. A study of Mediterranean history*. Oxford: Blackwell Publishers, 2000.

Hornblower, Simon. 'Introduction: summary of the papers; the story of Greek historiography; intertextuality and the Greek historians.' In *Greek Historiography*, ed. Simon Hornblower, 1–72. Oxford: Clarendon Press, 1994.

Hostetler, Laura. *Qing Colonial Enterprise. Ethnography and cartography in early modern China*. Chicago: University of Chicago Press, 2001.

Huppert, George. 'The Trojan Franks and their critics.' *Studies in the Renaissance* 12 (1965): 227–41.

Ingledew, Francis. '*The Book of Troy* and the genealogical construction of history. The case of Geoffrey of Monmouth's *Historia regum Britannae.*' *Speculum* 69, 3 (1994): 665–704.

Jacob, Christian. 'De l'art de compiler à la fabrication du merveilleux. Sur la paradoxographie grecque.' *Lalies* 2 (1980): 121–40.

Jacoby, Felix. *Die Fragmente der griechischen Historiker*. 15 vols. Berlin and Leiden: Weidemann and Brill, 1923–58 (cited as *FGrH*).

James, Simon. *The Atlantic Celts. Ancient people or modern invention?* London: British Museum Press, 1999.

Jantz, Martina. *Das Fremdenbild in der Literatur der Römischen Republik und der Augustische Zeit. Vorstellungen und Sichtweisen am Beispiel von Hispanien und Gallien*. Europäische Hochschulschriften. Reihe III Geschichte und ihre Hilfswissenschaften. Frankfurt-am-Main: Peter Lang, 1995.

Jones, Christopher P. *Culture and Society in Lucian*. Cambridge, MA: Harvard University Press, 1986.

Jones, Christopher P. *Kinship Diplomacy in the Ancient World*. Revealing Antiquity. Cambridge, MA: Harvard University Press, 1999.

Jones, Christopher P. 'Pausanias and his guides.' In *Pausanias. Travel and memory in ancient Greece*, ed. Susan E. Alcock, John F. Cherry and Jas Elsner, 33–9. New York: Oxford University Press, 2001.

Jourdain-Annequin, Colette. *Héracles aux Portes du Soir. Mythe et histoire*. Annales Littéraires de l'Université de Besançon. Besançon: Centre de Recherches d'Histoire Ancienne, 1989.

Kelly, Gavin. *Ammianus Marcellinus. The allusive historian*. Cambridge and New York: Cambridge University Press, 2008.

Kidd, I.G. *Posidonius III. The translation of the fragments*. Cambridge Classical Texts and Commentaries. Cambridge: Cambridge University Press, 1999.

König, Jason, and Tim Whitmarsh, eds. *Ordering Knowledge in the Roman Empire*. Cambridge: Cambridge University Press, 2007.

Krebs, Christopher B. '"Imaginary geography" in Caesar's *Bellum Gallicum.*' *American Journal of Philology* 127, 1 (2006): 111–36.

Krebs, Christopher B. 'Borealism. Caesar, Seneca, Tacitus and the Roman concept of the North.' In *Cultural Identity in the Ancient Mediterranean*, ed. Erich Gruen, 202–21. Los Angeles: Getty Publications, forthcoming.

Kremer, Bernhard. *Das Bild der Kelten bis in augusteische Zeit. Studien zur Instrumentalisierung eines antiken Feindbildes bei griechischen und römischen Autoren*. Historia Einzelschriften. Stuttgart: Steiner, 1994.

Kuhn, Christina T. 'Mythos und Historie in kaiserzeitlichen Smyrna. Kollective Identitätsstiftung im Kontext der Romanisierung.' *Scripta Classica Israelica* 28 (2009): 93–111.

Kuhn, Thomas S. *The Structure of Scientific Revolutions*. Chicago: University of Chicago Press, 1962.

Kunow, Jürgen. *Der römische Import in der Germania libera bis zu den Marko-mannenkrieg. Studien zu Bronze- und Glasgefässen*, Göttinger Schriften zur Vor-und Frühgeschichte. Neumunster: K. Wachholtz, 1983.

Lampinen, Antti. 'Narratives of impiety and epiphany. Delphic Galatomachy and Roman traditions of the Gallic sack.' *Studia Celtica Fennica* 5 (2008): 38–53.

Lane Fox, Robin. *Travelling Heroes. Greeks and their myths in the epic age of Homer*. London: Allen Lane.

Leach, Edmund. *Political Systems of Highland Burma. A study of Kachin social structure*. Monographs on Social Anthropology (LSE). London: G. Bell & Son Ltd, 1954.

Lee, A.D. *Information and Frontiers. Roman foreign relations in late antiquity*. Cambridge: Cambridge University Press, 1993.

Leerssen, Joep. 'Celts.' In *Imagology. The cultural construction and literary representation of national characters. A critical survey*, ed. Manfred Beller and Joep Leerssen, 122–3. Amsterdam and New York: Editions Rodopi, 2007.

Levene, D.S. 'Sallust's *Jugurtha*. An "historical fragment".' *Journal of Roman Studies* 82 (1992): 53–70.

Levick, Barbara. 'Morals, politics and the fall of the Roman republic.' *Greece & Rome* 29 (1982): 53–62.

Leyser, Karl J. 'Concepts of Europe in the early and high Middle Ages.' *Past & Present* 137 (1992): 25–47.

Lightfoot, Jane. L. *Parthenius of Nicaea. The poetical fragments and the 'Ερωτικὰ παθήματα. Edited with introduction and commentaries*. Oxford: Clarendon Press, 1999.

Lintott, Andrew. 'Imperial expansion and moral decline in the Roman Republic.' *Historia. Zeitschrift für Alte Geschichte* 21 (1972): 626–38.

Lund, Allan A. *Zum Germanenbild der Römer. Eine Einführung in der antike Ethnographie*. Heidelberg: Carl Winter Universitätsverlag, 1990.

MacKenzie, John M. *Orientalism. History, theory and the arts*. Manchester: Manchester University Press, 1995.

Malkin, Irad. *Myth and Territory in the Spartan Mediterranean*. Cambridge: Cambridge University Press, 1994.

Malkin, Irad. *The Returns of Odysseus. Colonization and ethnicity*. Berkeley, Los Angeles and London: University of California Press, 1998.

Malkin, Irad. 'Herakles and Melqart: Greeks and Phoenicians in the middle ground.' In *Cultural Borrowings and Ethnic Appropriations in Antiquity*, ed. Erich Gruen, 238–58. Stuttgart: Franz Steiner Verlag, 2005.

Malkin, Irad, ed. *Mediterranean Paradigms and Classical Antiquity*. London and New York: Routledge, 2005.

Marcus, George E. *Ethnography Through Thick and Thin*. Princeton, NJ: Princeton University Press, 1998.

Marincola, John. *Authority and Tradition in Ancient Historiography*. Cambridge: Cambridge University Press, 1997.

Martinelli, Giovanna. *Roma e i barbari. Dai Giulio Claudii agli Antonini*. I Quaderni di Mandala. Lecce: Edizioni Pensa Multimedia, 2005.

Marvin, Miranda. 'Copying in Roman sculpture. The replica series.' In *Retaining the Original. Multiple originals, copies and reproductions*, ed. Kathleen Preciado, 29–46. Washington, DC: National Gallery of Art, 1989.

Mastrocinque, Attilio, ed. *Ercole in Occidente*. Labrinti. Trento: Dipartimento di Scienze Filologiche e Storiche, Università degli Studi di Trento, 1993.

Mattern, Susan P. *Rome and the Enemy. Imperial strategy in the principate*. Berkeley, Los Angeles and London: University of California Press, 1999.

Matthews, John F. *The Roman Empire of Ammianus*. London: Duckworth, 1989.

Mattingly, David. *An Imperial Possession. Britain in the Roman Empire 54 BC– AD 409*. London: Allen Lane, 2006.

Mellor, Ronald. *The Roman Historians*. London: Routledge, 1999.

Merrills, A.H. *History and Geography in Late Antiquity*, ed. Rosamund McKitterick. Cambridge Studies in Mediaeval Life and Thought, Fourth Series, vol. 64. Cambridge: Cambridge University Press, 2005.

Merriman, Nick. 'Value and motivation in prehistory. The evidence for "Celtic spirit".' In *The Archaeology of Contextual Meaning*, ed. Ian Hodder, 111–16. Cambridge: Cambridge University Press, 1987.

Miller, D.H., and W.W. Savage. 'Ethnic stereotypes and the frontier. A comparative study of Roman and American experience.' In *The Frontier I. Comparative Studies*, ed. D.H. Miller and J.O. Steffen, 109–37. Norman: University of Oklahoma Press, 1977.

Millett, Martin. *The Romanization of Britain. An archaeological essay*. Cambridge: Cambridge University Press, 1990.

Mócsy, A. 'The civilized Pannonians of Velleius.' In *Rome and her Northern Provinces. Papers presented to Sheppard Frere*, ed. Brian Hartley and John Wacher, 169–78. Gloucester: Alan Sutton, 1983.

Moitrieux, Gérard. *Hercules in Gallia. Recherches sur la personnalité et le culte d'Hercule en Gaule*. Gallia Romana. Paris: de Boccard, 2002.

Momigliano, Arnaldo. *Alien Wisdom. The limits of Hellenisation*. Cambridge: Cambridge University Press, 1975.

Momigliano, Arnaldo. 'Athens in the third century BC and the discovery of Rome in the *Histories* of Timaeus of Tauromenium.' In *Essays in Ancient and Modern Historiography*, ed. Arnaldo Momigliano, 37–66. Oxford: Blackwell, 1977.

Morstein-Marx, Robert. 'The myth of Numidian origins in Sallust's African excursus (*Iugurtha* 17.7–18.12).' *American Journal of Philology* 122, 2 (2001): 179–200.

Mudry, Philippe. '"Mirabilia" et "Magica." Essai de définition dans l'*Histoire Naturelle* de Pline l'Ancien.' In *Mirabilia. Conceptions et représentations de l'extraordinaire dans le monde antique. Actes du colloque international, Lausanne 20–22 mars 2003*, ed. Olivier Bianchi and Olivier Thévenaz, 239–52. Bern: Peter Lang, 2004.

Müller, Klaus E. *Geschichte der antiken Ethnographie und ethnologischen Theoriebildung. Von den Anfängen bis auf die Byzantinischen Historiographen*. 2 vols. Studien zur Kulturkunde. Wiesbaden: F. Steiner Verlag GMBH, 1972, 1980.

Müller, Klaus E. *Geschichte der antiken Ethnologie*. Rowohlts Enzyklopädie. Reinbeck bei Hamburg: Rowohlt Taschenbuch Verlag, 1997.

Murphy, Trevor. *Pliny the Elder's Natural History. The empire in the encyclopaedia.* Oxford: Oxford University Press, 2004.

Murray, Oswyn. 'Philodemus on the Good King according to Homer.' *Journal of Roman Studies* 55, 1/2 (1965): 161–82.

Murray, Oswyn. 'Hecataeus of Abdera and Pharaonic kingship.' *Journal of Egyptian Archaeology* 56 (1970): 141–71.

Murray, Oswyn. 'Herodotus and Hellenistic culture.' *Classical Quarterly* 22, 2 (1972): 200–17.

Naas, Valérie. *Le projet encyclopédique de Pline l'ancien,* Collection École française de Rome 303. Rome: École française de Rome, 2002.

Nachtergael, G. *Les Galates en Grèce et les Sôteria de Delphes. Recherches d'histoire et d'épigraphie hellénistiques.* Mémoires de la Classe de Lettres. Brussels: Académie Royale de Belgique, 1977.

Nash, Daphne. 'Reconstructing Poseidonius' Celtic ethnography. Some considerations.' *Britannia* 7 (1976): 111–26.

Nenci, Giuseppe. 'L'occidente "barbarico".' In *Hérodote et les peuples non grecs.* Fondation Hardt Entretiens sur l'antiquite' classique, vol. 35, 301–21. Vandoeuvres and Geneva: Fondation Hardt, 1988.

Netz, Reviel. 'Greek mathematicians. A group picture.' In *Science and Mathematics in Ancient Greek Culture,* ed. C.J. Tuplin and T.E. Rihll, 196–216. New York: Oxford University Press, 2002.

Nicol, John. *The Historical and Geographical Sources used by Silius Italicus.* Oxford: Basil Blackwell, 1936.

Nicolet, Claude, ed. *Rome et la conquête du monde méditerranéen. 264–27 avant J.C.* Paris: Presses Universitaires de France, 1977.

Nicolet, Claude. *Space, Geography and Politics in the Early Roman Empire,* trans. Hélène Leclerc. Jerome Lectures. Ann Arbor: University of Michigan Press, 1991.

Nippel, Wilfried. *Griechen, Barbaren und 'Wilde'. Alte Geschichte und Sozialanthropologie.* Frankfurt-am-Main: Fischer Taschenbuch Verlag, 1990.

Nippel, Wilfried. 'Ethnic images in classical antiquity.' In *Imagology. The cultural construction and literary representation of national characters. A critical survey,* ed. Manfred Beller and Joep Leerssen, 33–44. Amsterdam and New York: Editions Rodopi, 2007.

Nippel, Wilfried. 'Anthropology.' In *Brill's New Pauly,* 2008.

Norden, Eduard. *Die germanische Urgeschichte in Tacitus* Germania. Leipzig and Berlin: B.G. Teubner, 1920.

Nutton, Vivian. *Ancient Medicine,* ed. Liba Taub. Sciences of Antiquity. London: Routledge, 2004.

Ogilvie, R.M. *A Commentary on Livy Books 1–5.* Oxford: Clarendon Press, 1965.

O'Gorman, Ellen. 'No place like Rome. Identity and difference in the *Germania* of Tacitus.' *Ramus. Critical studies in Greek and Roman literature* 22 (1993): 135–54.

Ong, Walter J. *Orality and Literacy. The technologising of the word.* London: Methuen, 1982.

Oniga, Renato. *Sallustio e l'etnografia*, ed. Maurizio Bettini and Gian Biagio Conte. Biblioteca di Materiali e discussioni per l'analisi dei testi classici. Pisa: Giardini, 1995.

Ortner, Shelley. 'Resistance and the problem of ethnographic refusal.' *Comparative Studies in Society and History* 37, 1 (1995): 173–93.

Pagden, Anthony. *European Encounters with the New World. From renaissance to romanticism*. New Haven, CT, and London: Yale University Press, 1993.

Parker, Grant. *The Making of Roman India*. Greek Culture in the Roman World. Cambridge: Cambridge University Press, 2008.

Petitjean, Patrick, Catherine Jami and Anne Marie Moulin, eds. *Science and Empire. Historical studies about scientific development and European expansion*. Boston Studies in the Philosophy of Science. Dordrecht, Boston and London: Kluwer Academic Publishers, 1992.

Peyre, Christian. 'Tite-Live et la "férocité' gauloise". *Revue des études latines* 48 (1970): 277–96.

Piggott, Stuart. *The Druids*. Ancient Peoples and Places. London: Thames and Hudson, 1968.

Pitts, Lynn F. 'Relations between Rome and the German "kings" on the Middle Danube in the first to fourth centuries AD.' *Journal of Roman Studies* 79 (1989): 45–58.

Polito, Roberto. 'On the life of Asclepiades of Bithynia.' *Journal of Hellenic Studies* 119 (1999): 48–66.

Price, Simon. 'Local mythologies in the Greek East.' In *Coinage and Identity in the Roman Provinces*, ed. Christopher Howgego, Volker Heuchert and Andrew Burnett, 115–24. Oxford: Oxford University Press, 2005.

Price, Simon. 'Memory and ancient Greece.' In *Religion and Society. Rituals, resources and identity in the ancient Graeco-Roman world. The BOMOS conferences 2002–5*, ed. Anders Holm Rasmussen and Suzanne William Rasmussen, 167–78. Rome: Edizioni Quasar, 2008.

Purcell, Nicholas. 'Maps, lists, money, order and power.' *Journal of Roman Studies* 80 (1990): 178–82.

Purcell, Nicholas. 'Becoming historical. The Roman case.' In *Myth, History and Culture in Republican Rome. Studies in honour of T.P. Wiseman*, ed. David Braund and Christopher Gill, 12–40. Exeter: Exeter University Press, 2003.

Purcell, Nicholas. 'The way we used to eat. Diet, community, and history at Rome.' *American Journal of Philology* 124, 3 (2003): 329–58.

Purcell, Nicholas. 'Romans in the Roman world.' In *The Cambridge Companion to the Age of Augustus*, ed. Karl Galinsky, 85–105. New York: Cambridge University Press, 2005.

Raaflaub, Kurt, and Richard J.A. Talbert, eds. *Geography and Ethnography. Perceptions of the world in pre-modern societies*. The Ancient World. Comparative Histories. Malden, MA, and Oxford: Wiley-Blackwell, 2010.

Rankin, H.D. *Celts and the Classical World*. London and Sydney: Croom Helm, 1987.

Rawson, Elizabeth. *Intellectual Life in the Late Roman Republic*. London: Duckworth, 1985.

Riggsby, Andrew. *War in Words. Caesar in Gaul and Rome.* Austin, TX: University of Texas Press, 2006.

Rives, James B. *Tacitus.* Germania, *translated with introduction and commentary.* Clarendon Ancient History Series. Oxford and New York: Clarendon Press, 1999.

Rogers, Guy M. *The Sacred Identity of Ephesos. Foundation myths of a Roman city.* London: Routledge, 1991.

Roller, Duane W. *The World of Juba II and Kleopatra Selene. Royal scholarship on Rome's Africa frontier.* London and New York: Routledge, 2003.

Roller, Duane W. 'Juba II of Mauretania (275)', in *Brill's New Jacoby* (online), Editor in Chief Ian Worthington. Leiden: Brill, 2010.

Romm, James S. *The Edges of the Earth in Ancient Thought. Geography, exploration, and fiction.* Princeton, NJ: Princeton University Press, 1992.

Roymans, Nico. *Ethnic Identity and Imperial Power. The Batavians in the Roman Empire.* Amsterdam Archaeological Studies 10. Amsterdam: Amsterdam University Press, 2004.

Rutherford, Ian. '*Theoria* and *Darsan.* Pilgrimage and vision in Greece and India.' *Classical Quarterly* 50, 1 (2000): 133–46.

Said, Edward. *Orientalism.* London: Routledge and Kegan Paul, 1978.

Sapelli, M., ed. Provinciae Fideles. *Il fregio del templo di Adriano in Campo Marzio.* Milan: Electa, 1999.

Scheid, John. 'Sanctuaires et territoire dans la Colonia Augusta Treverorum.' In *Les sanctuaires celtiques et le monde méditerranéen*, ed. Jean-Louis Brunaux, 42–57. Paris: Errance, 1991.

Schneider, Rolf Michael. *Bunte Barbaren. Orientalenstatuen aus farbigem Marmor in der römischen Repräsentationskunst.* Worms: Wernersche Verlagsgesellschaft, 1986.

Schön, Franz. 'Germanen sind wir gewesen? Bemerkungen zu den Tungri und Germani Cisrhenani und zum sogennanten taciteischen Namensatz (Tac. *Germ.* 2.2f.).' In *'Troianer sind wir gewesen'. Migrationen in der antiken Welt. Stuttgarter Kolloquium zur Historischen Geographie des Altertums, 8 2002*, ed. Eckart Olshausen and Holger Sonnabend, 167–83. Stuttgart: F. Steiner, 2006.

Schroeder, Alfredus.*De Ethnographiae Antiquae locis quibusdam communibus observationes. Dissertation.* Halle, 1921.

Scott, James M. 'On earth as in heaven. The apocalyptic vision of world geography from *Urzeit* to *Endzeit* according to the Book of Jubilees.' In *Geography and Ethnography. Perceptions of the world in pre-modern societies*, ed. Kurt Raaflaub and Richard J.A. Talbert, 182–96. Malden, MA and Oxford: Wiley-Blackwell, 2010.

Sedley, David. 'Philosophical allegiance in the Greco-Roman world.' In *Philosophia Togata I. Essays on philosophy and Roman society*, ed. Miriam Griffin and Jonathon Barnes, 97–119. Oxford: Oxford University Press, 1989.

Sedley, David. *Lucretius and the Transformation of Greek Wisdom.* Cambridge: Cambridge University Press, 1998.

Shapin, Steven. *The Scientific Revolution.* Chicago: University of Chicago Press, 1996.

Shaw, Brent D. 'The Elder Pliny's African geography.' *Historia. Zeitschrift für Alte Geschichte* 30, 4 (1981): 421–71.

Shaw, Brent D. '"Eaters of flesh, drinkers of milk." The ancient Mediterranean ideology of the pastoral nomad.' *Ancient Society* 13 (1982): 5–31.

Shaw, Brent D. 'Rebels and outsiders.' In *Cambridge Ancient History*, vol. XI: *The High Empire, AD 70–192*, ed. Alan Bowman, Peter Garnsey and Dominic Rathbone, 361–403. Cambridge: Cambridge University Press, 2000.

Smith, R.R.R. '*Simulacra Gentium*: The Ethne from the Sebasteion at Aphrodisias.' *Journal of Roman Studies* 78 (1988): 50–77.

Sordi, Marta. 'Timagene di Alessandria. Un storico hellenocentrico e filobarbaro.' In *Aufstieg und Niedergang der römischen Welt II.30.1*, ed. Hildegard Temporini and Wolfgang Haase, 775–97. Berlin and New York: De Gruyter, 1982.

Sperber, Dan. *Le symbolisme en général*. Paris: Herman, 1974.

Stewart, Peter C.N. 'Inventing Britain. The Roman creation and adaptation of an image.' *Britannia*, 26 (1995): 1–10.

Strasburger, Hermann. 'Poseidonios on problems of the Roman empire.' *Journal of Roman Studies* 55, 1/2 (1965): 40–53.

Stray, Christopher. '"Patriots and professors." A century of Roman studies 1910–2010.' *Journal of Roman Studies* 100 (2010): 1–31.

Sundwall, Gavin A. 'Ammianus Geographicus.' *American Journal of Philology* 117, 4 (1996): 619–43.

Swain, Simon. 'Plutarch's *De Fortuna Romanorum*.' *Classical Quarterly* 39, 2 (1989): 504–16.

Taub, Liba. *Ptolemy's Universe. The natural philosophical and ethical foundations of Ptolemy's astronomy*. Chicago and LaSalle, IL: Open Court, 1993.

Thébert, Yvon. 'Romanisation et déromanisation en Afrique: histoire décolonisée ou histoire inversée?' *Annales ESC* 33, 1 (1978): 64–82.

Thollard, Patrick, ed. *Barbarie et civilisation chez Strabon. Étude critique des livres III et IV de la* Géographie. Annales littéraires de Besançon 365. Paris: Belles Lettres, 1987.

Thomas, Nicholas. *Out of Time. History and evolution in anthropological discourse*. Ann Arbor: University of Michigan Press, 1989.

Thomas, Nicholas. *Colonialism's Culture. Anthropology, travel and government*. Oxford: Polity Press, 1994.

Thomas, Richard F. *Lands and Peoples in Roman Poetry: The ethnographical tradition*. Proceedings of the Cambridge Philological Society supplements 7. Cambridge: Cambridge Philological Society, 1982.

Thomas, Rosalind. *Herodotus in Context. Ethnography, science and the art of persuasion*. Cambridge: Cambridge University Press, 2000.

Thomson, L.A. 'Strabo on civilisation.' *Platon* 31 (1979): 213–30.

Trüdinger, Karl. *Studien zur Geschichte der griechisch-römischen Ethnographie. Dissertation*. Basel: Emil Birkhäuser, 1918.

van der Vliet, Edward C.H.L. 'The Romans and us. Strabo's *Geography* and the construction of ethnicity.' *Mnemosyne* 56, 3 (2003): 257–72.

Veyne, Paul. *Les grecs ont-ils cru à leurs mythes? Essai sur l'imagination constituante*. Paris: Editions du Seuil, 1983.

Veyne, Paul. *Did the Greeks Believe in Their Myths? An essay in the constitutive imagination*, trans. Paula Wissing. Chicago: University of Chicago Press, 1988.

Veyne, Paul. *'Humanitas*: Romans and non-Romans.' In *The Romans*, ed. Andrea Giardina, 342–70. Chicago: University of Chicago Press, 1993.

Volk, Katharina. *Manilius and his Intellectual Background*. New York: Oxford University Press, 2009.

Wagoner, Phillip B. 'Precolonial intellectuals and the production of colonial knowledge.' *Comparative Studies in Society and History* 45, 4 (2003): 783–814.

Wallace-Hadrill, Andrew. 'Greek knowledge, Roman power.' *Classical Philology* 83 (1988): 224–33.

Wallace-Hadrill, Andrew. 'Pliny the Elder and man's unnatural history.' *Greece & Rome* 37, 1 (1990): 80–96.

Wallace-Hadrill, Andrew. 'To be Roman, go Greek. Thoughts on Hellenization at Rome.' In *Modus Operandi. Essays in honour of Geoffrey Rickman*, ed. Michel Austin, Jill Harries and Christopher Smith, 79–91. Bulletin of the Institute of Classical Studies Supplement 71. London: Institute of Classical Studies, 1998.

Wallace-Hadrill, Andrew. '*Mutatas formas*. The Augustan transformation of Roman knowledge.' In *The Cambridge Companion to the Age of Augustus*, ed. Karl Galinsky, 55–84. New York: Cambridge University Press, 2005.

Wallace-Hadrill, Andrew. *Rome's Cultural Revolution*. New York: Cambridge University Press, 2008.

Washbrook, D.A. 'Orients and occidents. Colonial discourse theory and the historiography of the British empire.' In *The Oxford History of the British Empire*, ed. R.R. Winks, 596–611. Oxford: Oxford University Press, 1999.

Webster, Jane. 'Translation and subjection:. *Interpretatio* and the Celtic gods.' In *Different Iron Ages. Studies on the Iron Age in temperate Europe*, ed. J.D. Hill and C. Cumberpatch, 175–83. International Series 602. Oxford: British Archaeological Reports, 1995.

Welch, Kathryn, and Anton Powell, eds. *Julius Caesar as Artful Reporter. The war commentaries as political instruments*. Swansea: Classical Press of Wales and London: Duckworth, 1998.

Wenskus, Reinhard. *Stammesbildung und Verfassung. Das Werden der frühmittelalterlichen Gentes*. Cologne: Böhlau, 1961.

West, Stephanie. '"The most marvellous of all seas." The Greek encounter with the Euxine.' *Greece & Rome* 50, 2 (2003): 151–67.

White, R. *The Middle Ground. Indians, empires, and republics in the Great Lakes region, 1650–1815*. Cambridge: Cambridge University Press, 1991.

Whitmarsh, Tim, ed. *Local Knowledge and Microidentities in the Imperial Greek World*. Greek Culture in the Roman World. Cambridge: Cambridge University Press, 2010.

Whittaker, C.R. *Frontiers of the Roman Empire. A social and economic study*. Ancient Society and History. Baltimore, MD, and London: Johns Hopkins University Press, 1994.

Whittaker, C.R. 'Ethnic discourses on the frontiers of Roman Africa.' In *Ethnic Constructs in Antiquity. The role of power and tradition*, ed. Ton Derks and

N. Roymans, 189–206. Amsterdam Archaeological Studies 13. Amsterdam: Amsterdam University Press, 2009.

Wiedemann, Thomas. 'Between men and beasts. Barbarians in Ammianus Marcellinus.' In *Past Perspectives. Studies in Greek and Roman historical writing*, ed. I.S. Moxon, J.D. Smart and A.J. Woodman, 189–201. Cambridge: Cambridge University Press, 1986.

Williams, Jonathon H.C. *Beyond the Rubicon. Romans and Gauls in northern Italy.* Oxford Classical Monographs. Oxford: Oxford University Press, 2001.

Wiseman, T. Peter. 'Legendary genealogies in late-republican Rome.' *Greece & Rome* 21, 1 (1974): 153–64.

Wiseman, T. Peter. '*Domi nobiles* and the Roman cultural élite.' In *Les bourgeoisies municipales italiennes aux IIe et Ier siècles av. J.-C.*, 299–307. Naples: Editions du CNRS and Bibliothèque de l'Institut Français de Naples, 1981.

Wiseman, T. Peter. *Remus. A Roman myth.* Cambridge and New York: Cambridge University Press, 1995.

Wissowa, Georg. '*Interpretatio Romana.* Römische Götter im Barbarenlande.' *Archiv für Religionswissenschaft* 19 (1916–19): 1–49.

Wolf, Eric R. *Europe and the People without History.* Berkeley: University of California Press, 1982.

Wood, Ian. 'Defining the Franks. Frankish origins in early mediaeval historiography.' In *Concepts of National Identity in the Middle Ages*, ed. Simon Forde, Lesley Johnson and Alan V. Murray, 47–57. Leeds: Leeds University Press, 1995.

Woolf, Greg. 'Power and the spread of writing in the west.' In *Literacy and Power in the Ancient World*, ed. Alan Bowman and Greg Woolf, 84–98. Cambridge: Cambridge University Press, 1994.

Woolf, Greg. 'The uses of forgetfulness in Roman Gaul.' In *Vergangenheit und Lebenswelt. Soziale Kommunikation, Traditionsbildung und historisches Bewußtsein*, ed. Hans-Joachim Gehrke and Astrid Möller, 361–81. Tübingen: Gunter Narr Verlag, 1996.

Woolf, Greg. *Becoming Roman. The origins of provincial civilization in Gaul.* Cambridge: Cambridge University Press, 1998.

Woolf, Greg. 'Urbanization and its discontents in early Roman Gaul.' In *Romanization and the City. Creations, transformations and failures*, ed. Elizabeth Fentress, 115–32. Journal of Roman Archaeology Supplements 8. Portsmouth, RI: Journal of Roman Archaeology, 2000.

Woolf, Greg. 'The Roman cultural revolution in Gaul.' In *Italy and the West. Comparative Issues in Romanization.*, ed. Simon Keay and Nicola Terrenato, 173–86. Oxford: Oxbow Books, 2001.

Woolf, Greg. 'A distant mirror. Britain and Rome in the representation of empire.' In *Laudes Provinciarum. Rétorica y política en la representación del imperio romano*, ed. Juan Santos Yanguas and Elena Torregaray Pagola. Revisiones de Historia Antiqua, vol. 8, 135–47. Vitoria: Universidad del Pais Vasco, 2007.

Woolf, Greg. 'Cruptorix and his kind. Talking ethnicity on the middle ground.' In *Ethnic Constructs in Antiquity. The role of power and tradition*, ed. Ton Derks and N. Roymans, 207–17. Amsterdam Archaeological Studies 13. Amsterdam: Amsterdam University Press, 2009.

Woolf, Greg. 'Greek archaeologists in Rome.' In *Ruling through Greek Eyes. Interactions between Rome and the Greeks in imperial times*, ed. Elena Muñiz Grivalvo, Juan Manual Cortés Copete and Fernando Lozano. Leiden and Boston: Brill, forthcoming.

Woolf, Greg. 'Saving the barbarian.' In *Cultural Identity in the Ancient Mediterranean*, ed. Erich Gruen (Los Angeles: Getty Publications, forthcoming), 255–71.

Wörrle, Michael. *Stadt und Fest in kaiserzeitlichen Kleinasien. Studien zu einer agonistischen Stiftung aus Oinoanda*. Vestigia. Munich: C.H. Beck, 1988.

Wright, M.R. *Cosmology in Antiquity*, ed. Roger French. Sciences of Antiquity. London: Routledge, 1995.

Yarrow, Liv Mariah. *Historiography at the End of the Republic. Provincial perspectives on Roman rule*. Oxford and New York: Oxford University Press, 2006.

Zanker, Paul. *Augustus und die Macht der Bilder*. Munich: Beck, 1987.

General Index

Index of Main Passages Discussed